THE LADY SWINGS

MUSIC IN AMERICAN LIFE

A list of books in the series appears
at the end of this book.

THE LADY SWINGS

MEMOIRS OF A JAZZ DRUMMER

DOTTIE DODGION
& WAYNE ENSTICE

Foreword by Carol Sloane

UNIVERSITY OF ILLINOIS PRESS
Urbana, Chicago, and Springfield

The book is accompanied by a web page,
https:/www.press.uillinois.edu/books/supplement/_dottie,
that features supplemental material, as well as audio and
video materials. The symbol 🎵 in the text indicates a
reference to these materials.

Library of Congress Cataloging-in-Publication Data
Names: Dodgion, Dottie, 1929– author. | Enstice, Wayne,
    1943– author. | Sloane, Carol, writer of foreword.
Title: The lady swings: memoirs of a jazz drummer / Dottie
    Dodgion & Wayne Enstice; foreword by Carol Sloane.
Description: Urbana: University of Illinois Press, 2021. |
    Series: Music in American life | Includes bibliographical
    references and index.
Identifiers: LCCN 2020041538 (print) | LCCN 2020041539
    (ebook) | ISBN 9780252043598 (cloth) | ISBN
    9780252085512 (paperback) | ISBN 9780252052477 (ebook)
Subjects: LCSH: Dodgion, Dottie, 1929– | Women drummers
    (Musicians)—United States—Biography. | Drummers
    (Musicians)—United States—Biography. | Women jazz
    musicians—United States—Biography. | Jazz musicians—
    United States—Biography.
Classification: LCC ML419.D634 A3 2021 (print) | LCC ML419.
    D634 (ebook) | DDC 786.9165092 [B]—dc23
LC record available at https://lccn.loc.gov/2020041538
LC ebook record available at https://lccn.loc.gov/
    2020041539

From Dottie:

To Casey Silvey, a beautiful soul who inspired me to tell my life story and then provided the help I needed to make it come true.

To Wayne Enstice my coauthor for his years of research, determination, and devotion, to complete this book. Bless him.

From Wayne:

To Marie Frances, my wife of 53 years and bedrock to my sky.

In memory of John and Eleanor Enstice.

Contents

Illustrations follow page 152

Foreword

I . . . remember her as full of fun, a very
good drummer, as good as any of the men.
—Marian McPartland

I have no clear recollection of meeting Dottie Dodgion, but it most certainly took place in New York on or after 1958 when I first moved there. My vivid recollection is her effervescent personality, irresistible joie de vivre, and pride of place among the best of the best who were living and working in world-renowned clubs such as Birdland, the Five Spot, the Half Note, the Jazz Gallery, Minton's, and the Village Vanguard. At the time, New York City was THE home base for major jazz record labels, and jazz musicians were busy in the studios much of the time. I probably met Dottie and her then husband, alto sax player Jerry Dodgion, at the same time, and probably in a favorite hangout bar called Jim & Andy's. With clubs and record labels operating full time, there were also two popular television programs, each with its own "house band," which also kept a lot of musicians working. The Merv Griffin orchestra was led by Mort Lindsey and included famous jazz musicians Jim Hall and Bob Brookmeyer. The Johnny Carson Show house band was led by Skitch Henderson and later by trumpeter Doc Severinsen. That band included Tommy Newsom and former Duke Ellington star Clark Terry. To add to these incredibly fertile opportunities for a musician to secure employment, Broadway musicals used full orchestras, many containing string sections as well as traditional personnel found in swing bands. The truly offensive application of canned music had yet to rear its ugly head.

To read Dottie Dodgion's account of it is to understand some of the successful survival tactics of her heroic pursuit of a career in jazz, more particularly in the field of jazz percussion, which few women dared invade with any seriousness of purpose. Dottie knew she could do it and do it as well—in some cases even better than—her male counterparts.

Dottie Dodgion discovered the music world because of the atmosphere in her childhood surroundings. Her father was an accomplished drummer who inspired in his daughter a respect and curiosity for the music he loved and which she embraced with youthful enthusiasm.

In the 1930s and 1940s, Americans relied on the radio, movie musicals, and congregated in ballrooms to dance to the sounds of the big bands, all forms of entertainment that helped ease the anguish and genuine uncertainty of the Great Depression and on into the equally difficult years of WWII. The radio was a daily source of news of the world and cultural edification, i.e., broadcasts of live opera performances and symphonic concerts. Of course, one could also hear the popular big bands, such as Glenn Miller and Benny Goodman on live broadcasts, to name just two of the many popular aggregations of the day.

At the movies, brilliant scores by Irving Berlin, Harold Arlen, Jerome Kern, George and Ira Gershwin, Richard Rodgers and Oscar Hammerstein drenched the senses with glorious melodies, and because Dottie's parents loved all genres, the inclusion of jazz fit in perfectly as well. The sounds of the best jazz of the era, such as Benny Goodman, Tommy Dorsey, Duke Ellington, Count Basie, Jimmie Lunceford, and Louis Armstrong as well as singers Connie Boswell, Ella Fitzgerald, and Anita O'Day also engendered a fascination with jazz. Dottie was lucky enough to grow up during this period of densely textured, diverse music, so of course she wanted not only to hear more but to actually play the music. Mom and Dad applauded and helped in any way possible.

Her father was respected and admired for his musicianship, sense of fair play, and being a generally all-around good fellow, and he thought she was a good singer, suggesting she invest her energies learning songs from the so-called Great American Songbook. In those early days, she enjoyed vocalizing, never dreaming her true lifetime dedication would be the drums. The DRUMS? A violin or a harp or the piano, certainly, but the DRUMS? "Well, yes, why not?" asked Dottie and her Dad. Female drummers were not unheard of and, in fact, all-girl bands became popular when the men were away fighting in two world wars. In 1942, drummer Viola Smith sent shock waves through the jazz world by claiming in Downbeat magazine that "hep girls" could sit in on any jam session and hold their own. By the 1950s, a woman playing drums could expect a career in the lions' dens, competing with men in a world filled with sarcastic dismissal, scorn, and even fully realized resentment, attitudes too often undisguised. Dottie walked straight into the fray with sticks and brushes firmly grasped like weapons she would use to her advantage as she proved time and again that she was eager to learn and be recognized for her skills.

Dottie overcame unwarranted prejudices by using her keen intuitive abilities and unrelenting determination, while honing her skills at each opportunity she was given to demonstrate her prowess. In other words, she played her ass off. She never wavered, never lost faith in herself or in the music. To be sure, there were a handful of trusted male colleagues who were perfectly comfortable in their own skin and were willing to share insights with Dottie because they recognized she was so thoroughly involved and eager to learn. One such trusted, generous musician was bass player Eugene Wright who joined the Dave Brubeck Quartet for the group's U.S. State Department tours of Europe and Asia in 1958. Mr. Wright subsequently became a permanent member of the fabulously popular jazz quartet, which in 1959 also featured Joe Morello on drums and Paul Desmond on alto sax.

Dottie also gained a very large seal of approval from the notoriously mercurial bass player Charles Mingus who was almost as famous for his snarl and growl as for his prodigious prowess as a bass player. He was quick to recognize genuine talent when he saw it as well and was happy to nurture it. Mingus loved Dottie's playing, and I will not spoil the details of how they met.

Dottie has gained the respect and admiration she deserves but not without predictable obstacles thrown in her path, flung there by skeptical club owners and band leaders who refused to accept that a woman could play with the necessary muscle and stamina to propel a jazz group—whether a piano, bass, and drums or a full-scale band with five reeds, five brass, and a full rhythm section. She was gradually given more opportunities to put that fallacy to rest. When she was given the chance, her faultless sense of time brought additional praise and respect. With Dottie at the drums, the tempo never wavered. Her reputation began to grow and musicians accepted as fact the words of praise generously bestowed on Dottie by such jazz luminaries as Marian McParland or Grady Tate or Phil Woods or that notoriously hard to please curmudgeon Ruby Braff.

"The Lady Swings" is a riveting account of the twists and turns, convolutions, successes, adversities, failures, numerous and sometimes humorous opportunities to play—all of which were to become Dottie's triumphs. The male musicians who recognized her early potential were her early mentors. Many were colleagues of her drummer father. He tutored Dottie by example, and she, in turn, learned the valuable lessons of fortitude and resilience, qualities necessary to get on with it, no matter the obstacle. There were some moments of physical abuse and endless struggles for acceptance, which Dottie describes with brutal honesty. Her own vibrant spirit persevered, but not without the inevitable scars. Part of her remarkable stamina also derives from her mother's firm belief in her daughter's integrity and ability, combined with a natural, protective shield, a quality that never wavered.

An aspiring jazz musician dreams of working with or becoming a student of the most formidable of artists. Of course, one listens to recorded works and embraces any opportunity to hear the artists one most admires in live performance, but Dottie enjoyed several opportunities to actually work with some of the very best. Tellingly, these musicians recognized Dottie's skill, sincerity, and fixation on becoming among the best jazz drummers. She was never told, "You can't do that," and she wouldn't have believed it anyway.

Dottie Dodgion's rich life is set forth in vivid detail in this, the telling of her journey with all its colorful history. It is a story filled with revelations and courageous decisions. Mostly, this is a story of one woman's tenacious dedication to music and the playing of it. Dottie Dodgion is not only famous for her musicianship but for her fierce determination to always bring her "A" game to the job at hand, the natural instinct of a true artist. She continues to get behind that formidable drum kit at her regular Thursday night gig at the elegant Inn At Spanish Bay in Pebble Beach, California. If you are near the place, you should visit the lady and ask her to sign your copy of this book.

Carol Sloane, 2018
American Jazz Singer

Acknowledgments

From Dottie:

To Brian Gingerich, my friend since 1990 who opened every door he could for me so I was able to survive and play my music.

To Brendan Sullivan who declared himself my champion and backed it up.

To Susie Cecil, whose sincere warmth of friendship brought this "Last lap chapter" many smiles and laughs. So needed at age ninety-one.

To the entire staff at The Inn at Spanish Bay, from the valets who carried my drums to the head honchos upstairs, for my Thursdays for the last fourteen years of happiness playing music.

From Wayne:

In 2010 I got a call from Dottie Dodgion asking me to help with her memoirs. The idea was conceived at some point during 2008–2009 when Dottie recorded episodes from her life story in conversation with Casey Silvey, a Bay-area writer and editor who intended to adapt those sketches for a fictionalized screenplay. I am indebted to Casey for her unselfish gesture of sending me digital files of all twenty-four conversations.

Consummate vocalist Carol Sloane must be singled out for penning a foreword of such generous proportion and eloquence in celebration of a beloved colleague. Two readers of the manuscript in its early stages, Sean Gallagher, professor of art, Central Connecticut State University and Dr. Jeremy A. Smith, director, Archives of Appalachia, East Tennessee State University, merit special attention for keen insights and encouragement cheerily dispensed. Profound gratitude is extended to Dr. Furaha Norton, assistant professor of

English and comparative literature, University of Cincinnati, for her unfailing support and wise counsel. I would be remiss not to recognize freelance drummer, Chris C. Parker, for his contributions of music theory. Two reference librarians deserve particular mention: University of Cincinnati English Librarian, Rosemary Franklin, a veritable compendium of apt phrases and word choices, and Bryan Cornell, Recorded Sound Reference Librarian at the Library of Congress, who piloted me through the double-barreled maze of the National Mall and LOC protocol. This project benefited greatly from the dedicated advocacy of Joe Petrucelli, executive director, Jazz Foundation of America.

This book is the result of a decade-long collaboration between Dottie Dodgion and me, but countless other people aided in the task. Foremost among them are: Michael Weil, percussionist and jazz discographer; Thomas P. Hustad, author of *Born to Play: Ruby Braff's Discography and Directory of Performances*, Scarecrow Press; Professor Jennifer Barnes, director of vocal jazz, University of North Texas; Jason Tiemann, New York City–based drummer and educator; Bill Goodwin, jazz drummer; and Dick Vartanian, pianist and composer. Jazz writers who furnished crucial information include Brian Priestley, jazz author, broadcaster and pianist; Doug Ramsey, Rifftides: http://www.dougramsey.com; S. Duncan Reid, author of *Cal Tjader: The Life and Recordings of the Man Who Revolutionized Latin Jazz*; and Michael Steinman, JAZZ LIVES, writer, videographer, archivist. Invaluable leads and resources were provided by: lyricist, Iola Brubeck; Hank O'Neal, founder of Chiaroscuro Records; Donna Gourdol, Marian McPartland's granddaughter; Dennis McBride, director, Nevada State Museum/Las Vegas; Carol Chamberland, author and documentary filmmaker; Kathy Scobey, licensing manager, Sony/ATV Music Publishing; Rachel Domber, president of Arbor Records; Nancy Christiansen, personal assistant to Marian McPartland; Robert D. Rusch, founder and editor 1976-2018 *Cadence* jazz magazine; John Waters, American Video Cincinnati; and Phil DeGreg.

Dottie and I am grateful to the staff at the University of Illinois Press. Despite seismic disruptions due to the Covid 19 pandemic, the editorial and marketing teams rallied and with unfazed efficiency guided this project to completion. Many contributed in diverse ways. Particularly notable for their sustained commitment include Laurie Matheson, director; Jennifer Argo, senior editor; Angela Burton, rights and permissions; Kevin Cunningham, copywriter; Nancy Albright, copy editor; Jennie Fisher, designer; Michael Roux, marketing and sales manager; and Bob Repta, IT technical.

Boundless expressions of appreciation are reserved for my family. The wholehearted help of Kirsten Inquilla, Tim Enstice, and Nic Enstice, their timely doses of unaffected joy, commiseration, and benevolent critical judgments, were peerless. My wife, Marie, was beyond compare, displaying heroic reserves of patience and concentration in the face of exhaustive revisions and the elusive final draft.

Prefatory Notes

WAYNE ENSTICE

There is not necessarily a feminine aesthetic to
her playing anymore than there is from good male
drummers, which is why she was considered a
first in breaking through the gender barrier of the
instrument. . . . I completely recognize that I stand
on her shoulders, as [do] all the younger women that
came after me . . . whether they know it or not.

—Terri Lyne Carrington

Jazz drummer Dottie Dodgion is an unsung figure in American music despite a singular career spanning three-quarters of a century.

Dottie Dodgion commanded first-call respect in the fiercely competitive, almost exclusively gendered New York jazz world of the 1960s and 1970s. She was one of a very few women of that era[1] who assumed a mantle of pioneer by breaking into the circumscribed, hard-core male jazz fraternity on the drums, the most masculine of instruments.

Clearly, her mere presence at that time on that instrument in the big-league company she kept was consequential. Yet Dottie's achievement isn't defined solely by historical context or cultural symbolism. Comparable is her long-overlooked legacy as a player: How hard she swings, her artistry on the drums, and her rock-solid in-the-pocket accompaniment. Beyond the centerpiece of her drumming is Dottie's stature as a vocalist, including early performances that showcased singing wordless melodies in jazz.

Dottie Dodgion worked the New York jazz scene after the demise of the big bands, including the all-women orchestras, and before the rise of jazz studies in colleges and universities attracted unprecedented numbers of women pursuing careers in jazz. So, as a woman drummer and an entrenched member of the New York jazz community at the middle of the twentieth century, she bridged a gap between two eras and then disappeared.

Dottie Dodgion's prominence among her peers in sophisticated East Coast jazz cliques has not been matched by either public or critical currency. During her peak years she appeared on only a handful of recordings, and even jazz insiders more often than not sense only the barest outline of a distant memory at the mention of her name.

One of her closest friends and fellow drummer, Vince Lateano, made these observations about Dottie's chronic obscurity and her grit in the face of it: "Dottie has never stopped, she just plugs away. . . . She keeps doing it but she's still scuffling, as she has probably for most of her life. It's a sin that someone with her talent and stature is so unappreciated considering the music she's brought to the world."

At ninety-one, Dottie Dodgion remains quietly active, with regular Thursday night gigs at a luxury hotel in Pebble Beach, California. She soldiers on despite frequent bouts of sciatica. To alleviate intense pain when she plays, Dottie sits behind the drums on a bicycle seat covered by a pillow. Because the bike seat is indented on both sides, causing her to wobble back and forth "cheek to cheek" as she plays, Dottie threatens to use velcro to keep her firmly planted on the throne. Plainly, her resolve, not to mention her sense of humor, remains intact.

This memoir aspires to an eleventh-hour rescue of Dottie Dodgion. It is not lost on her localized West Coast circle of fans and supporters that this is the last best time to widen that circle. Her distinctive story deserves nothing less. As the world-renowned jazz bassist, Eugene Wright, succinctly described Dottie: "She's one of a kind."

* * *

A few words are in order about how this book was developed and organized. The stories that constitute Dottie's memoir are drawn primarily from her storehouse of memories. I can vouch for Dottie's exhaustive attempts to recall each episode in detail, but her ability to pin down precise dates and to be certain about the sequence of linked events suffered regular lapses. That's mostly due to age. No doubt another reason is that some parts of her life were so painful for her to experience at the time that she either banished them to a shadowy recess in her mind or purged them altogether.

Dottie's stories are arranged into three sections and divided into thirty-nine topics, designated as either "Scenes" (the sequential narrative) or "Behind the Scenes" (pauses in the sequential narrative). Although the organization is chronological, the narrative progression of a Scene may include digressions that blur strict chronology. This method allowed Dottie the freedom, as needed, to improvise her stories thematically whether or not the calendar function of her memory would cooperate.

Supplementing the text are personal quotes from musicians and friends of Dottie that were drawn from a pool of approximately forty interviews that I conducted by phone or through correspondence. Complementing Dottie's story is video footage of her in performance and a series of instrumental and vocal recordings including rare and unreleased sides, all of which are accessible through the press website.

Some incidents in the book want corroborating sources because most of the principals who figure prominently are deceased or, in a few cases, because a subject declined to participate. Where intimate personal relationships were concerned, we shied away from digging too deeply into the past, preferring to avoid any distress that might occur in the wake of chasing down leads and asking pointed questions. Pseudonyms or generalized descriptions were used to shield some identities. Realizing that despite this degree of propriety some innocent relations of protagonists in Dottie's life may, by virtue of this book, confront unwelcome revelations is already a high enough price for her to pay.

Every time I was with Dottie
I came away and my face was sore
because I was smiling so much.
—Richie Cole

Introduction

Hi, honey, it's me, Dottie D.

I'm a jazz musician and this book tells the story of my life, the unvarnished highs and lows. My soul at birth had passion, common sense, and fearlessness built-in. A tool set for survival that from the start has served me well. Between the ages of 5 and 16 I did a lot of living. A lifetime in eleven years.

As a child I was given a head start—a love of music—and it became my world. I was born with rhythm in my nursery rhyme. As a youngster, I wouldn't go to bed without the radio on and to this day I awaken with a song.

At sixteen I took my first steps professionally and then spent the next fifteen years mostly on the West Coast paying my dues and little by little literally piecing together my craft. From early 1961 until the mid-1970s, I was part of the New York scene, which included touring with several first-class bands led by men, bands flush with heavy male cats, big names from the big-band and bebop eras. My acceptance as a woman drummer in that exclusive circle of all-male jazz bands may have been a rarity at that time, but I never asked my peers to acknowledge me. My entry into the Big Apple brotherhood of jazz was always by invitation.

I wasn't self conscious about blazing new paths in the jazz world, I was just too damn busy answering other people's ads. Today, with the benefit of longevity kicked in, I can appreciate that what distinguished me back then has, with the passage of time, taken on a luster of importance.

My success in that male-dominated culture didn't come easy. The guys were not going to give it up—the drummer was the balls of the band—and I really had to prove it. When I first started playing, musicians would call the slowest ballad they could to show me up, to prove that a girl can't swing at that tempo, but I would have died before giving up on a ballad.

As a female, I wasn't expected to be strong or positive. One time a drummer in a club I was working stepped on the stand at the end of a tune and blustered, "Okay, I can take over now." I blustered right back: "Take over what? Get your own gig!" That was a hard pill to swallow for some musicians in New York.

Cooking with many of the best rhythm sections in the history of the music has been glorious, yielding many high points in my life that have nourished me spiritually if not always materially. Many low points in my life were beyond my control, from kidnapping to rape to devastating illness.

Unsavory bits, such as a suicide attempt, abortions, and ill-fated unions, were more often the outcome of questionable judgment. Those dark corners pack content sensational enough to inspire potboiler fiction, but I feel it's important to recount and understand them in the context of my struggle to survive and somehow succeed as a working-class Italian female in early-twentieth-century America. That slog was so intense it seems that missteps were inevitable.

I persevered through gender prejudice that typecast me according to my looks and laid roadblocks in my path to becoming a professional jazz musician. Those roadblocks came in two flavors: blatant sexist behavior, or the more subtle ploy of invoking chauvinist cultural values that defined what was and what was not dignified work for a woman. My first husband, bassist Monty Budwig, tried to steer me away from drumming because it wasn't ladylike. He preferred that I work as a vocalist. My second husband, reed player Jerry Dodgion, supported my drumming but wisely discouraged me from doubling as a singer to protect my reputation in New York as a serious musician who specialized on one instrument. I like to kid that I divorced them both and threw caution to the winds, playing drums when I wanted and singing when I wanted!

My style was not an audience magnet. Never a flashy drummer—to this day I'm not a "paradiddle Josephine"—and I'm not really a soloist. I play the melody. I used to kid that I'm not a real drummer! It was the swing, the division, the flow of one note to the next, that excited me. My conception is based on keeping good time, on being the glue that holds the overall sound together.

Despite my "low profile" on the bandstand I always felt that I had a voice of my own on my instrument. I was thrilled by remarks made about me by the late, great tenor saxophonist, Frank Wess: "She's one of my favorite people. She's very unique. I like her sound. I like her hi-hat. . . . She's got a unique sound."

By 1990, my withdrawal from the jazz capital of the world was complete. I relocated to the West Coast where I gigged and eked out a living in California towns and cities that were not, to say the least, humming with "America's classical music." Nevertheless, one of the joys of putting this book together has been to learn that, although I have been absent from the mainstream jazz world for a considerable time, vestiges of my reputation survive and my name still circulates among succeeding generations of women drummers. I am truly humbled by that.

> "Dottie's influence is probably something that
> she doesn't even realize. . . . So, thank you Dottie."
> —Phil Woods

Principal Voices in My Story

Important voices in my story are my daughter, Deborah Dodgion; my ex-husband, Jerry Dodgion; and bassist, Eugene Wright. As I was quoted years ago in a *Down Beat* profile by Carol Sloane, "If it hadn't been for J.D. and Eugene, I would probably be a plain housewife today. They are the reason I'm a drummer, because they taught me everything: dynamics, color, texture, discipline—everything."[1]

I am indebted to Jerry and Deborah for their help rummaging through more than fifty years of memories, salvaging details that were crucial to the narrative of my life.

Other Contributors to My Story

I extend my gratitude to all the musicians and friends who were part of this project, including those who have enriched this memoir with their recollections and testimonials. Sadly, some of those listed below have been lost to us.

Kenny Barron
Randy Brecker

Iola Brubeck (1923-2014)
Sonny Buxton
Terri Lyne Carrington
Ron Carter
John Coates Jr. (1938–2017)
Richie Cole (1948–2020)
Bob Cranshaw (1932–2016)
Sylvia Cuenca
Jay Daversa
Bob Dorough (1923–2018)
Eddie Erickson
Ahnee Sharon Freeman
Dave Frishberg
Eddie Gomez
F. DeWitt Kay, Jr (c. 1937–2015)
Vince Lateano
Mike Longo (1939–2020)
Gus Mancuso
Dee Marabuto
Sherrie Maricle
Turk Mauro (1944–2019)
Marian McPartland (1918–2013)
Allison Miller
George Mraz
Anne Phillips
Vicki Randle
Sandra Reaves-Phillips
Mickey Roker (1932–2017)
Ron Rose (1930–2014)
Louise Sims
Carol Sloane
Scott Steed
Francesca Tanksley
Grady Tate (1932–2017)
Frank Wess (1922–2013)
Phil Woods (1931–2015)
Eugene Wright

PART I

THE CALIFORNIA YEARS

On the Road

I was born on September 23, 1929, a month before Black Tuesday and the start of the Great Depression. The world and I were headed for a roller-coaster ride. The only difference was mine lasted longer.

Christened Dorothy Rosalie Giaimo (I am of Sicilian descent on my father's side), my birthplace was the southern California city of Brea but I spent most of my childhood up north in the Bay Area. My father, Charles Giaimo, was born July 27, 1907. A self-taught drummer, he loved jazz. At twenty-one, he was on the road in the Smoky Mountains of Tennessee when he met my mother, sixteen-year-old Ada Martha Tipton. Born April 12, 1912, she was an exotic mix of Cherokee and Irish. My parents married the year I arrived and didn't live happily ever after. In two years, my father was gone. He dumped my mother and yours truly at my Sicilian grandmother's house in Los Angeles and took off touring with his band.

My earliest memory, at age four, is plugged into my ethnicity. I was playing with the boy next door, making mud pies after a storm. He got mad because my mud pie was larger and had a better shape, so he flung some mud at me, dirtied my dress and yelled, "Go home, 'Wop!'" Boy, that made me mad! I aimed that huge mud pie of mine and really let him have it. He ran home crying and I did the same. Swallowing my sobs, I told my mother how that brat called me a Wop. I wasn't sure what that meant, but it didn't matter. "I'm not a Wop, Mom," I insisted. "I'm Sicilian."

I eventually learned from my paternal grandparents that "Wop" was a derogatory word; it just wasn't said. I can remember Grandfather Giaimo coming home raving because neighbors across the street had yelled, "Get out of here, Wop." He wanted to be an American so bad. I think he's the one who put the second "i" in our name so it would be pronounced "Jy-mo" and sound American.

I don't remember too many good times with my Sicilian relatives. Somebody was always yelling orders at somebody else so endless upset was in the air with lots of grumbling under breaths. My grandmother was the worst of the lot. Like me, my mother couldn't stand living with her and the feelings were mutual. My grandmother hated my mother for one simple reason: She wasn't Italian. Grandmother Giaimo hated anybody who wasn't Italian, but even if you were Italian it still wasn't enough. You had to be Sicilian; if you weren't Sicilian you weren't really Italian, so she hated you anyway. She was Sicilian through and through.

After my parents divorced, my father had visiting rights. When I was about five-and-a-half, Mom and I were staying with the Giaimos and one day my father stopped by. He asked my mother if he could take me for a little ride and buy me some ice cream. That was the last time I saw my mother for two years! He kidnapped me and the next thing I knew I was on the road with him. My entrance to show biz!

My father worked a lot of different jobs, on cruises and some hotels, but his most steady work was in roadhouses and strip joints. After he abducted me, roadside clubs were my home until I was seven years old. A roadside club was a nightclub that was a good distance outside city limits. They usually had a dance floor and the entertainment was typically a trio or a quartet. The gigs would last three days—over a weekend—and because it was too far to drive back and forth to whatever city was nearby, the roadhouses had rooms for the musicians. That's how we lived, moving from one roadside club to the next, each time with me upstairs in our room in the evening while Dad played downstairs.

Most times I didn't mind being alone because I could hear the music, but now and again, having an urge to see what was happening, I'd sneak down a few steps and watch. If one of the club staff or a musician saw me I'd be carried down and plopped on top of an upright piano. Someone would say, "Sing a song, Dottie," and I'd let loose with some dumb cute little tune like "Itty Bitty Fool" or "Three Little Fishes." I guess that because my father was a drummer it was expected that I could sing, and it was okay with me. I had my first taste of performing and it went down easily.

I was so distracted at first with the novelty of my new lifestyle that I didn't worry about seeing my mother. Besides, my father told me that what we were doing was all right with her: "Momma said I get to take you on a little vacation." So, at first I didn't question it, and, best of all, I was away from those testy Sicilians. After a couple of months, though, I really started missing my mother and wanted to see her but my father ignored my pleas. "Not yet," he'd tell me.

We traveled by car across the country, my father at the wheel since the guys in the band were usually too drunk to drive. All that time, little did I know the anxiety my poor mother was suffering. My father never told me how long we were going to be gone, and I never dreamed that my mother didn't know. She had the police looking for my father in state after state, but because we were constantly on the road they couldn't find him.

After two years I was a different child. No longer the cute Shirley Temple doll that everybody adored, tweaking my cheek, I had become a gangly seven-year old. Caring for me got more awkward, especially when people asked: "What school does she go to?" Complications like that probably got my father to start thinking twice about his little girl tagging along, but what really put the brakes on was the drama that unfolded one night with me at the center of the plot.

We'd been at a roadhouse for several days with the usual arrangement: My father was working nights in the club downstairs and I was upstairs unafraid in our room because I could hear the band playing. One of those nights, while I was waiting for my father to finish his first show of the evening, some joker knocked on the door.

Now my father warned me to always keep the door locked, to never open it for anyone unless it was the owner of the place who would check every once in a while to see that I was alright. When I heard the knock I asked who it was, and when there was no reply I got confused. I mean, I couldn't be sure it wasn't the owner so I opened the door. It wasn't the owner! There stood a man I'd never seen before. He said he was a friend of my Daddy's and that Daddy had sent him because he forgot his keys. What do I know? He walked in and I sat down to watch. At first he just casually glanced around, but when he began opening drawers and rifling through Daddy's things I got suspicious. "Daddy doesn't like anybody going through his drawers," I told him.

Sensing I might make a fuss, he mumbled, "I don't have time for this," and with his hand over my mouth, he shoved me into a clothes closet and locked the door. It didn't take long before I got panicky, flailing my arms searching for a pull string, until it dawned on me that there was no light in that closet to turn on. In the dark I was quaking with fear, but I waited until I heard him leave before I started screaming, banging my feet on the floor and beating my fists furiously on the door. It was no use. The band was still playing and no one could hear me. I had to wait for what seemed an eternity until intermission for my dad to come up, and by then I was a wreck.

It took me a long time to get over that. Into my thirties I couldn't sleep at night without a light on. God bless the guy who invented night lights.

The trauma I suffered was so intense it made me paranoid. I became suspicious and fearful, harboring irrational feelings that I tried to keep private. The incident disturbed my father, too. Now, whenever he left for work he was anxious about my welfare, and that took a toll on him. He got so jittery he couldn't concentrate on performing, and because he let nothing stand between him and his music, my father returned me to my mother.

That was some homecoming. Right away I was blown away that my mom had remarried! All the time I was gone she looked for a man who would be a good father for me, and the guy she chose, Ed Jensen, owned a chicken farm in Colusa County, about forty miles from the city of Woodland. My mother thought Jensen a decent man, and at first I thought so, too. Boy, were we wrong! Jensen was a brute and before long his true colors emerged. His first move was to get rid of me. Calling me unruly, he convinced Mother that I needed the discipline of a convent school, so I was enrolled in Holy Rosary Academy in Woodland.

Although I had missed kindergarten and first grade, I tested at my age level so they put me into second grade. I stayed at the Academy until I was nine, boarding at the convent during the school week. I didn't like it much. The nuns could be harsh; my nickname for one of them was "Iron Pants." My attitude wasn't helped by getting punished pretty regularly for mischief. It's not that I was a bad kid—I never swore at any of the nuns—but I got lots of slaps on the hand for misdemeanors that, really, were more the fault of my curiosity. I remember putting a frog in a classmate's desk to see the reaction I'd get. Of course it backfired. Another time I found a ladder in the hall outside the nun's lounge and, since I was dying to know what was under the headpiece the nuns wore, I climbed up the ladder and peeked through the transom. I was on my knees in the chapel at play time for the next four weeks.

I wasn't proud that my antics triggered a steady stream of reports to my mom, but there was a silver lining: The strictness of the nuns paid off for me in the classroom. I had good grades, pretty much straight "A's" with the occasional B+, and a few years later when I went to a public junior high my GPA at the convent enabled me to skip a grade. Despite my unhappiness, I got a good education at that convent.

On weekends I went home to the chicken farm, but it was as grim as the convent. Our ramshackle house had a wooden floor that was dotted with large knot holes. One night I got into bed, stretched my legs under the covers, and my feet landed on a large snake huddled for warmth. Intuitively, I felt that episode paralleled my life: no control over lots of unwanted surprises. Thankfully, I got a temporary reprieve whenever my mother would drop me off to spend a Saturday or Sunday at my maternal Grandma Tipton's place.

Grandma Tipton lived just outside the city of Colusa, California, on a tiny farm with a few chickens, not far from a high levee out by the watermelon patches. On a sunny day I'd walk up to the levee with my "Aunt" Mary, one of Grandma's daughters who was only a year older than me. In the crevices of the levee were the strangest plants I had ever seen. Mary and I called them "levee pumps." I know now they were common cattails, but back then they were mysterious flowers that stirred my imagination. Levee pumps shot up on a tall, slender stem and had a long cylindrical top, medium brown in color. They looked like a hot dog on a stick! Even though the tops were soft like velvet, they were firm enough for us to color them with crayons. The hours would fly by as I sat decorating those pumps from morning through practically the entire afternoon. When supper was ready, my mother put her two fingers between her teeth and whistled; I can still hear that high-pitched trill, that little melody calling me home.

The fun I had with Aunt Mary, away from adult supervision and transported by the exotic world of the levee, was in stark relief to the bookends of the dour convent and Jensen's homestead. Most days I was a very glum little girl. Trying her best to cheer me up, my mother bought me a dog. We named him Spot.

SCENE **TWO**

Spot

Spot was a small mixed-breed dog with a lot of terrier in him. Set against his wiry white coat were two, large, dark brown spots. My mother was right: Getting that dog was a lovely distraction for me. At least for a little while.

I had Spot for a week when my stepfather, Ed Jensen, discovered that he was a chicken killer. I didn't know it at the time, but that sealed Spot's fate as far as Jensen was concerned. About two weeks later he made me get in the family car, holding Spot on the front seat, and the three of us headed to town. When we reached Main Street, busy with cars whizzing by, Jensen reached over, grabbed Spot, opened his door and threw my beloved dog into the traffic! I watched Spot get killed instantly. Jensen kept driving as I sat there frozen with shock. I couldn't believe he did that! One day I had a dog that made me happy and then it was brutally taken away. I don't think I ever felt so helpless in my life.

When the full impact hit me, I started sobbing. Sobbing over the fate of poor Spot and sobbing out of pure panic. After all, if he'd do that to my dog I might be next. Jensen was a big man, six-foot two and easily two-hundred pounds; to a little girl he was mammoth. When we got home and my mother learned what had happened she gave him hell. Jensen responded by throwing my mother against a wall and beating her up. That was my second glimpse in quick succession of who Ed Jensen really was: a violently abusive man.

Their relationship never recovered. Jensen was drunk a lot of the time, my mother would blow her top, and he would slap her around. I couldn't stand it when the fights started so I'd run away and hide. I turned inward just like after I was locked in that roadside club clothes closet. I had to disappear in order to survive, and they were so busy fighting they never missed me.

In an effort to save their marriage, my mother and Ed decided to sell their place and move. It wasn't doing very well anyway and my mother was tired of working that damn chicken farm. We moved from the Woodland area and got a house in Berkeley, not a particularly nice one, but it was better than what we had on the farm. The house was in a downgraded area just this side of the tracks behind a Heinz pickle factory. My mother got a job as a waitress at Woolworth's, Jensen worked for a time in a factory as a steamfitter, and at age nine I started public school in the fourth grade at Columbus Elementary.

Not long after we moved, Ed got laid off. Bitter and angry, he drank up their income and hurt Momma an awful lot. He threw her up against walls so hard that she suffered broken ribs and a busted collarbone. Feeling desperate, I found a way to escape and music was at the heart of it.

After my father returned me to my mother he found work in San Francisco at a local strip joint called "Streets of Paris." He rented a room at the Padre Hotel in the Tenderloin and settled in the city. When I learned he was back in the Bay area I began lobbying my mother to see him. It took my mother about three months to forgive him for leaving her and kidnapping me, but in the end she decided that he had a right to see me. I also think the hard life she was having with her second husband softened her anger at my father. So, at age nine, I began making bus trips alone to San Francisco for weekend visits with him. I would stay over on Saturday night and leave Sunday evening.

Looking back, I suppose I should be surprised that my mother approved of my "solo flights" so far from home at such a tender age, especially since so many of our relatives shook their fingers and scolded her, but I think my mother made a calculation. Considering the nightmares I was exposed to at home, she opted for me getting away despite the risks of my traveling alone.

And it's not like my mom didn't prep me in advance. She told me to walk fast when I got to the bus station, making it difficult for somebody to accost me. She also taught me that when I was on the bus not to let anybody, and certainly no strangers, approach me and insinuate themselves with lines like, "Hi, little girl." To prevent that from happening, I made a beeline to a window seat on the bus and glued myself to it, looking out. Although I followed my mother's advice, I was, of course, wonderfully oblivious to the dangers, and, in a way, that was a good thing. I could focus my full attention on the education in life and music my father was giving me.

Father was a charmer, to say the least. Five-foot-ten inches tall, trim and handsome, he had dark, curly hair with a slight widow's peak and gray on the sides. Twinkling eyes, a good-looking Sicilian nose, and a devastating smile completed the picture. Dad was a very fastidious man, in his dress and his habits. His hotel room was spotless; shoes lined up in his wardrobe closet; magazines evenly stacked, including back issues of Vargas Pin-Ups; pens and pencils in his desk drawers arranged in orderly file. He smoked a pipe in the daytime and allowed himself one cigar after dinner. He wasn't a big drinker, but each night before dinner he raised a glass of his own concoction. Called a "Passion Drink," he made it with brandy in a sweet vermouth float topped by a cherry.

The bus ride from Berkeley across the bay took about thirty minutes. Most times I'd take a Saturday afternoon bus and arrive in the City before my father went to work. He'd meet me at the station, we'd grab a taxi to the Tenderloin, and taking my hand we'd walk his neighborhood. If I arrived after my father started work, I'd take a taxi by myself straight to the Streets of Paris where I'd get a friendly reception from the club's doorman. I was too young to officially go inside, but the doorman would scout around and when the coast was clear he'd whisper, "Okay, duck down," and I'd scramble under his legs and through the door.

As my father and I strolled the blocks near his hotel, he'd introduce me to people in the neighborhood, on the street and in the shops. Dad was king at Original Joe's Restaurant, so whenever we went there for lunch or dinner someone would shout: "Chuck's here and that's his little girl!" In a short time it stuck: I got the handle, "Chuck's Little Daughter." After that, anytime I left his hotel by myself—it was only three short blocks to the "Streets of Paris"—the first newsman I passed would say, "Hello, Chuck's little daughter." If some guy came up behind me and wondered aloud, "Whose little girl is that?" people on the street would chime in, "That's Chuck's little daughter." My father worked the Streets of Paris for probably four years and I was the community foster child.

On Saturdays, after dinner, we'd go up to my father's hotel room where I'd grab a nap as he showered, shaved, and put on his tux for work. On the way to the club he'd drop me at the RKO movie theater for the last show. When I'd get out, about 11:30 at night, I'd walk to Golden Gate Street, down one block on Turk to the Streets of Paris where the strippers would take me into their dressing room in the basement. I'd sleep for a bit and then the girls, standing around nude, would put makeup and powder on my face, dress me up, and make me laugh. It was great fun and I felt protected.

When it was time for the girls to go on, I would walk upstairs to a corner of the club and listen. Although Streets of Paris was a strip joint full of sailors whistling at the girls, my father led a band that had some of the greatest jazz musicians in San Francisco playing tunes for the strippers, like Dizzy Gillespie's "A Night in Tunisia" and "Mood Indigo" by Duke Ellington.[1] Daddy had that powerhouse band in part because there wasn't a lot of work for musicians at that time, but also because he was a real swinging drummer and all the musicians said he was fantastic. His excellent time attracted all the best strippers, like burlesque queens Sally Rand and Tempest Storm, and he taught a lot of young strippers because they couldn't keep time at all. He'd gently instruct them, "No, honey, you bump on 2, you bump on 4."

Hearing the compliments about Daddy's playing made me proud to be his daughter, but I never thought seriously about playing the drums. All I knew at the time was that he thrilled me. I was fascinated by how he sang as he played; for a long time I thought all drummers could do that. Nevertheless, and although he didn't school me—he didn't teach me one lick—by listening so much to what he did at the drums (I was there for rehearsals as well as the evening shows) I must have absorbed a certain amount of rhythm from him. The rhythm was in my ears and recorded in my head.

After my father finished his two sets at Streets of Paris we'd head back to the hotel where we talked and played records until four or five in the morning. Listening to a rush of music with my father was always the highlight of my excursions across the Bay. His room had two beds. He sat on one and I'd sit upright on the edge of the other bed, listening intently with hands clasped and legs dangling. He always had great music on the phonograph: Billie Holiday (my favorite), Duke Ellington, Count Basie, Woody Herman—he played me all the big bands, and because we listened to them so much, to this day I can sing almost every part of those old tunes. They all had so much soul it used to just reach right down deep inside of me.

We listened to music using one of those little travel record players. We played it soft so I'd put my ear right up next to it to make sure I wouldn't miss a note. As night crept slowly toward daybreak, while I was eating an avocado he'd cut in half and dipped in olive oil and vinegar, he might put

Benny Goodman on. "Listen to this, honey," he'd say, and as the trumpet section would blare and my eyes would get big, he'd shake his head as if to say, "Isn't that wonderful?" My dad gave me a marvelous start in music.

One of the most valuable lessons he taught me was respect for the music. My father would never say anything while the music was playing. I learned that you can talk before a record is on and you can talk after it's finished, but you never open your mouth and ask a question about anything when the music is being played. My father listened so hard that his example made me listen.

I carried that high standard with me into New York and was respected for it. In a club I'd find a corner to sit, listen, and keep my mouth shut. If you wanted to succeed as a woman in this business, that's exactly what you did. You observed, you listened, and you didn't say dumb-ass silly things that women usually say to get attention.

Sometimes my reputation for listening intently preceded me, like one evening when Ron Carter, the great bass player, was working Sweet Basil, the Greenwich Village jazz club. Ron had Ben Riley on drums and Kenny Barron at the piano—God, what a great group it was. Each night I'd make my way to the back of the club to sit near the drummer and concentrate on the music. Now Ben at that time was good-looking and he'd flirt with the girls, so up on the stand maybe his attention would be momentarily diverted. I remember when I overheard Ron say, "Here comes Dottie, Ben. You better be on your toes!"

Those late-night sessions on weekends with my father continued through my teenage years. In contrast to all the upset I suffered in the company of the other adults in my family, I can honestly say that listening to records with my father was the most wonderful part of my childhood.

As I got older, Dad used my visits as an opportunity to teach me about the facts of life. One night the subject was strippers. He said that "just because strippers take their clothes off doesn't mean they're whores, that they were bad. No," he said, "It's because they weren't educated and they had to do this kind of work to make money for their kids." His word to the wise was: "Never be a snob!" He went on to describe how some of the girls got in trouble, how sailors would drop a pickup line, like "Honey, this might be my last day on earth" to talk a lady into having sex and when she wound up pregnant he would split leaving her alone to raise the child. The Streets of Paris visits were an important part of my education about how men and women really treated each other. The word ugly comes to mind.

Not all my "classes" on learning to be a grownup were at the Padre. One night in the mid-1940s, at a club in San Francisco, I had a dramatic lesson about self respect and the advantages of being a lady in all situations. Trumpet player, Howard McGhee, was the billing; bebop was just starting in California and Howard was one of the first to introduce that way of playing a phrase. Dad had been raving about Howard, and when he learned that Dizzy Gillespie was in town and would be joining Howard that night we made a beeline for the club. My father had played Dizzy's records in the hotel, so he leapt at the chance for me to hear those trumpet giants in person.

Dad knew everybody in all the clubs, so he had no trouble sneaking me in. I was scooted under the hinged service door and stood behind the bar in front of where all the booze was lined up on shelves. Dizzy and Howard were the first beboppers I ever heard and it was thrilling to see their expressions as they played and to be swept up by that pulsating rhythm. At the end of the first set, a ruckus diverted my attention from the music.

A woman, noticeably drunk and mad as a hornet, charged out of the ladies' room and slapped a guy hard sitting right in front of me at the bar. I was dumbstruck. When the guy turned around and belted her, I really got scared. My father saw I was alarmed so he calmed me down, and then he used that real-life situation as a teaching opportunity. He was very hip that way.

Daddy broke the scene down to tell me, first, why the guy hit his woman back: Since he was sitting with all his buddies and she embarrassed him, he hit her back to save face—he might not have hit her if she'd been ragging on him when they were alone. Second, he told me that no man likes a drunken broad. Third was the rule of thumb that a woman should never hit a guy because he can hit a lot harder and he will win. Finally, he had me look at the action from a different angle by describing how, if the guy had slapped his woman first and she still stayed with him, then she really was a dumb bitch!

Eventually, I realized that my father was teaching me how to be one of the guys. So, I put his pearls of wisdom in my little bonnet upstairs and sure enough some of them forecast experiences I had later in my career. Like when I went to New York and wanted approval without losing my dignity, I took my father's advice to never use the "F" word. If I wanted to cuss somebody out I'd say, "faccia cocuzza," which sounds bad but really means "squash face" or "pumpkin face" in Italian.

The big city excitement of those early San Francisco trips, all the growing up I was doing, and the freedom I felt on the weekends, made it tough for me to return to the cheerless existence I faced each week in Berkeley. Mom was still working long hours on her day shift at Woolworth's, trying to make ends meet. Jensen, out of work, stayed in the house. Most days he started drinking early in the morning, and in the afternoon when I'd come home from elementary school he'd show what I thought was affection by giving me hugs. He bounced me on his knee, shook my body and tossed me about. In my innocence I thought he loved me, but later on I wondered for a minute, "Was I sexually precocious at the time, did I encourage him toward some prurient interest in me?" Clearly I didn't. I wasn't even thinking about sex. I was ten years old and everything was love with me. He was the one thinking about sex.

The rape happened in the daytime. He busted my cherry and there was blood on the walls and smeared all over the sheets. My mother walked in about fifteen minutes later; I was passed out cold and Jensen was gone. When she saw the blood and me unconscious on the bed, she went berserk. She rushed to my side to be sure I was breathing, and then she dashed to the kitchen, grabbed a butcher knife, and burst out of the house to go after him. She caught sight of him when he was almost on San Pablo, about two- and-a-half long blocks away. A neighbor, stunned by the sudden appearance of my mother running, screaming furiously, and wielding a large knife, yelled, "What's wrong, Ada?!" My mother pointed the knife at the fleeing figure and shrieked, "That's what's wrong!" She chased and chased Jensen but couldn't catch him.

The rape erased much of my memory of succeeding events. About all I can recall is based on what my mother told me. She had Jensen arrested and hauled into court and later divorced him. I was in no condition to testify at the trial, but on the strength of evidence given by my mother, along with a neighbor's corroborating testimony, it was an open and shut case. Jensen got twenty years. It goes without saying that my mother was devastated; a few weeks later she suffered a nervous breakdown. When she collapsed, I thought her breakdown was all my fault. I carried that guilt for a long time.

The Giaimos

My father, Charles ("Chuck") Giaimo was born in New Brunswick, New Jersey. He had a brother named William (Bill) and two sisters, Sally and Antoinette (Toni). When Dad was twelve, the family moved to Lincoln Heights in Los Angeles.

My paternal grandmother, Concetta (Katie) Sanfedele, was from Catania, Italy, and she was a fantastic cook. When she was a young girl but old enough to work, she started as a kitchen helper in some of the castles in Catania and Palermo. She worked her way up to become a sous chef before she married my grandfather, Frank Giaimo. Even though Sicilians are known for sardines, I never saw her serve even one to her family. There was no low food of that sort, no cioppino (a fish stew that originated in San Francisco). Food like that was for fishermen, for poor people. She had been taught to cook first class. The only time she was happy was when she was cooking.

I learned a lot about cooking from Grandma Giaimo, but it wasn't easy. She was guarded about the secrets that made her cooking special. She gave me many of her recipes, but often she left out a key ingredient. Her attitude was, "this is my kitchen, this is my kingdom," so she never encouraged me to learn. Quite the opposite in fact: if I got too nosy about a certain recipe, she would promise to show me and then put her back to me. There was a time, though, when I broke the code of one of her cooking mysteries: the way she sweetened her sauces.

One of her rules of thumb was that she would never use sugar, even though in those days pretty much everybody used at least a pinch in their recipes. I knew that sometimes she would use the cut-off tops of anise, the Italian celery, to sweeten a dish, but her sauces were sweetened in a different way. I didn't know exactly what it was until one time when I caught her off-guard. After she put all the main ingredients in the pot I watched as she added a peeled potato that was cut in two. "Aha!" I thought, the potato will take out the acid left from the tomatoes and make the sugar. That's why her sauces were so sweet!

Born and raised in Palermo, Italy, my paternal grandfather, Frank Giaimo, was skinny as a rail despite gorging on his wife's cooking. Grandpa loved Grandma's food so much that he went out of his way not to eat at the better places in southern California! Like the time he was working in downtown Hollywood. Grandpa's trade was stonemasonry and he had his own construction company. He was one of the contractors who built a new wing onto the Hollywood Roosevelt Hotel, which is right across from Grauman's Chinese Theater, and on his midday break from that job he'd sometimes find a spot in the hotel to sit and eat his packed lunch. One day a few hotel staff saw my grandfather as he got settled to eat and offered to have the kitchen fix a hot meal for him. The Roosevelt Hotel served wonderful Jewish food including a delicious borscht, but since my grandmother always made veal cutlet sandwiches on French bread for my grandfather, he replied, "No, no thank you, my wife, she-a-fix-a my lunch."

My paternal grandparents had two daughters: Antoinette (Toni) and Sally. Aunt Toni was an inspiration to me. Although crippled by polio at the age of two, Aunt Toni was very self-reliant and very strong physically; she had powerful arms from wielding her crutches and from lifting herself off her bed onto a wheelchair. She didn't let illness or my Grandmother Giaimo stop her from being happy and doing as much as she could for herself. My grandmother would pressure Toni, "Don't do that," "I'll do it," but she always resisted so Grandma couldn't control her.

My Aunt Toni fought hard to be independent. When she wanted a car, she didn't wait for permission, she just got it! Because her legs were paralyzed, she had to have a mechanic move the gas pedal and brake up on the steering rod. Running errands with her, I'd watch in amazement as she slid sideways onto the seat, hoisted her legs up and over, and away we'd go! I was very impressed by my Aunt Toni's courage. During that era, few victims of polio would have dared to be that liberated.

My Aunt Sally was a different story altogether—or so I was told, because Aunt Sally died when I was four years old. One thing I do know, because I've seen pictures, is that she looked nothing like the rest of our family. Aunt Sally was considered the beauty among the Giaimo women, and I'm the one who is supposed to look just like her. (Aunt Sally was the only one on my Sicilian side who didn't have a big hook nose. When I was small, my mother used to press on the bridge of my nose while praying that it wouldn't develop that aquiline look. I guess her prayers were answered: I got Aunt Sally's nose.)

Evidently, Aunt Sally was very sweet to me, buying me expensive little fur coats and pretty dresses, but while Aunt Toni was an active, even dominant, figure in the Giaimo household, Aunt Sally was passive and subordinate, with tragic consequences.

For most of her short life, Aunt Sally let Grandma bully her. When she finally rebelled, their relationship collapsed. Aunt Sally's "crime" was that she wanted to marry outside of the Sicilian family. Worse yet, her fiancé wasn't even Italian! My grandmother felt she had no recourse but to forbid the marriage. That made Sally even more determined, but, as fate would have it, she contracted pneumonia and the drawn-out, bitter fight with Grandma Giaimo weakened her dramatically. Aunt Sally deteriorated mentally and physically at such an alarming rate she developed double pneumonia. Despite the seriousness of her condition, my grandmother refused to call a doctor. She confined Aunt Sally to her bed and tried to heal her with rest, steam, and Vicks. It didn't work. Aunt Sally died on her wedding day. It was also her birthday. She was twenty-two.

My paternal grandparents had two sons: my father, Chuck, and his brother. William (Bill). Grandfather Giaimo wanted to turn over his construction business to one of his sons but neither my Uncle Bill nor my father wanted it. Maybe it was for the best, because both of them wound up a disappointment to Grandpa. Uncle Bill was a racetrack man; when I was nine he took me to the races and I picked his horses. He was also a hustler who made a series of misfired investments, including a bowling alley that failed and then a florist shop, but he lost that, too. Uncle Bill always had a scheme, always had a dream, and was always borrowing money from my grandfather.

Dad never took a penny from his father, but it didn't matter, because Grandpa didn't like what my father did for a living. Grandfather Giaimo had no respect for musicians; he called them gypsies. I remember as a youngster how he'd scold me for singing around him: "Ah, so you're going to be a gypsy just like your father!" That snooty remark stuck with me; it was a vivid illustration of how controlling the Giaimo clan was.

All my relatives on my dad's side were by nature very upper-hand, very bossy, very interfering. Really interfering! In other words, they were very Italian. Even my Aunt Toni, bless her heart, would stick up for me when I had a skirmish with her mother, but then she'd turn around and heavily blue-pencil my school work. But it was all for my own good, you see, or at least that's what I was told, so to get along I was compliant. Each time I was rebuked or snubbed I wouldn't take offense. "Okay," I'd say, yielding just enough to make it seem like they were the boss. I knew not to talk back, not to sass.

My father exerted the most control over me. Like a Svengali, he pretty much had me brainwashed as I was growing up. His wishes were always the rule, what he thought I should be, how he thought I should act. When I was living with Mom, he insisted I call or write him a couple of times a week to let him know everything that was going down. If he didn't hear from me, he'd royally bawl me out. I didn't risk not being in his good favor because of an unspoken threat that hung over my head: If I crossed him, he'd cut my music privileges and I wouldn't get to hear him or other bands in the Bay Area.

An example of how Daddy manipulated me occurred when I was a kidnapped little kid on the road with him. One afternoon, as I was contemplating some deep thought sitting on the floor of our room upstairs in a roadside club, my father burst in, took one look, and his stern reaction startled me: "What are you pouting about?!" Well, he made it clear that from then on, boy, as soon as I saw him I was supposed to crack a big smile, flashing my pearly whites to brighten the room! I'll never forget that; I was so innocent, just blissfully daydreaming, and bam! The appearance of being happy was one of his selfish needs, and with me he could control the situation. It had to be his way, always his way.

The Giaimos exerted a measure of control over me as long as my father lived. Even when I was an adult, everyone on that side of my family expected I would write them a few times a year, send cards on appropriate days, and visit at least two or three times a year—or shame on me. It didn't stop until they all died. I can't tell you how happy I am that I don't have one living relative!

Eleanor Powell's Shoes

Once the pain of the rape receded a bit, Momma and I moved out of the Heinz Pickle Factory house and into a rental place on Delaware Street in Berkeley.

That was the beginning of very lean times; Momma had little money and we seldom had enough food. She'd bring stuff home from Woolworth's every chance she'd get but it wasn't enough, so in desperation we started a garden in the backyard. The tools we used were kept in a little shed, and one afternoon, while poking around in a shadowed corner of that shed, I accidentally cornered a huge rat. Before I could run it lunged at me, biting me good on my left arm just above the wrist. I carry that scar and a fear of rats to this day.

We planted a variety of vegetables in our garden, but the only crop that Momma and I could get to grow was zucchini. We had this whole big yard of nothing but zucchini so we ate it every which way: fried, baked, stewed, boiled, you name it. Contending with a zucchini glut injected our lives with a touch of dark comedy. Looking back, it was also a godsend because poor as we were, that modest squash was our salvation; and strange as it may seem, I still love to eat zucchini!

Momma was a good cook, but she learned to hate cooking because she was so tired in the evening from her long shift at Woolworth's. To lift her spirits, I decided to surprise her by baking a cake for her birthday. At this time, Mom had a girlfriend named Pinky. They worked together at Woolworth's and, for a while, Pinky took one of the rooms in our rental house. Pinky was going with a Marine and so I figured with four of us available a birthday party was in order, with my cake as the centerpiece.

When the day arrived, I was proud as punch about how beautiful the cake looked, but I was mortified moments after Mom and our two guests took their first bite. Looking perplexed, they each choked down their mouthful, then politely placed their forks on the table. It was clear that they'd had enough, thank you very much. I was mortified and clueless, but the mystery was solved in minutes when my mother put two and two together. A few days earlier she had poured salt in the sugar bin and, blissfully ignorant of the switch, I put two cups of salt in the batter! Momma felt bad, but of course she never dreamed that I would bake a cake. I broke down and cried. She took me in her arms and told me it was the thought that counted, but my heart was broken. I never baked again.

The botched birthday cake was a minor bump in the road compared to the revulsion I felt at another celebration, this time in a Catholic church. During those Berkeley years, my mother never went to church, and I hadn't been since I left the convent school. So, I surprised her one day when I expressed an interest in returning to the church. "No, No, No!" she insisted. Eventually, though, she relented, understanding my need for an escape from the drudgery of our lives, and I went to Mass every Sunday until the time drew near for my first communion. In preparation to receive the Holy Eucharist I went to church on a Saturday for confession.

When I knelt down as a penitent in the confessional box the smell of liquor was overwhelming. The priest was drunk! Out of his head on wine! That sickeningly sweet odor brought back lurid memories of the rape, and my head swam with images of Ed Jensen. Hysterical, I bolted the church. Mother told me I didn't have to go back, and I didn't: no confession, no first communion. From then on I was done with organized religion. I didn't need a church to find God; somewhere I had read that "God is with you all the time. He's inside you." I liked that idea.

To soothe my soul, I joined a tap class at Columbus Elementary and was a natural. I had good time and rhythm, convincing me that deep inside I had an affinity for dancing; it was like I was supposed to do that. I used to take my tap shoes and pretend to be Fred Astaire; the clarity and rhythmic drive of his taps really impressed me. Later on, when I became a drummer, I'd dance my ass off sitting behind the traps to get a good swing feel.

I lived for those tap classes. I had no other creative outlet and tap dancing released so many of my pent-up fears. I started to dream of becoming a professional tap dancer, and, more and more, when I made that trip across the East Bay to watch the shows at Streets of Paris, I found myself captivated by how the girls moved to the rhythms my dad played. It wasn't lost on him that I liked to dance but he couldn't spend the time to help me. So, it was providential that I met Hoppy.

Hoppy was the MC and opening act for my father at Streets of Paris. He was also a tap dancer! One afternoon I was out with my father when we bumped into Hoppy. He was headed to his studio to work on a routine. "Mind taking Dottie along?" Dad asked. "Sure," Hoppy said. "C'mon." This arrangement cleared some space for Dad so he was happy, and I was ecstatic! For the next year there was a new highlight in my weekend schedule: a side trip with Hoppy for a dance lesson.

Hoppy lived in a hotel. Whenever he tried to rehearse in his room, tenants on the floors below would scream bloody murder, so he rented the basement in another building. There was a lot of clutter and storage in that basement, but Hoppy cleared out a living-room-sized space in the center. A piano sat along one wall and next to it was a travel-box record player just like the one my dad kept in his hotel room, and just like with my dad, I learned from Hoppy by listening.

To begin my lessons, Hoppy would play a rhythmic pattern on the piano until I had it in my ears. Then we'd dance it together. He'd lay out another rhythm and immediately dance it with me. I didn't try any wing-nut shenanigans, throwing my arms all around. It was strict timekeeping and Hoppy loved my time!

After a while, I could pick out each rhythmic pattern so quickly I almost knew where he was going next. That helped me later on in playing the drums. When a piano player would kick off the beat, almost immediately I could tell what rhythmic pattern he wanted. If the piano player started a transition between two different patterns, I knew how we were going to resolve it. I've been told that I have big ears, and it's true. Just like with Hoppy, I can hear it almost before they hit it.

More than anyone else, Hoppy was the one who encouraged me to dance. "She really has it!" he told my dad, and it wasn't long before I scored a childhood coup that justified his praise. In February 1939, the World's Fair opened in San Francisco Bay on a 400-acre, artificially constructed strip of land, fancifully named "Treasure Island." One of the exhibit halls along the midway featured a children's dance competition, and I am everlastingly grateful that my elementary school registered all us kids from the tap class for that contest. Dressed in top hat, little tuxedo tails, and black stockings, I took first prize—a pair of Eleanor Powell's dancing shoes.[1]

Winning that contest lifted me out of my doldrums, and more than ever I wanted to build my life around dancing. That is, until my dad brought up the subject at one of our late-night chats in his hotel room. Sounding a lot like his own father, he said, "Nah, You'd better be a singer, gypsies don't make any money." He called dancers *gypsies* because in those days dancing jobs were very few and far between unless you were a fan dancer or a stripper.

I was really disappointed when my father steered me away from dancing, but I knew he was right. After all, I would have had to wait a long time to get into a chorus line, do ballroom dancing, or be allowed to work in clubs. My dream was impractical so I gave it up, but that didn't stop me from dancing. I had time and I had rhythm and my flair for dance was one of the most natural ways for me to express my physical intelligence. Another was sports.

I made the basketball team when I entered sixth grade at Burbank Junior High in Berkeley. Playing forward, I was quick and sure in my footwork. I owe a debt of gratitude to Hoppy's disciplined coaching for my execution on the court, and I have no doubt that the attention I paid to refining my motor skills at that stage of my life repaid me later when I found it so easy to coordinate a cymbal with a hi-hat.

After completing the sixth grade at Columbus my excellent record from Holy Rosary Academy enabled me to skip seventh grade and jump directly into eighth. I was twelve and my scholastic advancement coincided with a noticeable change in my physical appearance. I had been an A cup for a long, long time so at ten, even eleven, I still looked like a child. Then I sprouted up and got pretty well developed.

Others noticed my budding maturity, too. Next door to my father's hotel in the Tenderloin was Romaine's Photography Studio. Karl Romaine was a glamour photographer. I think of him as the Vincente Minnelli[2] of photography; the way Romaine helped Hollywood hopefuls reminded me of the way Minnelli revamped Judy Garland's image on the big screen.

Romaine's assistant spotted me one afternoon as I passed by the studio with my father. He pitched the idea of a photo session and Romaine welcomed me with open arms! The shoot was in 1941, just before Pearl Harbor. Dressed elegantly, with full makeup and in a seductive pose, I looked for all the world like a young woman of eighteen. Mentally and emotionally I was a teenager, but my appearance argued that I had skipped puberty entirely. That contradiction would play out, sometimes uncomfortably, over the next several years, starting with my tryout at the Coconut Grove.

In addition to the time we spent together in San Francisco, my father and I would travel occasionally to Los Angeles on the Sunset Limited passenger train to visit my paternal grandparents. The return trip was always the best part. That's when we feasted, just like Grandpa used to do, on Grandma's veal-cutlet sandwiches. Grandma would wait for a leg of veal to thaw to just the right point where she could cut and keep intact a bunch of slivers that were thin like paper. Then she dipped each one into her special bread crumbs, mixed with garlic and oil, and fried them for barely a minute at low heat on her wonderful gas stove. Thin and tender, the sandwiches would virtually melt in your mouth.

Before one of our excursions to L.A., my father heard that popular pianist and bandleader, Vincent Lopez,[3] was auditioning singers for an extended engagement at the Coconut Grove, a room in the Ambassador Hotel on Wilshire Boulevard. Dad was tempted to have me tryout but hesitated because of my age. As he thought about it, though, he figured it was worth a shot. After all, gussied up I looked like an eligible voter and, since the audition was in the ballroom of a first-class hotel where food was served, there likely wouldn't be an age limit anyway. So, we pressed forward only to learn when we arrived that the club management was searching for a new sensation, a young unknown prodigy to sing with the Lopez band! Suddenly it appeared that my school-kid stature would actually answer their ad!

That was my first real shot at the big time and I was excited! My excitement dipped when we walked into the Coconut Grove. The size of the ballroom intimidated me and it was so cold my goosebumps doubled. The clincher was when I heard Lopez's band: It didn't swing. To me, it was a "Mickey Mouse" band, and I couldn't imagine how I would fit in, anyway, anyhow. I wanted to back out, but my father wouldn't hear of it, so after being introduced to some bigwigs, I sang a trial run with the band in front of an early afternoon crowd. Much to my chagrin, I won the audition and got the job, but it was an empty triumph.

We stayed with my grandparents and I started doing two shows a night, but it didn't take long before the club owners got suspicious. Based on my physical endowments, they had assumed I was around seventeen or eighteen. When they found out I was twelve there were shrieks of "oh, God, no!" Management was looking for a young protégé, but not *that* young. With preteen me they would have had child labor laws down on their heads.

I had mixed emotions when I got booted. Not because I was rejected—I was almost happy to leave that lame band—but it all happened so fast my world was turned topsy-turvy. I remember sitting on the bandstand overwhelmed by the commotion. One minute I was a big hit and the next I was out. My brief time with Lopez left a sour taste in my mouth about the music business; I thought everybody was phony and I didn't trust anybody. I took some consolation in my grandmother's sandwich on the way home.

In 1941, home was still the rental house on Delaware Street in Berkeley. Mom and I had moved there two years before, secure in the knowledge that Ed Jensen was serving a long sentence behind bars. We lived there for two more years, except for one brief but ghastly interruption. Our living room had a large, square picture window at street level, and since we couldn't afford curtains our privacy was sacrificed to the weekly budget.

One evening after dark I was sitting alone in that room doing my homework. Deep in a book, I suddenly felt a presence. I looked up, glanced out the window and saw a figure dimly defined by street lighting moving toward the house. It took a moment to register, but as his face got close to the window I recognized Ed Jensen, standing there staring at me! The evil look in his eyes seemed to say, "Here I am, the big boogeyman, and I'll never go away. You'll never be safe." He made no attempt to come in; he didn't even move, but I froze. I just froze! My heart in my throat, I whimpered, "Mom, Mom, Mom, Mom." Somehow she heard me, rushed in, took one look, and yelled, "You son of a bitch, get away from here!" When she picked up the phone he split. Moments later the police came but they couldn't find him. He had disappeared.

I never learned how that happened. If Momma got an answer she didn't tell me; I was just a kid. Jensen showing up like that was creepy, that much I knew, and for Momma it was a blatant threat. Worried that Ed would return to exact his revenge, she filed a restraining order, and while waiting for it to take effect, we moved temporarily to a rooming house kitty-corner to and up a few blocks from our rental place.

The rooming house was convenient: close enough so we didn't have to move all our things but far enough, we hoped, to throw Jensen off the track. Two weeks later the coast seemed clear so we doubled back to Delaware Street. Our fear of impending doom gradually eased, although for months after I kept where we lived a secret. Maybe that worked because I never saw Ed Jensen again. At least in daylight. My sleep was haunted by his ghost waiting in pitch-black closets or lurking in shadows with giant rats.

The Tiptons

My maternal grandmother, Betty Louise Clemmons, was of Irish descent; she bragged that she was a first cousin to Samuel Clemens, or Mark Twain, and it became part of our family mythology. Grandpa Tipton was a full-blooded Cherokee Native American. His birth name was "Running Bear." I remember his advice to me as a little girl: "Make sure you are three silent steps ahead of your enemy!" My daughter, Deborah, recalls that the first time she visited her great-grandfather in Eureka, California, he "had a real tepee pitched in the back yard where he slept at night by a small stream" and he taught her how to whittle a stick to spear trout and "cook it the Cherokee way."

My maternal grandparents met in the Great Smoky Mountains of Tennessee, outside of Knoxville. Before their wedding could take place, my grandfather had to change his name. Her people wouldn't accept a marriage license with the name "Running Bear," so he adopted the fully anglicized, John Henry Tipton. Tipton was a very common name at that time in the hills—like Smith and Jones these days—and it went comfortably with Clemmons.

My grandparents stayed in the Smokies for a few years after their marriage, and Grandpa Tipton took a job as a train brakeman working the cabooses in Tennessee. When he was transferred, the Tipton clan wound up in California.

Grandma Tipton was an unschooled housewife and a study in contrasts: she could be kind and easygoing with a glint of devilment in her eye. She was also a crier, a whining "nobody-loves-me type." I brought out her even-tempered side so we got along fine. I never gave her any flack and she didn't want to deal with any from me; she had four sons and they were trouble enough. Grandma Tipton, like Grandma Giaimo was a good cook, but she was strictly Tennessean: fried chicken that was out of this world, biscuits and gravy, flapjacks, dandelion greens, cornbread. The best of Appalachian cuisine.

I didn't see much of Grandpa Tipton, but whenever I did bump into him he was such a large, poker-faced mystery he frightened me. My jitters around Grandpa Tipton were worse when I tempted fate. Like the time my Aunt Mary and I snuck some cigarettes and hid behind the house to smoke. Grandpa Tipton got a whiff and when we saw him bearing down on us we ran like hell. He quickly caught Mary, and, boy, she got it good, but he couldn't find me, down low behind a couch. He tried to coax me out. In his Indian-inflected speech and an unruffled tone he repeated, "Doddie, Doddie, where are you?" Well, that confused me: I was afraid of getting spanked and yet I felt I should show him respect. After a few minutes I gave in. "Here I is, Grandpa," I said meekly and unwittingly dodged a bullet. Momma said Grandpa Tipton laughed so hard and was so touched by my innocence he couldn't whip me.

Grandma and Grandpa Tipton had ten children. Only seven survived childhood: four sons and three daughters (including Momma and Aunt Mary). Since Grandma Tipton kept having babies, and since Grandpa Tipton was gone most of the time on a caboose, it fell to my mother as the eldest to help my grandmother by riding herd full-time over her brothers and sisters. My mother never talked much about her early years except to bitch about her siblings. The entire brood ran to her with their problems so Momma had to be the family referee. When my hot-looking, drummer Daddy came to town it didn't take much wooing to convince her to leave all that behind.

The few times I saw my aunts and uncles on the Tipton side was when we were kids, and since we were all about the same age I must confess that calling them either "uncle" or "aunt" was just a formality. The youngest boy, my "Uncle" Jackie, was three years my junior; I bought him his first pair of long pants. I recall an extended visit with the Tipton family shortly after I was raped by Ed Jensen. To keep our sanity, Mother and I moved out of the Berkeley house and stayed for a time with her parents. The memories I've retained of that family circus are sketchy but indelible since my uncles could be rowdy, even nasty, and I was a convenient patsy.

Like the morning the boys hatched the bright idea of using the family's wood-burning stove—the kind that had a cast-iron holder on top that you'd lift off to put the wood in—as a prop to scare me. Grandma had a regular stove, too, so this wood stove didn't see much use. As luck would have it, though, on that fateful morning it had been going most of the night before and was red hot. My uncles, assuming the stove was cold, grabbed me as soon as I entered the kitchen in my flimsy nightdress and held me fanny down on that scorching stovetop. I howled and they laughed. They thought I panicked because I was afraid of that big, ugly stove, and by the time they let me scramble off, my ass was burned really bad.

The Tipton family lived an isolated existence in the hills of Tennessee. Half of the Tiptons didn't finish high school and none of them went to college. Mother was one who had no formal education. Any learning she got was self-taught and that bent her family's nose out of joint. They thought her, "Oh, so smart, oh, so uppity" because she read a lot, consuming books one right after the other and traveling in her imagination across time and space.

Mother certainly didn't want to be ignorant; dignity and self respect were essential to her. As a young adult she shed the Tennessee twang in her speaking voice, and she liked to forget that she was half Cherokee because of the prejudice against Indians who were considered below Appalachian hillbillies. During the war, Momma volunteered as a nurse's aide at a Veterans Hospital and got training similar to the Red Cross. She worked to broaden her horizons while narrow interests stunted the rest of the Tiptons. Even as a little girl, I could see how different she was from the rest of them.

Momma was an amazing woman in many ways, although she could be incredibly naive about worldly things. Like when she was pregnant with me she worried how in the world I would be born because she thought my body was spread through hers, that my arms and legs were in her arms and legs! Then there was her relationship with men. In the hills, Momma had no real experience with the opposite sex, which left her wide open to male vultures. The proof is that if she'd had any common sense about men she wouldn't have married my father!

Just like me, my mother wanted to be a dancer, but having a baby so young meant she never had the chance to spread her wings and make that dream come true. Then when my father dumped us at my grandparents' house to go on the road, she had to contend by herself with my paternal grandmother who hated her and wanted her gone! Fortunately, my Aunt Sally stepped in. She befriended Momma and helped her win at least a taste of her ambition. Sally, who loved to dance herself, got Momma out of the house, into clubs, and back into social dancing.

That mission accomplished, Aunt Sally started taking my mother to dance studios, and on one of those occasions auditions were being held. However it happened, Momma impressed the right people and got an offer to go with the DeMarcos,[1] a nationally known exhibition ballroom dance team, but it wasn't to be. She was a very pretty lady who really could dance, but with me in tow taking the offer was out of the question.

Momma knew how I felt about music—with both my parents in love with music, my genes had no choice—and since she was deprived of a career on stage she didn't want to be the one to stand in my way. I will always be grateful that she didn't get jealous when I took bus rides to the big-city clubs and started on a path to do all the things she would have loved to have done in her life. Momma was bigger than that: she defied her family's wrath to encourage me. Her trust in me to do the right thing meant a lot.

The Eight-Day Clock

In September 1942, the war had been raging for ten months, I turned thirteen, and Mom and Pinky, her girlfriend from Woolworth's, found diversion going to Marine Hall dances in San Francisco and sometimes Oakland. One of those evenings, Mom met a wonderful Marine named Sammy Sampson. She finally hit the "jackpot" with a beau and the attraction was mutual. Mom and I had always been poor, but all that changed when Sammy came into our lives. He was from a wealthy Boston family, but it wasn't the money that made us happy. It was Sam. We just loved him, and I swear there was a halo around that man's head as if he'd come from heaven.

Sammy moved in with us on Delaware Street, and for the next year Momma was laughing and smiling all the time. I never saw her that happy again, ever. Ever! Sammy opened up a fairyland for Mom and me, took us places we'd never seen and introduced us to things we'd never done. The only catch in those carefree days was the highfalutin attitude of Sammy's upper-crust Boston family. They didn't like my mother at all and they made no bones about it. To them she was trash and that insult didn't sit well with Momma; she was a proud woman. The chutzpa really hit the fan when Sammy's mother demanded to know about my mother's background, where she came from. When Sammy told her Tennessee, she nearly busted a blood vessel: Tennessee?!!!

After his mother's put-down, Momma had very little patience with her. The two never met, and the one time my mother talked to Sammy's Mom on the phone she was probably too aggressive in her tone because Momma didn't kowtow to anybody. For his part, Sammy just ignored the objections of his family; he told us, "We don't need their money." Not long after, Sammy and Mom decided to get married. I was thrilled and began planning what to take on their honeymoon. I went along because Mom didn't want to leave me with any of her relatives.

We honeymooned in San Diego where Sam was stationed in the Marine Corps. I got to see a lot of San Diego, and I remember one evening in particular when we went to the Grand Hotel for dinner and a Marine dance. After we finished eating, I was sitting quietly in my finery looking much older than I was, when a seventeen-year-old Marine recruit appeared at our table. "Excuse me, Sir," he said to Sammy, "may I ask your daughter to dance?" Sammy, looking slightly bemused, replied, "I'm sorry, son, but she's only thirteen." Shocked, and obviously a soldier from Brooklyn, he spluttered, "thoiteen?!! and walked away crestfallen.

The honeymoon was wonderful, but back home our feet touched ground because Sammy's orders to Guadalcanal were waiting in the mail. After Sammy was shipped overseas it was just Momma and me again on Delaware Street. One of the few prized possessions we had in our modest house was a charming eight-day clock that sat prominently on the mantel. Sammy had made a regular practice of winding that clock so in his absence we took over the ritual. Every eighth day we wound that clock.

One day, several months into Sammy's tour, my mother walked into the living room and said, "The clock is slow." Actually, the clock had stopped, and the instant we realized it the phone rang and Momma got the news that Sammy had been killed in action. The day that clock stopped was the day that Sam died. His death hit my mother so hard. It hit me hard, too, but not like her. They had only one year together. It saddened me that after all she'd been through, the love of her life was so abruptly and brutally extinguished.

When I graduated from middle school, my mother and I moved north from Berkeley to Albany, but the new surroundings didn't lift my mother's spirits. Gloom was just as thick in our new home, and her depression became my depression. I still visited my father in San Francisco on weekends, but seeking solace in music wasn't an option for me during the school week because my mother wasn't into playing records and I was afraid to put on the radio. Despondent, I turned to cigarettes, three packs a day. I remember smoking "Spuds," a mentholated substitute for the real cigarettes that were shipped to the boys at war.

Our new place was just a couple of blocks over the line that divides Albany from El Cerrito so I enrolled for the ninth grade at nearby El Cerrito High. In contrast to my excellent record in the convent, I was a "C" student my first two years in high school. Most of the subjects just didn't interest me. As in junior high, though, I was into sports, once again playing forward in basketball and pitching for the El Cerrito High girls' softball team.

Since I was an indifferent student, my mother made me take typing. I'm glad she did. Typing was a physical thrill. The rhythm of typing came so naturally to me that I got straight A's in that course. I could do 72 words a minute on an old standard typewriter and that was very fast. My mother also insisted I take a business course in high school. She could see that I was on a path to become a musician and she wanted to be sure I had some kind of practical training to rely on if I fell on hard times.

My father, on the other hand, always advised against the deceptive security of a day job. After I got out of school and turned professional full-time in the music business, he was behind me 100 percent. Until, that is, I ran into the kind of rough patch my mother had worried about. When I told him, "I'm going to try and get a day job," he was adamant in his disapproval. "Don't do it! If you get a day gig you'll be corrupted; you'll get caught in that money trap and you won't ever get back to your music, you'll never have your dreams come true."

The reason he thought that way was because of my "Uncle" Emo, who was really Grandfather Giaimo's uncle. Uncle Emo had a grocery store and my father was forced for a time to abandon his music and work in that store. He hated every moment of it so he was trying to save me from a similar fate. And he succeeded: My whole life I've worked less than a year in the daytime! My karma has been kind and I've most often found a way to pay the bills. Like the time I was weighed down with worries before a gig because I was so broke I didn't know how I was going to cover my rent. Well, the room was packed and at the end of the evening waves of people came up to the bandstand to tell me how happy I'd made them. Those good wishes translated into $82 apiece in tips for my trio! So, in one night, as my father used to tell me, the phone can ring and change your whole life as a musician. If you have an eight-to-five there's no chance.

The despair in my home life made escape on the weekends necessary as never before. I took in more and more of the diverse Bay Area music scene, and, despite the discouraging Vincent Lopez episode, I hadn't lost my ambition to be a singer. Then, as if it were all planned, opportunities started to arrive. Now, it didn't hurt that I was Chuck Giaimo's daughter and had on occasion sung with my father's band during rehearsals in front of cream-of-the-crop San Francisco musicians. So, my name quickly circulated as a new singer in the city, and before long I was a hot commodity, hired for private parties and weddings, and when I wasn't working I was sitting in with somebody.

Like the times I sat in and sang with the Eastman Trio, fronted by clarinetist Teddy Eastman. I knew all three of the guys: Eastman, his bassist, and his accordion player, Gus DeWorth, who jammed with the finesse of a jazz pianist—there was never anybody like him. The Eastman Trio worked at the Tahitian Hut in Oakland, which was around the corner from the Hula Shack where my father sometimes played. Whenever he was booked at the same time I was sitting in, I would go back and forth between stages.

At the Hula Shack my father seated me right next to him on a high-rise stage where I watched and listened to everything he did. When I heard a certain sound he made on the drums, I could see immediately how he got it. Everything he did at the drums made sense to me: When to use the tom-toms, when to use the mallets, how he changed the color of the music. As I said earlier, I wasn't aware that all this was taking root in my DNA because my focus was on being a singer, but it's clear to me now that magical things were happening when I shadowed my father at countless sessions around the city. The constant attention to music every day erased any remaining doubts I might have had about my future professional direction. I knew then that music was for me. That's what I had to do. Since then, it's always been music!

At that point in my life, singing was still at the center of my ambition. My father couldn't miss how serious I was, and since he was the one who had urged me at age ten to give up dancing and be a singer, it was only right and natural that he arrange some professional instruction for me. The vocal coach he chose didn't teach me how to sing; he just honed my skills. At my first lesson he told me to put my hand on my stomach and feel the muscles moving when I talked. He wanted those same muscles going when I sang. His theory was that singing should be as natural as speaking, and because I breathed right when I talked, he said I should talk when I was singing and not worry about the diaphragm.

A bonus was that by breathing right I could tell the story better. So, he was the first one to school me about phrasing and how to divide a tune without separating the syllables of words, something that Fred Astaire knew so well. Astaire, who didn't have much of a voice, sang with clipped phrasing, as if he, too, was speaking the words. His example gave me confidence as I developed my style because, like him, I didn't have the chops to hold long notes. Gradually, because of the way I altered phrase lengths to benefit the story, my delivery grew more personal.

I also recall the colorful advice my vocal coach gave me about hitting high notes. He explained that when a high part in a song was coming up, I should make believe that the highest note is going to come out of the top of my head; that I should reach for the top of my head with my throat. After about a year my studies with him ended, and so did my formal education as a singer.

Although I was appearing a lot in the city as a vocalist, I had not, by a long shot, retired my dancing shoes. At about age fourteen, I met Lou Ghillioni who was two or three years older than I was and already out of high school. He wasn't my boyfriend but we hit it off because we both loved to dance. On Friday or Saturday nights Lou and I would go to Sweet's Ballroom, the East Bay home of the big bands, and dance to whatever famous swing unit was playing: Count Basie, Gene Krupa, Artie Shaw, Tommy Dorsey, or Harry James. Lou and I were in the same "pocket" all the time so dancing with him was purely for pleasure. My competitive juices as a hoofer, the side of my nature that got me Eleanor Powell's dancing shoes, didn't shift into high gear until I met the first real love of my life in a storybook high-school romance.

Polio

Meanwhile, there was romantic light at the end of the tunnel for my widowed mother. Pinky's boyfriend, the Marine at Momma's party who suffered through my briny birthday cake, had a good buddy in the corps, Bob Musselman. Musselman had the big stripes: He was a staff sergeant who trained cadets for commissioned posts. Pinky and her steady introduced Bob to my Mom and that was it for him. Momma wasn't so quick on the trigger. She was lonely, but they had nothing in common; she was from mountain people, and he had a very conservative upbringing in Valparaiso, Indiana.

Bob really had to work at it. In the end, though, Momma recognized that Bob was a good man, that he wouldn't be chasing skirts on her like most service men, so finally she surrendered and they married in 1943 when I was fourteen. Although it was always clear to me that he loved her more than she loved him, their marriage (her fourth) lasted until her death in 1982.

I was a tough sell, too, but my hard-nosed attitude gradually softened as Bob's affection for my mother played out in front of me. What clinched it was one incident in particular that got me to see Bob in a new light.

Although I had made weekend visits to my father for several years, my mother, still smarting from the kidnapping, would not allow him reciprocal privileges to visit at her house. Each passing year the pressure mounted as my father got more insistent about visiting and I grew increasingly tired of having to choose between parents for the holidays. The stalemate seemed interminable. Until Bob broke the ice. Secretly, I think my mother was curious to see if Dad had changed, but it took Bob to declare a peace offering: "Let's have Chuck come here for Thanksgiving!"

I bonded fully with my stepdad on the road. Bob had mustered out from the Marines to be with Momma and me, and he took a job driving big rigs hauling produce. On at least two occasions, I made runs with him from Oakland, over the Donner Pass, to Bakersfield or Los Angeles. Touring long stretches of highway was brand new to me and it piqued my interest in getting behind the wheel. So, at fourteen, my stepdad taught me how to drive, and I remembered him fondly years later whenever I had to handle small packed cars driving in blizzards to far-flung gigs.

Back at El Cerrito High, I may not have been popular with the girls but I sure was with the guys. I dated some of them, but they were lame—corny as hell with no finesse, nothing. They just wanted to get into a chick's pants. Maybe a grain of salt is in order because my opinion of boys at the time was probably warped by being raped at ten. Another tip-off about my frame of mind was that as soon as I would get a boy to like me I'd drop him. That was a common response when girls were sexually abused at a young age, or so I was told years later by my "head doctor." As I understood it, part of me deep inside was trying to get even for what I had suffered at the hands of Ed Jensen.

All that changed when I met a boy who was different, one who had respect for me. His name was Harry Bossi. Harry was Italian, he was a star basketball player, and he was gorgeous without knowing it. A strong, silent, but actually very shy type that other girls swooned over. Little by little as we became friends I noticed how guarded he was and how he didn't want commitment of any kind. So, I took it slow, launching a plan I had learned from somewhere that if you want a guy you get in good with his best friend. Enter Poncho.

Poncho was from the street and Harry wasn't, so Poncho, knowing what a beautiful soul Harry had, protected his naive friend. When a girl approached Harry wiggling her tail Poncho acted as the referee, telling the girl to "Get lost!" and telling Harry, "No, no, not her, you don't want anything to do with her, Harry!" When Poncho met me he changed his tune: "Now, that's her! She's the one, Harry!" Evidently, Harry felt the same way because of all the girls that wanted him, he picked me.

Poncho was in my corner from the first, but dancing cemented our friendship. Poncho loved to jitterbug and I was a jitterbugging fool. The three of us would go to school dances. Even though Harry didn't dance, knowing how badly I wanted to go he'd sit at a table and smile as Poncho and I danced and danced. Harry had no reason to be jealous. He was sure I was in love with him, and besides, Poncho, who was a true friend, never once made a move on me. I still danced at Sweets with Lou Ghillioni on weekends, but during the week and on special weekend occasions, like at school socials and proms, Poncho and I would steal the spotlight, sealing our reputations at El Cerrito High as the "Jitterbug King and Queen."

The chemistry between Harry and me was intense. We'd neck in his car and when it got too hot and heavy, Harry would be a gentleman and tell me, "Dottie, cool it!" He was mindful about how young we were and I loved him all the more for it. Even though Harry and I were an item throughout high school there were only a few times when I was in his house. That was because his mother hated me. She was a very jealous Italian mother and I was a threat, and it didn't help that I was a nightclub singer who evidently associated with the lowlife.

My mother, on the other hand, was very fond of Harry and that worked to my advantage when in my senior year Harry and I couldn't wait any longer and we made love. It was the first and only time we had sex. He was so gentle, he opened me like a flower. My mom was unfazed and supportive the next morning, telling me, "You're not a girl anymore, you're a woman and the rules have changed. From now on be selective and have respect for yourself." Those indelible words have stayed with me throughout my life.

During high school, one of my singing gigs around the Bay Area was with the Howard Fredericks band. When I was fifteen, Howard offered me a chance to go on the road in the summer, but Mother nixed the idea, insisting I get my diploma first. That was all the motivation I needed; I went back to cracking the books to be sure to graduate and join Fredericks the following summer. But, as per usual in my life, there was a snag in my straight-ahead and this time it was a big one.

Shortly before graduation, when I would be "free-free-free" to get on with my music, I did something I had never ever done before: I ditched school for a day and went swimming in a Berkeley lake with some of the gang. Two days later I was running a relay in gym class and my legs gave out; I fell down and couldn't stand up. Rushed to a hospital in Berkeley, the diagnosis was polio!

To confirm the diagnosis doctors gave me a spinal, which meant drawing out a sample of cerebrospinal fluid to check for the virus. It came up negative, so the test was repeated. The result was inconclusive so more spinals were drawn, eventually eight in all, but because the results went back and forth between negative and positive, they were no help. The doctors knew I had polio but they couldn't figure out why the tests weren't consistent. It was a new disease at that time—way before Dr. Salk—and the doctors were stymied. I thought my life was over, and as if more alarm bells were needed, when they wheeled me into the isolation ward and I looked through a window into the room next to mine, I saw the body of a young girl. Her skin was blue and she was bent in two; she had just died of spinal meningitis. I thought for sure that would be my fate, too, so I "stuffed that down"—I buried it inside me. To make matters worse, images of Aunt Toni flooded my thoughts.

Aunt Toni was also on the minds of my Sicilian grandparents. Years before, when Toni was diagnosed with polio, my grandparents had spent thousands of dollars trying to find a cure. Now, faced with the prospect of their granddaughter crippled by the same disease, they covered the cost for trial injections of an experimental serum at something like a thousand dollars a shot. The second one took!

With the help of the serum, the doctors were able to catch the polio in the early stages before it settled in. The lead doctor told my mother the good news that I was cured, but I didn't believe it. The successive shocks that had hammered me in the hospital broke my spirit, so although I had recovered physically and was capable of walking, psychosomatic fear took over and convinced me that I was going to wind up like Aunt Toni.

Looking back, my emotional collapse boggles me because I had that much-cherished gig waiting for me with Howard Fredericks at Guerneville River Park, about seventy-five miles north of San Francisco. It was going to be my first official chance to sing with a big band, and Howard Frederick was the band to be with. He had the best musicians, and to be hired for the summer, to be singing every night with that band, amounted to a real coup. I was devastated that the job was lost.

A crack of light penetrated the dark before I was discharged. One of the doctors told my mother that if someone helped me get around for a few weeks he was sure I would overcome my stress-induced mental barrier against walking. That advice inspired Momma, God bless her. She called and explained the situation to Howard Fredericks, and, God bless him, too, he assured Momma they'd find a way at the Park to get me from the cabin to the bandstand for each of my performances.

Incredible as it may sound, good karmic strings continued to be strummed because the boy singer on the band was none other than my Sweet's Ballroom dancing partner, Lou Ghillioni! God love his heart, Lou carried me every night and sat me in a chair in front of the microphone stand. When it came time for me to sing, I held onto the mike and pulled myself up. By summer's end, and as the Fredericks gig came to a close, the doctor's prediction came true: I regained full use of my legs!

I was lucky. Instead of polio, all I had was a little scar on my leg and I was back to swimming, playing tennis, and jitterbugging to my heart's content. Now I was truly ready for the road!

Jail Bait

When I got back to the Bay Area from Guerneville I went almost immediately into rehearsals as a vocalist with Nick Esposito's band. Nick Esposito was well respected in San Francisco. He wrote a lot of his own music, was very advanced, and by the early 1950s he was a recognized figure on jazz guitar. His biggest hit, "Empty Ballroom Blues"[1] was released in 1946 on the Pacific Records label in Berkeley.[2]

When I joined Nick he had a new sextet that included Claude Gilroy on tenor, Buddy Motsinger at the piano (Buddy was replaced a couple years later by John Marabuto), Ralph Pena at the bass, and John Markham (who later worked with Charlie Barnet and Benny Goodman) played drums. That band really swung, and in keeping with this new adventure for me as the vocalist in front of a progressive modern jazz combo—and also because I figured Giaimo was too hard to pronounce—I started calling myself "Dottie Grae." I picked the spelling *Grae* instead of the more conventional "Gray" because I wanted it to be original.

Hiring a vocalist was not Nick's first choice for his new group. He had actually written arrangements that included a second horn, but because he didn't have the money to cover it, he and Claude Gilroy got the idea to get me as a cheaper substitute to sing what in essence was a horn part. So, when I came on board, my job was to sing notes not words. Instead of words, I used vowels or consonants to hit the notes.

Nick called this style *phonetics*. The difference between scatting and phonetics is that scatting is off the top of your head, you spontaneously pick your own notes off the chord that you're hearing and then you improvise your own melody from that. With phonetics, Nick would write in my part just like for a horn; he would write out a definite melody line and I couldn't take any liberties with the notes. I sang the lead and learned how to blend with the harmonies laid down in Nick's charts.

It was gutsy of me to take on Nick Esposito's charts since I had sung lead in a group only once before, and that was the result of pure happenstance during a Sunset Limited trip to Los Angeles to visit the grandparents. One afternoon I stopped in at the musician's union and bumped into the drummer for the Mel-Tones (a vocal quintet formed by jazz singer, Mel Torme). He knew that I sang, so after visiting a bit he invited me that afternoon to watch the Mel-Tones rehearse for a radio show. I no sooner entered the hall to listen from the sidelines when they recruited me as a sub for one of the singers who had taken ill! That singer just happened to be the lead, and thank God for that because I couldn't harmonize. Someone singing the lead and me singing second does not come easily to me at all. I'm definitely a top-of-the-head-note lead singer.

Another complication with Nick's charts was that I had never learned to read music! Dad could read anything but he didn't encourage me to learn. When I came up it wasn't expected that singers could read. Ordinarily the only things they needed to know were the key and the tempo they wanted for a song, but doing phonetics with Nick Esposito wasn't by any stretch an ordinary singing gig. What helped me master his arrangements was my ability to listen and my music memory. For years my father had played me records of great singers—Ella Fitzgerald, Peggy Lee, Anita O'Day—and I memorized them, boom, boom, boom. It was easy. So, by the time Esposito's band finished going over and over a piece during rehearsals I'd have learned my part completely.

I was sixteen when Nick hired me in 1945 so before we went on the road he had to take out guardianship papers on me. That way he could legally travel across state lines with a minor and I could work the clubs. As my guardian, Nick was personally responsible for me, a role he took very seriously because he wasn't blind to my image as a bit of a "Lolita."

That image was only enhanced when, at seventeen, I returned to Romaine's studio for a modeling job. Most of the photographs Romaine took were advertising shots that I was able to exploit for my budding career, including the only one I still have, which is a head shot with me as a platinum blonde. But for one of the shoots, I wore a gown that dropped off the shoulder showing the top of my bosom. That picture turned up in a "girlie" magazine. It was quickly squelched because I was so young, but that episode confirmed for Nick the jeopardy I represented. As an underaged girl who looked like a glamorous twenty-something starlet, I was the very definition of "jail bait."

Nick was like the father in his band, so with my welfare in mind he tried his best to educate me about how some men, who would see me in the clubs and restaurants where we worked, were "jail baiters." To protect me on the road, Nick kept the reins tight. At each gig he would personally escort me to my hotel room after our sets were finished, check that I had locked my door, and warn me not to unlock it if some man started talking to me from the other side. Nick didn't have to put too fine a point on that warning!

Nick's band worked pretty steady, and it wasn't just one-nighters. We'd appear for two weeks—gigs didn't last longer than that as a rule—and then move someplace else. On a typical evening in the clubs we'd do two shows, an hour-and-a-half each. I'd sing at least four conventional songs—songs with words—followed by an instrumental by the boys, and then I'd do two or three numbers singing phonetics with the band.

We made bigger money out of town. So, after working the Bay Area in 1946, we toured the Midwest. On our return trip we drove through a bunch of little stopover towns in Idaho. By that time I had become, by default, the designated driver for the band. Nick couldn't do it because he suffered from migraine headaches, and the rest of the guys were usually too drunk or too stoned to get behind the wheel. I was elected, and I was a very good driver, putting to use what my stepdad had taught me.

Driving on the back roads outside Boise, I ran a gauntlet of sorts that seared in my mind an unforgettable series of images, traumatic and darkly absurd at the same time. It all started shortly after sundown as we sped along a vast empty landscape. Suddenly I heard a "bump!" Then another and another, until, in the headlights, I could see—"oh, my God! . . . oh, my God!"—bunches of baby jackrabbits attracted by the lights jumping up and slamming into the front of the car! In disbelief that I was killing all those baby rabbits, I slowed way down and tried to dodge them. Finally, John Markham said, "You can't slow down for every one, you've got to plow right through them." Taking deep breaths, that's just what I did. Oh, my God—"bump, bump, bump"—I died a thousand deaths.

That wasn't all that rattled me as we traveled between gigs. Listening to the guys "lama, lama, lama"[3] about women was gross. Nick didn't take part in the chatter, but some of the other band members gave me an earful. I learned the truth and nothing but the truth about what men really thought about the ladies.

Cloaked in shadow driving that band bus, I was all but invisible but wide awake and listening; my male counterparts had no idea how closely I was paying attention! Of course, my father's stories in the Padre Hotel had started my education about relations between the sexes, and I had witnessed and endured undiluted ugliness in my personal life, but this was yet another tutorial about how men think. Listening to my bandmates I was surprised at how such demeaning vulgarity was so casually expressed.

One of them would mention a girl they all knew and how much of a good looker she was, and another would chime in about do's and don't's when you fuck her. It was mean, it was graphic, and it was lewd, like talk about some girl's panties—"she has dirty pants." Lord knows I never thought that men talked quite that way. They were almost laughable, blathering for hours like a bunch of little old ladies gossiping.

Listening to the men in Esposito's band may have helped me understand the "guys' point of view," but I lost respect for them personally. Not as musicians—I never lost respect for them as musicians, because that was the only time I felt they told the truth. On a personal level, I said to myself, "You know, Dottie, you don't have to get involved with these guys," and I crossed them out mentally, even if they flirted with me. But I was flirty anyway. My attitude was happy and men were attracted to that. It was a natural happiness with me because I was playing music.

TD&L

At seventeen I fell in love with a bouncer. He worked at the original Facks, a San Francisco jazz club on Bush and Grant, where Nick's group was the house band. In his early twenties, my bouncer was "tall, dark, and lethal"— "TD&L." I got the "tall and dark" parts right away; the lethal part showed up a little later when I realized what a whopper of a bad move I had made.

I fell for all the wrong reasons. Aside from his looks, "TD&L" had a big Cadillac, he had his own booth at Enrico's Cafe, a San Francisco haunt that was featured decades later in the movie, "Bullitt," and he hung out with North Beach Sicilians, sons of the owners of bars and restaurants on Columbus Avenue, which was Little Italy in San Francisco. Clearly, I was still young enough to be attracted by that sort of razzle-dazzle, and I was especially vulnerable because at the time I wasn't thinking I was worth that much. I guess that's why I picked the bad boys, because their swagger made me feel that I was important, too.

This bouncer guy had everything going for him, he could have had any-body. And he liked me? It was hard to believe. True, I wasn't bad-looking—at 106 pounds with a good figure I was a little cutie—but despite the allure I projected in Romaine's photos, I was no bombshell. Except to TD&L; when he saw me he liked me right away. Part of it was definitely a sexual attraction. I also figured it had something to do with my local celebrity. Some of his kicks were that I was performing in one of the best West Coast jazz clubs, and that I was good enough to be respected as a musician. So, I guess I sort of was somebody, and that to him was seductive. As people came in the club he would brag in his Italian dialect, "She's a-mine." Back then I thought that was a compliment!

TD&L took me once or twice to his house. He lived with his mother, a little old Sicilian lady who didn't like me at all. I was the first girl he'd brought home so his mother assumed our relationship was serious and that I was about to steal her son away. I remember watching him iron his shirt collars with a steam iron. His mother ironed his shirts but not the collars; he did touch ups on them to make sure the collars were starched just right and would roll properly so they lifted and didn't just lay flat. Having a high collar on the neck was very important to Italian men of that era.

All in all, he was immaculate when he dressed and that obsessiveness carried over to our relationship. We were together for only six months but it seemed like forever because in pretty short order he started to scare me to death. I had no idea somebody could switch on a personality and then instantly switch another way. He was such a "Jekyll and Hyde" it made me wonder if he was seriously mentally ill.

He got crazy possessive, worried that somebody was going to take me. Whenever I went out, say to a show, he had some of his gang tail me to make sure I went where I said I was going, and when I got back he'd quiz me about what I saw. It got to be a nightmare; doubly so because despite his bizarre behavior I was still starry-eyed about him. My feelings were in such conflict that when he told me, "I want you to take a ride with my brother and do what he says," I wasn't strong enough to resist.

Little did I know what his twisted mind had concocted: TD&L planned to pimp me for money! My man was trying to make me into a call girl and in the end I agreed to it! He told me there was nothing wrong with it, but I had no idea. Finally, I talked myself into it. I told myself it was a sophisticated thing to do, like in movies I'd seen, and that I'd do it and it wouldn't mean anything to me. My God, I sometimes wonder why I even considered it, but the truth is I wanted to please TD&L because I was afraid of him. He intimidated me, like some of the men in my family did at that time in my life.

One of them was my Sicilian grandfather. He had such an irritable disposition that you never knew when he'd explode. He slapped me on occasion, like TD&L did, so I always tried to please him, too. I was also afraid of my dad. He hit me a few times (and just like with my grandfather, I never knew what I did wrong), so even the threat of courting my father's displeasure was something I wanted to avoid at all costs. With both my grandfather and my father, I learned how to get around tempers, how to see trouble coming, how to be humble pie, but still keep my confidence. A happy medium; the balance of a Libra.

Eventually, I developed an aversion to groveling. That's why, when I became a mature adult, if anybody, male or female, tried to control me, tried to dictate to me or show me how irritable they could be because I wasn't doing what they wanted, then, boy, I'd get fierce. It all came from feeling so uneasy and having to be so on guard when I was younger.

Pimping me out as a "working girl" was a snap for TD&L. His younger brother was a pimp who had his own cathouse! His brother was also a regular at Facks. One night, not long after I was introduced to him, I told his brother that I was ready to give it a try at his brothel, so he drove me to a building that was a combination Japanese laundry and mahjong parlor. We used the back door. The first room we entered was dimly lit, quiet and scary. The heat was oppressive and as my eyes adjusted I saw a few sweaty men playing mahjong. As we crossed the room I was so afraid that I couldn't feel my feet touch the floor and yet I was trying to keep up the pretense of being so sophisticated.

Deep in the building I met some of the whores. They huddled around to welcome me, like Streets of Paris strippers used to do, and then, along with TD&L's brother, they led me into a private room to meet the Madam. After giving me the once-over, the Madam seemed a bit uneasy. Turning to the brother, she was candid: "I don't think so. I don't think this is going to work." Even though I had been doing my best to act like I could pull it off, I'm sure she could see right through me, but TD&L's brother insisted. Then he returned to the parking lot and the Madam pushed me into a small room filled with beds and curtains. A guy was standing off to one side, waiting; he was short, fat, ugly, and glistening with sweat. The Madam yelled to him, "here, this one's yours" and promptly left.

It was so disgusting I couldn't believe it. Impatient for some action, the guy barked, "Get undressed!" Once I stripped, he ordered, "Get down there!" and pointed to his "thing," for me to give him head. I tried to do it, but it gagged me. I got sick, vomited all over the guy, and then completely flipped out! Grabbing my clothes, purse, and coat, I ran out crying. "No, no, I can't do it, I can't do it!!" I shrieked as I passed the Madam, who was waiting right outside the door. "Get in the car," she yelled and followed me out. Leaning into the car window she scolded TD&L's brother, "it's not for her!" "Yeah," he said, "what the hell was my brother thinking?!" I thought the same thing about myself.

I was a complete flop as a call girl. Seeing me all shook and crying as we drove back, TD&L's brother asked, "Why in the world did you do this?" "Because it's what TD&L wanted," I moaned. That made him fume: "My brother's stupid, he's really stupid! I should never have let him talk me into it; he had no goddamned business doing this to a girl like you."

I was worried. "He's gonna be mad," I told him. "Don't you worry about it," he said, "My brother's not going to touch you." Good as his word, when we pulled up to the club and TD&L ran up to the car, his brother laid into him: "Listen, I'm taking her home and I'll kill you if you ever try to put her through this again!" After that scene, I thought sure as hell once TD&L got me alone he was going to beat me. He didn't. Turned out he was scared to death of his brother! He might have been the younger brother, but guys who were pimps were tough.

My celebration was premature. Before long TD&L's psychotic tendencies intensified. Each day I was putting up with more and more crap from him, and each day I was more and more frightened. His personality shifts were extreme: One moment he was sweet and then, bam! he was angry, vile, and out of control. Lord knows what it was; I couldn't help but think he was going full-tilt crazy. Knowing what a violent temper he had, I never did anything to egg him on. Secretly, though, I decided that the first chance I had, I was going to leave him. In the meantime, I sneaked out of my apartment where he had visited me and quietly moved in with Nick and his wife. That way I could hide after hours, but he still knew where I worked, he knew the places the band hung out, and he had his spies everywhere.

As I got more scarce, TD&L got more suspicious. His rage shoved him over the edge. He started punching, slapping, and shaking me, but he was cunning about it. TD&L didn't want to be known as a bad guy to his buddies, so he made sure that whenever he attacked me we were by ourselves. That is, until the final straw broke the whole thing wide open.

The band had finished an extended gig at Facks and we had a couple days off before leaving for a job Nick had booked in San Luis Obispo, two hundred miles south of the city.

TD&L had heard the buzz about us finishing at Facks and was enraged that I hadn't told him. Then he couldn't find me. He didn't know where I lived and I wasn't at the club, so he was embarrassed in front of his friends that I'd gotten out from under his control. I can imagine how they must have teased him about letting me get away.

His fury gathered into a storm cloud that burst the night after we closed at Facks. To celebrate, I went with Nick and the guys to a waffle shop across from the Drake Hotel. We took our seats in a horseshoe booth; I sat in the back, at the deepest part of the horseshoe curve, the other musicians arrayed like bookends on either side of me. Even though TD&L knew we liked that joint, I thought I'd be safe, surrounded by my bandmates in a public place. No way! Alerted by his spies, TD&L charged in and made right for our booth. Fixing his glare on me, he growled, "where you been?"

Insane with anger, TD&L reached over the table, grabbed me roughly by the shoulders, and started pulling, trying to lift me out of my seat! I begged the four musicians to "Help me, help me!" but it was futile. The guys got up and let him yank me out. Looking back, I can't blame them. I wasn't their old lady to be protected from this monster. Why should they take a chance on getting their hand or lip broken just because I was dumb enough to bring that maniac into their midst? I must admit that at the time I wasn't so forgiving; even years later it was very hard for me to do.

TD&L shoved me through the crowd at the front register, dragged me out the doors and into his car in front of the waffle shop. On a big city street with people walking by he really beat me, whacking me sideways right and left, bloodying my lip, shouting, "nobody leaves me!" After several minutes, my face was numb from the blows and he was temporarily spent. I took the opportunity to calm him down a bit—I don't know how I did it, probably fed him some lies—and convinced him to take me home.

I could sense his anger refueling as we drove, and when we parked at Nick's place, TD&L, cigarette hanging out the side of his mouth, hauled me out of the car, strong-armed me up the steps to Nick's front door, and rang the bell. Nobody answered; Nick and his wife were out. I took the house key out of my purse and put it in the latch, shaking like hell. Right then, TD&L ripped the burning cigarette from his mouth, hissed, "Here's something to remember me by," and stubbed it out on my bare arm. As I winced in pain, he warned, "Don't even think about leaving me! Don't even think about it!"

Despite the clinch he had me in I managed to open the door. Straight ahead of us, across the foyer, was an open closet with a big light cord dangling. Memories of other small dark spaces with rats inside or a thief outside sent a rush of adrenalin through me. I fought to get free of his grasp, but at six-foot-two, and twice my weight, he easily held me a couple feet off the ground while he wrapped the light cord around my neck. When the cord was tight he released his grip and let me hang for a few moments. As I struggled to breathe, he leaned menacingly against my face and spat, "make no mistake, I'm very serious." Then he loosened the cord, dropped me down, and went out the door. He could have killed me and, clearly, he got within an inch of doing it!

A short time later, Nick's wife came home and found me in the closet just a bundle of nerves. She was outraged when she saw the intense discoloration on my arm and the abrasions circling my neck. I had to wear high collared and long-sleeved tops for quite a while to cover those nasty welts. Nick was shocked by what had happened; he didn't see the beating I took in front of the waffle shop and so he had no idea TD&L was that dangerous.

Nick was still my legal guardian, so he and his wife decided to keep me in their house until the band headed south. Twenty-four hours later I stole safely out of town and was on the road with the band. That San Luis Obispo gig was a stroke of luck, arriving just when I needed to get far away from TD&L. It seems that whenever I get into something that's really bad for me, angels come to my rescue.

Speaking of angels, the night we opened the club for a two-week engagement in San Luis Obispo I met this wealthy young guy, Ricky. He was so darling, and so lovely to me, and he took to me right away. Compared to TD&L he was a little guy, but he had a big Cadillac. The next night he came in again. This time he brought me a green, velvety suede jacket. We sat down to talk at intermission, me in my plush new jacket. I learned that he owned a huge ranch and that he was a pilot who worked as a crop duster. I also learned that he had fallen in love with me and wanted to get married! When I picked myself up off the floor, I accepted.

Next day I called my mother. "Dottie, that's awful fast," was her very reasonable response. So, I spilled the beans to her about TD&L, how he'd lost it with the cigarette burn, and how he'd hung me in a closet. I explained that I needed to get far away from him, but living and working in the same town made an escape seem impossible. Then what drops into my lap but love at first sight with a crop-duster kid. The good news, I told her, is that "I really do love Ricky and he'll give me anything." She relayed my version of events to Bob, and, reluctantly, I think, they accepted my decision to marry.

But where my parents were skeptical, the guys in the band were delighted. They said, "great, he can fly us to all our gigs!"

Happiness was mine until the fourth night of the gig. At intermission, Ricky and I were standing next to his car outside the club having a cigarette. I was leaning against the front fender when suddenly an apparition snapped me out of my nicotine daze. TD&L was marching down the street headed directly for us, looking mad as hell! Ricky didn't know TD&L from Adam, and I hadn't told him my waffle-house horror story. Still, he noticed how I'd tensed up, so he asked, "Who's that?" "This guy's going to try and kill me because I left him. He's very dangerous, Ricky." "Really?" was his one-word response. Very cooly he reached in his glove compartment and pulled out a gun. He told me later that he kept a gun as insurance when making trips to the bank with large amounts of cash to deposit.

Ricky put the gun behind him and out of sight just as TD&L got within range. Looking straight at me, TD&L snarled, "Get over here!" With that, Ricky leveled his gun at TD&L and warned, "You better leave her alone or I'm going to take you out! Now, turn around and go back where you came from and if I ever see you bother her again, I'll kill you!" It was straight out of a movie, and I couldn't believe it when I looked into TD&L's eyes. He was scared to death! That big coward, I could hear him whimpering and I just loved it! I loved it! Boy, I really wanted to marry Ricky now! That little guy wasn't afraid at all.

It wasn't to be. When Ricky asked me to marry him, telling me that I wouldn't ever have to worry about anything again, there was just one condition: I had to meet his grandmother. Well, I didn't have a good track record in that department and, sadly, this time was no different. Ricky's grandmother objected to me because I was in show business. She took me aside and told me, "You're not for him: you're an entertainer, you're a gypsy (shades of my grandfather!) and that kind of life won't do. As Ricky's wife, you would have to be right here with me, and me only, helping take care of his business. That's the kind of woman he needs." She talked turkey and I feared she was right.

At the end of the first week of the band's gig in San Luis Obispo, Mom and my stepdad, Bob, came down from Berkeley for the wedding, bless their hearts, but as our nuptials got closer and I saw Ricky every day, the complaints about his grandmother giving him a bad time went into overload. We drove to his ranch again, and while he was crop-dusting I looked into the future, envisioning what my life would be like. I looked at it hard to see if it was for me. I couldn't pretend and ruin both our lives.

At the end of the second week, the band was ready to make the return trip to San Francisco and I had to make a decision. Turns out Ricky had developed some misgivings, too, as he tried to grasp how he would fit into my musical world. He wound up so confused that I had to make the choice for both of us. I broke up with him. "I'll always love you for what we had," I told him, "but this is not going to work." He was so understanding but still so over the moon about the "Dot" that it tore me up. I carried a torch for a while, but never saw him again. A few years later, Ricky crashed his crop-duster plane and was killed.

Mingus

I was with Nick Esposito from 1945 until 1949, but we weren't working all the time so I took jobs with other bands whenever I could. One of those jobs was an eye-opener.

In 1947, I went to hear a jam session in an Oakland club featuring a new jazz-world sensation, bassist Charles Mingus. Mingus had temporarily settled in the Bay Area with an ambition to break the color line of the San Francisco Symphony, to be the first Black musician accepted into that conservative institution. He was a genius on his instrument but the symphony people didn't care—they wouldn't let him in. When I got to know Charles better I heard him describe that incident with one-word: bigotry.

That evening at the jam I was so completely lost in the music that my recognition of racial politics, along with any other markers of my immediate reality, faded away. I was so absorbed that it startled me when late in the set someone on the stand yelled, "Hey, Dottie, come up and sing!" I left my seat with the jitters—I mean, singing impromptu with a musician of Mingus's caliber was daunting—but it didn't stop me. As my father had told me years before: "That's not the time to fold. It's the time to pour it on!"

Jamming with Charles that night it was obvious that our time agreed. I figured that maybe the way we hit wasn't lost on him either and that maybe he filed it for future reference. And maybe he did, because the second time was the charm. In 1948, I rejoined Nick Esposito at Facks and a few nights after we opened, Mingus came into the club. He nodded, I smiled, and the band kicked off one of my wordless features.

Hearing me do phonetics with Nick was probably as unexpected for him as it was fortuitous for me. At the close of the evening an intrigued Charles asked me to a rehearsal, and after we met up a few days later he expressed his confidence that I could handle the vocal parts he was experimenting with in his band. In fact, Charles never doubted me at all, even though I couldn't read. Charles was always inventing and soon I was to become one of his inventions.

When I started with Charles he had Buzz Wheeler on piano and Kenny McDonald at the drums. The guys were deep in rehearsal even though there wasn't a gig on the horizon. I guess, since he was in the Bay Area by himself with nothing else to do but wait on a decision by the city symphony, why not rehearse? Rehearsals continued for several months after I joined, and they made a lasting impression on me because we worked five hours a day, three days a week. Charles was a perfectionist and it was clear to all of us at the rehearsals that whenever we did get to play on a gig, there wouldn't be any second chances to correct mistakes; we had to get it right the first time. If you didn't want to practice for five hours you were out of the band.

Mingus could be a sweet huggable bear one moment and very intimidating the next. You arrived and there was no small talk. He wasn't interested in our personal lives; he wasn't rude, but there was no doubt that Charles, at twenty-six years old, was the Big Daddy. He treated all us young kids like beginners at a lesson every time we played with him. He told us what to do, what and when to play—he had everything figured out. You had to pay close attention or he wouldn't have any use for you.

Similar to what I did with Nick, I performed like a horn in Charles's band. I had specific notes to sing in both bands and I sang them within the chords exactly. I never sang words with either of them. Instead, I vocalized the set melodies using the sounds of vowels and consonants. The difference between the two bands was that with Nick it didn't matter which vowels and consonants I used, but it did with Charles. Sometimes he'd want me to sing B's, sometimes he'd want D's. I sang an instrumental part in both bands, but I did that with Charles by repeating a set vowel or consonant sound to blend as he bowed the harmony on his bass. Charles didn't use the term *phonetics* to describe what I did with him; it was closer I think to *vocalise*, which may be defined as using the same vowel or consonant to sing the exact notes on a chart every time a tune is played.[1] (*Vocalise* is distinct from *vocalese* as practiced by, for example, King Pleasure, Eddie Jefferson, or Jon Hendricks, where lyrics are added to preexisting instrumental jazz solos.)

Since Charles knew I couldn't read, he didn't write out parts for me. Once again, I did it by ear, memorizing the music as we rehearsed it over and over, so by the time the rest of the guys got it, I had it down, too. The one tune I definitely remember doing with Charles was an arrangement he wrote on a popular song, "The Gypsy."[2] I was thrilled to do that tune, given its jazz pedigree: it had been performed the year before by Charlie Parker during his so-called "Lover Man" date for Dial Records. All that work paid off when Charles's bowing parts and my vocalise finally meshed and a grin appeared on his face. I loved seeing that great big grin!

Around Christmas, 1948, Charles landed an extended gig at the Knotty Pine, a biker bar on 18th and San Pablo in Oakland.[3] I remember this because it was at the same time that a nearly year-long recording ban, enforced by the American Federation of Musicians, was lifted. Even with the gig, we continued to rehearse several days a week and our band was hot, it was together, and as word got around I was proud to be a part of it. My dear friend, Dee Marabuto, whose husband, John, was in Nick Esposito's band with me, heard us at the Knotty Pine, and she remembers that "it was the talk of the town within the musicians' circle that Dottie was going to be with Mingus."

We played New Year's Eve at the Knotty Pine and, as the evening wore on, Charles got more and more exasperated with his drummer, Kenny Mc-Donald. McDonald kept messing with the time and Charles kept warning him, "If you don't quit looking at the bitches and concentrate I'm going to throw you off the stand!" Well, later in the set, that's just what he did! We were on a high stage and Charles took McDonald by his lapels and threw him clean off! McDonald plummeted down a flight of stairs behind the drum chair and—God!—I thought Charles had killed him! (McDonald survived but Charles had to scramble to replace him, finally hiring Johnny Berger.)

Mingus disbanded our group after the Knotty Pine gig and left the Bay Area. I didn't see him again until maybe fifteen years later when he came into the famous Half Note jazz club on Hudson Street in New York City where I was playing with Zoot Sims. When Charles spied me on the stand he stared quizzically; up to then he'd had no clue that I played the drums. He made his way over to the stand and shouted at me while we were playing: "Dottie, is that you?" I yelled back, "yeah," and Charles told Zoot, "I want some!" Charles sat in and it was fun as hell; all the while we played he shook his head and repeated, "Damn, Dottie, Damn!" That was cute.

After Charles left town early in the new year, 1949, I was back with Nick Esposito's house band at Facks. Shortly after my return, jazz piano giant, Art Tatum, played opposite us for a week. During Tatum's sets everybody in the house was absolutely mesmerized; this was late in Tatum's career, but he was still untouchable at the keyboard. Once he'd finish a set everybody wanted a piece of this blind genius.

Except me. I listened closely to the music, but when it was done I was very good at stepping back to leave the man alone. I wasn't fascinated by fame. My daughter, Deborah, once said to me, "Oh, you're afraid of becoming famous." I said, "Yeah, you're damn right, I don't want to be a household name." Those people don't have a life of their own and they don't know who loves them. I like incognito. I want to be cool, but underneath; I want to come from underneath and have the fun, which I did.

A few weeks after Tatum left, tenor saxophonist Charlie Ventura brought a combo to play opposite us at Facks, and the music was right in my bag. Ventura, who had gained fame as a soloist in Gene Krupa's band, led a bop septet that included the relatively new vocal duo of Jackie Cain and Roy Kral. I hadn't heard of Jackie and Roy, but the first time Jackie sang at the club I was in awe—on some numbers she was doing phonetics and that was the first time I ever heard anyone else do it.

The more I listened and learned about Jackie and Roy the more I felt that, next to them, I was back in junior high. Before their appearance opposite us, they had made a series of recordings with Ventura and played L.A. They were getting bigger and bigger and bigger. When Esposito's band took the stand, Jackie and Roy heard me sing in that same new style, but since we never traded stories I don't know who got there first. What I do know is that I didn't copy Jackie Cain. I sang wordless melodies before I knew she existed.

In May 1949, an unexpected gift fell in my lap. I entered a recording studio for the first time and waxed two sides with the Nick Esposito Boptette, an expanded group that included Nick on guitar; plus tenor saxophonist, Claude Gilroy; pianist, Buddy Motsinger; Vernon Alley at the bass; Joe Dodge behind the drums (a few years later, Dodge was part of an early edition of the Dave Brubeck Quartet); and Cal Tjader on bongos.[4] Tjader had played in Brubeck's octet three years before this date. As Dottie Grae, I sang phonetics on two tunes: "Dot's Bop" (written especially for me by Nick Esposito and pianist/composer Dick Vartanian), and "Penny," by Shelton Smith. ▶ * The band also cut two instrumental numbers. All four selections were recorded in San Francisco and released by 4-Star records.[5]

Not long after the recording date, I left Nick's band, at least temporarily. I can't remember if work had dried up or if I got restless for something new. In any case, I was at loose ends so I went down to Los Angeles and stayed with my paternal grandparents in Hollywood while I looked for work. I was surprised to learn that my name had gotten around among L.A. musicians. Known as a pretty good singer who was reliable, stayed in tune, knew her keys and her tempos, I was hired for different local gigs—a Saturday night here, a weekend there—and was introduced to the "Grandfather of Film Music," David Raksin.

Raskin took a liking to me and circulated my name among various agents. His recommendation carried weight; I was hired a little bit more, and I sat in some, too. Pretty soon I was appearing regularly on the streets in Hollywood. I started running with the L.A. crowd and hanging out at Billy Berg's on Vine. That's where I first heard Anita O'Day. Her time was so great; oh, God!—her vocals were like tap dancing to me.

I was in my element in Hollywood, surrounded by a jazz scene filled with new faces and sounds. Somewhere in that excitement, someone told me that the comedian, Roscoe Ates, was looking for a singer who could feed him straight lines to take on the road. I decided to audition. Another shot at touring was too good to miss!

---

*This book is accompanied by a web page, https://www.press.uillinois.edu/books/supplement/_dottie, that features audio and video material. The symbol in the text indicates a reference to these materials.

Apple Pie, Apple Pie, Apple Pie

I'd heard of Roscoe Ates. Before I met him he was a name in the entertainment business. He'd done a lot of films, you'd see him playing a sidekick in low-budget cowboy movies. In the 1930s, Ates was popular as a stuttering comedian, and that's how he was billed when I worked with him in 1949. By then his movie career was on a down slide, and his move to the small screen was maybe a year away.[1]

I aced the audition and was thrilled to get the gig, even if Ates was as corny as his jokes. We went on the road immediately to the Midwest. I was with him for about three weeks but I remember very little about it because the chaotic aftermath of our split has blunted my memory. I do recall that for my part of the act I got to choose my own songs, like "Blue Skies" or "Blue Moon," and I'd be accompanied by the house band, usually a pianist and bass player.

Ates and I didn't see each other much—only for a brief time each night before we hit—but that was enough. He was a dirty old man, but he made such lame passes I stopped them with one line. Frankly, I was more upset about not getting paid; by the end of the second week Ates hadn't come through with a nickel. When I pressed him about my money he promised to fork over everything he owed at the end of the third week. He was a dirty old man and a cheat. After we closed in Omaha, he took all the money, lost it gambling in one night, and skipped town. Not only was I left high and dry in the hotel unable to pay my bill, I was stranded with no way of getting home. Thank God, my angels were literally around the corner!

While I was appearing in one club with Ates, the Mary Kaye Trio was working the sister club two blocks away. I hadn't heard of Mary Kaye, but during my first week in town Mary and the members of her trio came in to see me and introduce themselves. Right from the start we got along famously and it wasn't long before they invited me over to their rooms. I jumped at the chance. My hotel was very lonely—it wasn't high class, it was a traveler's hotel—and from then on, I hung out with them every night after the shows.

In that short time the four of us became very good friends. We got so close I considered them "my family away from home." When Ates abandoned me to the wolves, Mary and company bailed me out, but paying off my hotel bill left them so broke they couldn't afford to send me home. Taking pity on a hapless trouper, they took me under their wing: Mary said, "We close tomorrow night, baby, and then we're going to Springfield, Illinois, to play the Black Orchid Lounge for a whole month. You come with us and we'll figure something out." The Mary Kaye Trio saved my life.

Mary Kaye was a gorgeous Hawaiian woman who played guitar and sang with a powerful four-octave voice. Her trio, which was a popular jazz and lounge act in the 1950s until it disbanded in 1965, included her brother, Norman Kaye, on bass and vocals, and Frank Ross, comedian, accordionist, and tall-tom drummer. When the group, with me in tow, got to Springfield, Mary cooked up a scheme to get me enough money for the trip back to the West Coast. She convinced the owner of the Black Orchid to feature a "spin-off" of her regular trio, a one-time-only act that had me on a stand-up drum and singing at the same time. Oh God, I was lucky! Aside from me, this newly minted trio had Mary's husband, Jules Pursely, playing bass and Norman Kaye's wife, Mary, on piano.

The only flies in the ointment were that I wasn't a drummer and the stand-up tom was a completely new instrument to me and I had precious little time to get acquainted. That's when Frank Ross, bless his heart, stepped in. Frank took me aside during rehearsal and assured me, "You can play a stand-up drum, it's easy." First he had me repeat the words, "apple pie, apple pie, apple pie." Then he handed me a pair of brushes and told me to duplicate that sound on the stand-up tom. Translated into strokes on a drum, that phonetic pattern became a series of triplets played in a standard swing rhythm.[2] I followed his instructions to the letter and it was like dancing when I got it into my head. That very simple bit of schooling is really the reason I started drumming. Honest to God, that is how I started playing drums and I have Frank Ross to thank for it!

Our makeshift unit with me and the two spouses played several shows nightly opposite Mary's regular trio. And it wasn't just a little bit of playing; I had to play full sets. All I really had to play was the simple apple pie pattern, but after I got some confidence I started experimenting, playing "apple pie" all kinds of different ways. "Apple pie" is really about the division of the bar—where you place your division—and every drummer's signature is how he plays his triplets. Some drummers get hired over others because of the subtlety of their division.

Later in my career, when I played in big bands I'd thrill to how the lead trumpet player put an accent on the last note of a triplet. In that case, the drummer will know to make her division wide, to make it real long, but that can also cause her to drag. If that happens, she has to shorten her apple pie on the ride cymbal. It's a matter of minute adjustments that are so intangible it can be difficult to explain, but it's how you keep the time, and it comes natural to me. My ears are way out there.

Working in a jazz trio at the Black Orchid Lounge was the result of pure serendipity, but looking back I sometimes wonder if fate had decreed it. I mean, in addition to the novelty of performing on the floor tom, I sang while I played. Sure, I had been singing since I was five when I did my Shirley Temple imitation on top of a piano in one roadhouse after another, and sure, I started working as a professional vocalist at fifteen, but this was the first time I mimicked my dad by doing vocals from behind a drum.

After Springfield, I didn't repeat that routine for several decades, but the experience stuck with me. Ditto my introduction to brushes. I had watched my father use brushes so it doesn't surprise me that I pulled it off at the Black Orchid. Later, when I got to New York, I checked out how legendary jazz drummer, Papa Jo Jones, would swish them around. On a calf head, not a plastic head, you swing the right brush to the left and the left brush to the right, while alternating them underneath one another. As the wires of the brush spread, you get a "shoosh, shoosh, shoosh" sound. I loved Papa Jo. Boy, he could swing! He knew how to put a crisp edge to his brushes; he'd shorten his division and make it come alive.

As I came up, brushes were an essential part of jazz drumming so I honed my drum-brush technique to follow in the footsteps of my idols. As esteemed pianist Kenny Barron remarked: "She was very good with the brushes—that's one thing that I noticed because not every drummer's good with brushes. You know, there are people like Papa Jo, who was a master, Dottie, Kenny Clarke, and Ben Riley."

Today, things are different; you can hardly find drummers, male or female, who play brushes. Everything is sticks, and loud, nothing subtle at all. Music today has gone from rock, with a back beat, to heavy metal—how are you going to play brushes behind heavy metal?

Brushes are great for ballads, but ballads are seldom played anymore because it's so easy for drummers to rush a ballad. A secret I learned was I'd think in 2 when I'm playing a ballad. I'd double up the tempo in my head to put a little lilt in it and make the ballad walk. It seems that drummers today have lost the art of playing just a single stroke with the brushes and letting it breathe. "The music breathed easily on the ballads when she played," said John Coates Jr., the long-standing pianist at the famed Deer Head Inn jazz club in the Poconos.[3]

Returning to the Black Orchid Lounge story, I played for two weeks with Mary and Jules in our trio which was tailor-made to get me solvent and back on my feet. Then my appendix burst and I was literally knocked off my feet! It happened midday. I was listening to the Mary Kay Trio rehearse when suddenly an intense pain hit me on my right side. Frank, seeing me doubled over clutching my stomach, drove me to the Springfield Catholic Hospital.

Close to death, I went right into emergency surgery. When the surgeon opened me up he removed my burst organ and treated me for gangrene that had started to set in. The next day, when I'd recovered from the anesthesia, I was told that I needed a second surgery to remove my ovaries because their proximity to the diseased appendix might have gotten them infected. But since I was underage they had to call my mother, over two thousand miles away, to get her permission.

The doctors, trying to cover their asses, told my mother that if they didn't remove the ovaries, "She might die." Much to the doctor's surprise, Momma said, "Don't do it." "No!" she insisted, "I don't believe it's necessary so I'm not giving you my permission for a surgery that could damage my young daughter's future." She obviously was trying to protect my childbearing interests, but, still, I was amazed that she said, "No." Months later, when I questioned her about the danger I might have been in, Mother explained that she had felt pretty confident about the decision because of her medical training during the war. From what the docs told her about my case, she knew that a second surgery wasn't necessary for me to survive.

She was spot on! I lived with my ovaries intact, but I had a hell of a scar—14 inches from below my belly all the way up to my sternum. Plus, I endured two weeks recovery time in the hospital, a stretch that coincided with Mary Kaye's gig at the Black Orchid. I was grateful the trio wasn't stuck waiting around for me, but I got restless cooped up in my hospital room, impatient to move forward with my life and aching to get back to music.

Frank Ross was my only antidote; he visited every day, looking like he'd escaped from Barnum and Bailey. I'd hear him as he strolled down the hall, bells on his shoestrings jingling merrily. He'd enter my room grinning and gesturing broadly like the physical comedian he was, his clothes decked out in a zany array of pencils stuck in his hat band and balloons taped to the cuffs of his pants. Holding my stomach, I'd tell him, "Don't make me laugh, Frank," and then I'd guffaw so hard at his antics I'd have to beg him to stop for fear my stitches would split. He was wonderful to me.

On the heels of my discharge, Mary and her entourage, with me tagging along, headed for the West Coast, our travel budget beefed up with some gigs along the way. Back in Los Angeles, I went straight to stay with my paternal grandparents in Lincoln Heights and introduced them to Mary Kaye, Frank, and Norman. That was the first of many visits the trio, my "second family," made to the home of my Giaimo elders. One of those visits was a knockout.

Frank Ross was close to the renowned jazz promoter and record company executive, Norman Granz. One evening Frank brought Norman, along with Mary and her brother, to my grandparents' house for dinner. Granz, bowled over by my grandmother's cooking, could not contain himself: "Mrs. Giaimo, you've got to open a restaurant!" He even offered to personally open one for her! That balloon popped when, true to form, my grandmother shrugged and told him, "No, no, no. Too big and too many people I don't care about. I cook for friend and family around the house, that's all."

Those visits were the high points; otherwise, living with my grandparents was a daily source of frustration. I was a good granddaughter, but they hadn't changed—still high-handed quibblers—but even in the best of circumstances I didn't want to be with them in Lincoln Heights. I wanted to be out on my own, but I had no money and was dependent on them to survive.

Another problem was my aversion to Los Angeles. Saying I'm not fond of the City of Angels is putting it mildly; I get close to suicidal in L.A.! That's why I gave it the epithet, "Death Valley." Partly it's the weather, it eats up your brain. Just as bad was the phoniness, phony like a Hollywood "kiss-kiss"; it was "Movie-Land" all the time. It was tough for me to keep my emotional balance in that city, but physically, despite the operation and the long trek back from the heartland, I was pretty much back to normal. At least I thought I was.

I spent a lot of time looking for work, landing the occasional gig. Walking the club circuit one evening, I was about to cross the intersection at Hollywood and Vine when I passed out cold on the sidewalk! A bystander must have called an ambulance because I was rushed to a hospital where I died for a minute or more! Evidently I was in and out of consciousness when I was admitted, but when they slid me onto an operating table I was clinically dead.

Hearing that, my poor mother and Bob hurried down at night in their rickety old car. They started out with only one headlight but it burned out shortly after they left. Terrified, my parents drove a "black hole" almost four hundred highway miles from Sacramento only to be told when they arrived that the seeming finality of my condition had been reversed, and that the doctors had revived me before I suffered any permanent damage.

All the ruckus was caused by a delayed complication from my bout of appendicitis. Abdominal adhesions, or bands of scar tissue, had slowly wrapped around my lower bowel, and the obstruction got so severe it took all the air out of me and knocked me out not far from the Hollywood Walk of Fame.

When I was well enough to leave the hospital, Mom and my stepdad drove me to their place in Albany to fully recover from death's door—for the second time in a matter of months! After my convalescence, I went back to singing. The first gig I had was at the Blue Moon club in San Francisco, accompanied by my friend and former Esposito bandmate, pianist John Marabuto. On Mondays I started going regularly to hear my father's rehearsal band at the Musicians' Union Local 6 building, and it was a spin-off of those visits that reawakened my interest in the drums.

A Little Help from My Friends

I soon was a Monday fixture at the Musicians' Union; after my father's band finished, there was the added attraction of jam sessions that were always cooking downstairs in the bar. I'd hang out and soak it all up and sometimes the guys would ask me to sit in—they all knew Dad so they automatically figured I could do it. I'd play whatever was set up. One time there'd be a snare, a snare stand, and the throne; next time somebody would have left a hi-hat or a cymbal alongside the snare. Each time I jammed I taught myself piecemeal about different parts of a drum set. By the time I bumped into a bass drum it was a walk in the park because I'd already gotten all the rest.

The musicians helped me, too. "Don't be a 'leadfoot,'" was one thing they drilled into me. A leadfoot, is a drummer who plays too hard on the bass drum. The bass drum is supposed to be underneath, to be felt more than heard. You don't want to play the bass drum too loud and drown everybody out. I learned how to play the bass drum softer than the bass player, to let the bass be the bass—it has notes and melody. I also learned how to accompany on the drums by listening closely at those sessions to what the guys were playing. When they hit a rhythmic lick, I'd pick it up immediately, just like I caught the patterns Hoppy danced in his rented basement. A few months later when I started as the house drummer at Jimbo's Bop City, I had put it all together.

The serendipity of my learning curve at the Musicians' Union epitomized my identity as a musician: a self-taught drummer who got help along the way. Fate sprinkled my path with unexpected teachers, discovered influences, and the occasional embrace of jazz-world camaraderie. My father's example was paramount, but the accidental teaching moment of Frank Ross in Springfield was well-timed for my development. Then there was John Markham, the drummer I first met in the 1940s working in Nick Esposito's band.

In 1955, John gave me an invaluable lesson on how to properly hold my sticks and he schooled me on getting the best performance out of the calf heads on my bass and snare drums. He told me never to tune my snare drum before I play. Wait, he said, until after the first set because then the calf head will have had time to get acclimated to factors in the environment: The number of people in the room, the warmth and humidity—all that makes a big difference on the highs and lows of the snare. He warned me that if I played a place that was real cold, a natural calf head could get very tight and split.

John also taught me to tune my drums low, to a G, to fit the sound of the bass and piano; that is a pitch that works nicely with the keys of all the horns, too. As famed bassist Ron Carter recalled, "one thing that stuck out in my mind was how well she tuned the bass drum and the floor tom. Usually those are the two drums that guys always either don't tune at all or mistune according to how the bass is sounding at that moment. She seemed to understand that the better tuned were the floor tom and the bass drum she had the chance to hear the bass player better and, for me, my range of the bass wasn't limited by the pitch of the bass drum and the floor tom."

I took lessons from Tony DeNicola, long associated with clarinetist, Kenny Davern, in Vegas in the late 1950s. Tony schooled me on how to use my wrists and fingers so I wouldn't get tired while playing. Drums don't require that much strength. What matters is the total eye-hand coordination with the four appendages, but I was never a "basher" anyway. My favorite drummers were listening musicians, above all the Bop innovator, Kenny Clarke, because he understood the drummer's role as part of the total sound not as a separate entity.

Kenny Clarke's versatility inspired me. When I came up in the early 1940s through the mid-1950s, a lot of drummers I heard were known as either small-combo drummers or big-band drummers. To be able to play hard and loud in a big band and with great feeling, and then to be able to play soft in a quartet and get the same definition, the same awareness, was very unusual. They both took an awful lot of energy, but in different forms—one largely physical, the other mental—so I hardly ever found a drummer who was really good at both. Kenny Clarke was the first drummer I heard who could do that. With Clarke as my model, I played with small groups and then was equally confident when I would drive a big band. I loved that I could do that; that I was fearless enough to not even think about it. It was really special whenever I made the switch to a big band because it was out of the ordinary for me and also because the drummer in a big band is a workhorse—a workhorse because a big-band drummer has to accommodate such a variety of approaches to the beat.

In terms of division, all musicians have their own little spot to play and a big band has a large collection of those differences. The lead trumpet player gets up and the drummer's supposed to fit. The tenor player plays his solo and the drummer has to adapt. When the bassist takes a solo the drummer's role is to play a little bit underneath the bass. The drummer never gets time off!

The mental demands on a big-band drummer are compounded by the sheer physicality of the job. In a small group you have brush work which gives you a little break, but in a big band it's usually all sticks so you really have to lay the wood down all the time. I had to shift into another gear; I had to raise my arm a little bit more for volume and in general play harder, using all my 123 pounds! When I say "harder," I mean I had to hit my cymbal with more force and my hi-hat had to be crisp enough on two and four so it could cut through the ensemble and everybody in the band could hear it. Instead of intimate, it's more definite, but I kind of play like that anyway; I make it clear where I'm placing the time. That's what the guys love!

Kenny Clarke was also the first drummer I ever heard play with another drummer (British jazz drummer, Kenny Clare). That impressed me because as far as I'm concerned on any bandstand there's room for only one drummer. There have been only two exceptions to that in my experience. The first time was in the mid-1960s when I played a series of informal jams with one of my favorites, Albert "Tootie" Heath, master drummer and brother of tenor saxophonist, Jimmy Heath, and bassist, Percy Heath.

No other musicians were involved when I played with Tootie; no piano, no bass, just the rhythm. I'm not sure how I first met him, but I remember sitting with Tootie in some nightclub when he said, "You know, you should come up to my loft. I have two drum sets and I'd love to jam duets with you." "I'd love to do that, too," I replied, and it was full speed ahead because I didn't doubt at all that I could live up to whatever Tootie would throw at me.

We met about once a week for maybe two months, always at his loft, always with the same arrangement: Tootie had one complete drum set facing the other on a platform so we could look into each other's eyes as we played. When I agreed to jam with Tootie I instinctively knew it wouldn't be about tossing sticks in the air or showing off with paradiddles; it would be about placing our time. Still, it was competitive; he'd set a tempo and play an 8-bar solo. Then something would come to me that I'd probably heard in a big band, or I'd get a hit tune in my head, and I'd play an 8-bar solo, hitting my cymbal like I was tap dancing. I always stuck to the melody and that cracked Tootie up.

The second and most recent occasion was in 2004 when I played with legendary drummer and veteran of the Duke Ellington Orchestra, Louie Bellson, for his eightieth birthday celebration at Clint Eastwood's Mission Ranch. It came about when Louie, who was very frail by then and couldn't play a full set, needed someone to open for him at his celebration. "How about getting Dottie?" he asked one of his crew. "Have her bring in a group to open for me." I jumped at the offer and got a quintet together that included bassist, John Wiitala; pianist, Eddie Mendenhall; guitarist, Bruce Forman; and alto saxophonist, Paul Contos.

When Louie and I met to make arrangements I asked, "Since I'm going to open for you is it okay if I play on your drums?" I figured when my quintet finished the set Louie and his group would take over the stage, but he surprised me by saying, "No, I want you to set up your own drums, I want to trade eights with you!"

On the day of the celebration, after my group took its bows, Louie and his band played three numbers and then he invited me back on stage to join his band for several tunes. As we played, I had my head turned to look at Louie and we both kept smiling because we fit like a glove, our apple pie divided in the same exact spot, and we were swinging, really swinging. It was exhilarating because we felt the same width of the strokes. The rhythm where we played wasn't a gnat's ass out of sync; it was like we were melting into one another.

My destiny as a drummer got another proof one afternoon in late 1949 when my father ran into my Mingus bandmate, Johnny Berger, on the street. Johnny by then was a junkie, and he was trying to sell his drums cheap, his whole set that probably cost three hundred dollars, to get money for the junk.

Johnny said to my father, "Hey, Chuck, you need a drum set? I'm selling them for seventy-five bucks." Dad, feeling his pain, said, "My God, Johnny, I'll give you a hundred fifty." Well, the outcome of my father's generosity was that he got me a beautiful Slingerland set with a maplewood shell on the snare and, best of all, I picked up my precious 18-inch Zildjian ride cymbal.

That cymbal is the only piece from that original set that I still have. It's my baby; I've had that cymbal for over seventy years! After all that use, the metal is so thin that it gets a soft and tasty sound, and like an old codger who's lost his teeth, all the rivets that used to circle the rim have fallen out. In its heyday, those rivets gave that cymbal a "sizzle," an added brightness; now, even though they're gone, I swear you can still hear them. It's their ghosts! Every drummer I know wants that cymbal, but I will never give it up until I go.

Heading into the 1950s, I had my first full professional drum set. Drumming was back on my mind but singing remained my focus. As word got around that Dot was back from her medical furloughs, my vocal career started to take off in the Bay Area. After the Blue Moon, I hooked up for the last time with Nick Esposito's band for a job in Oakland, on Broadway over by the Paramount Theater. The joint was called the Paradise Club, and when I met Bob Bennett, the club bartender, paradise was where I thought I was.

The Drummer Was Always Late

My vocal career was picking up but I was down. Recent setbacks were finally getting to me. Maybe it started back when Charles Mingus left town; he was a genius who cared and losing him bothered me more than I probably knew. The ordeal with Ates left me disillusioned; the surgical catastrophes that had me twice near death in quick succession further darkened my outlook. Feeling alone and out on a limb in my ambitions, I was searching, likely without realizing it, for guidance, for structure, even distraction.

Then Bob Bennett entered my life and I thought he was a teacher. He introduced me to what, for me, was a new social circle: the after-hours crowd. That was his world and the cast of characters he mixed with. Some of them were working-class waitresses and bartenders—straight-shooters from the business. Some were hangers-on looking for an angle—most of them were unsavory crooks.

The Paradise Club was an extended gig so Bennett and I had a lot of time to hang out, to flirt, and for me to be flattered. I got to know him, or at least I thought I did. He was so charming, a fast talker who was the coolest. He won over Mom and Bob, too. He gave them a complete set of expensive bar glasses, from sherry and martini glasses to beer mugs. They thought that was wonderful. None of us knew that he had stolen every one of them!

With my self-esteem scraping bottom, I was susceptible to Bennett's seductive manner. I had him on a pedestal, way above me, so when he decided we should get married I was knocked out and followed him blindly. We said our vows in a chapel, and I remember thinking during the ceremony, "Yeah, this is it!" After the wedding, the place we moved into was furnished, but—I can almost laugh about it now—he and his friends had stolen all the furniture!

In addition to club dates, I took a day job to help us make ends meet. That was one of the few times I broke my father's rule. I worked for a lawyer, operating a steno machine and typing a lot of legal work—although I couldn't take shorthand I could still type 72 words a minute, so my boss adored me.

Each evening after Bennett got off and I finished my gig, we'd split from the Paradise and go to some other bar to shoot pool, drink booze from a cup, and mingle with his buddies who, unbeknown to me, were all con-men. At first I was comfortable socializing with his cronies, and Bob always treated me like a lady, but I was naive about the shadowy world I'd entered.

My eyes were opened one night when I was in a saloon with Bob and one of his grifter friends. A milkman came in and he must have been a regular patsy of theirs because it didn't take long before they conned the guy out of his money using the old shell game.[1] I had never seen Bob do that. I blurted, "My God! You cheated him!" His flip response was, "Listen, baby, if I don't do it somebody else will. He's a sucker."

Infatuated with Bob, and needing to believe in him, I shut my eyes to how sordid he was. Night after night I watched as Bennett and his circle of hustlers took chumps to the cleaners. Night after night I stayed in denial, but the longer I had my face rubbed in their "take what you can get and forget the other guy" mentality, the more the con game Bob and his buddies were playing ate at me. I felt complicit, and that really ate at me.

Then Bob's moods began to change. I had never known him to be a bully, so when he started blowing his top and browbeating me I clammed up and caved to almost every demand he made. That is until I'd had enough. One night, parked in front of our house, I remember trying to sweet-talk him out of swindling more unfortunate boobs. Deja-vu TD&L, he hauled off and slapped me repeatedly across the face! Stunned, I shrunk back and screeched "I'm gone!" "That's the last time you'll do that to me, ever!"

My defiance only enraged him more and I got frightened. He pulled me out of the car, up the stairs, and into the house. Inside, I got free and he barked, "come back here!" "Don't you dare touch me again!" I spit back, but once the shock subsided I knew that for my own good I had to calm things down. I took it slow with Bennett and as his anger cooled I slipped into another room, quietly gathered up my purse and a few other things, and before he knew what was happening, I left him right then and there.

He couldn't believe it! He thought I'd give him another chance to make up, but I slammed the door, literally and figuratively. Maybe not giving him any warning didn't show much tact, but I never cried wolf and I was very proud of that.

The next day at work I told my lawyer boss what had happened. His advice was short and sweet: "You can get it annulled." I didn't hesitate and the job was done. Eight months, that's how long the marriage lasted, but, sadly, that wasn't the end of the story. Not long after I left Bennett I took a hotel room to face the fact that I was pregnant. I was determined to make my own way and not go crying home to Momma. I did it myself with a coat hanger in the bathroom, and in the aftermath I was in terrible pain, bleeding all over and frantic.

Desperate for help, I broke down and called my mother. She came with my stepdad, Bob. "Come on home, honey," Momma said, and they took me back to Sacramento where she fixed me up. I knew at the time that what I did was dangerous; but it would have been more dangerous to have Bennett's child. I didn't want his baby. I'd just gotten away from all that.

I recovered quickly and went back to working the Bay Area as a vocalist. Many jazz clubs had opened since the war and at the center of the progressive music scene was San Francisco's Fillmore District, the so-called "Harlem of the West." When I wasn't working I hung out at a new Fillmore District joint, Jimbo's Bop City.

Bop City (which today is a San Francisco landmark) was run by a prominent African-American businessman, John "Jimbo" Edwards.[2] Edwards opened a cafe, "Jimbo's Waffle Shop," at 1690 Post Street, but musicians convinced him to turn the large back room behind the cafe into an after-hours hangout. In 1950, "Bop City" was born and before long this popular jazz club was attracting world-class innovators who were coming through San Francisco, from Bird to Diz to Miles, as well as iconic mainstreamers like Basie, Duke, and Tatum.

Tall and in his fifties, Jimbo had a huge smile with perfect pearly teeth. When the doors opened, he sat at the entrance to the back room and collected money from customers as they filed in. I think the entry fee was a dollar. A cigarette always dangled in the middle of Jimbo's mouth and without moving his lips he'd say, "Hey Sweetie," when I arrived.

An after-hours jazz joint, Bop City's doors were open from two to six a.m. to accommodate all the "big cats" who hung out after their gigs had closed for the night. I became a regular at Bop City, and it wasn't long before I started sitting in, singing and socializing with the musicians—we'd have coffee with a shot of brandy served in coffee mugs.

One memorable night in 1950, a whole crowd of top musicians wound up at Bop City. The place was roaring when I took the mic for a song and I'd no sooner finished when somebody yelled, "Hey, let's get everybody up on the stand and take a picture!" I tried to get off but one of the guys stopped me, "No, Dottie, stay up." So, there I stood, the blonde chanteuse at the mic. Dizzy was doodling on the piano behind me, and I was surrounded by other giants like Miles Davis, Milt Jackson, and Percy Heath. But it didn't mean anything; it was a set-up picture to get a group shot of the musicians for publicity purposes. Years later I saw that picture reproduced in a book, *There and Back*, by Roy Porter.[3] In the caption I'm identified as "Betty Bennett." The Bennett part was left over after the annulment; "Betty" was Jimbo's invention. He had nicknames for everybody, and since I looked more like a "Betty" than a "Dottie" to him, that's what he called me.[4]

One night, not long after that photo was snapped, Jimbo was in a tight spot. He couldn't find a drummer to start at two a.m., probably because the musicians in town who otherwise might have been available couldn't get out of their regular gig early enough to make the start of the set. So, Jimbo walked up to me, cigarette clamped between his gleaming white teeth, "Hey there, Betty." he started. "It's DOTTIE," I said. "Oh, yeah, right, right, right, right," he backpedaled. "Dottie, I need a drummer, you want to play this gig? I can only give you five."

Now, although at the time I was known primarily as a singer in the city, I had been drumming informally at the Local 6 jams and occasionally I'd sit in on brushes at some other session. Those impromptu affairs happened when I'd be hanging out at a rehearsal and the drummer was late. The guys would ask me to fill in, so I'd join them, playing apple pie on a magazine, pushing the brushes on the cover to give them some rhythm. That's all the guys wanted. They didn't want a soloist. Musicians hate soloist drummers; they want rhythm, and I loved doing it. I couldn't worry about having an ego because I wasn't really a drummer, I was a helpmate.

When Jimbo offered me the one night he must have known that the musicians approved of me, and once he heard me play a little brushes on the snare drum he was fine with it. After I subbed that night, I didn't want to risk missing a chance to do it again so I started carrying a pair of Kung-Fu shoes just in case I got asked to play. (My prep for vocals was similar: I always carried a list with the keys of the tunes I sang on a folded piece of paper in my wallet.) My Kung Fu shoes were flat slip-ons that folded up in my purse; if I was in high heels I couldn't play, and I didn't like playing in my bare feet because I wouldn't have enough control over the pedals. (I stopped wearing Kung Fu shoes around 1985 when I pulled a muscle under the arch of my left foot.)

I didn't have to wait long for an encore at Jimbo's because the drummers were always late! After I subbed a few more times, Jimbo gave me a short-term gig as the house drummer. I still made five bucks a night but that didn't bother me because I was backing a lot of those same bebop cats who were in that publicity picture, not to mention a lineup of major players in town with various swing bands who sat in during sessions when I was at the drums. I was comfortable playing with all of them because I adapted easily to both swing and bop. The evolution of those styles felt natural to me. With Bop, the compositions got more clipped, but the major change for me was how I handled my triplets. In swing bands, triplets would be wider, a little broader; I shortened my triplets with beboppers like Dizzy.

On the bandstand at Jimbo's was a piano, a bass, and a "never knew what you were going to get" raggedy set of drums. One night I went in and found the bass drum, the snare, and the hi-hat, but the cymbals on the hi-hat were gone. There are supposed to be two cymbals on the hi-hat, one on the bottom and one on the top. A rod runs through both cymbals; the top cymbal is connected to the rod by a clutch that you use to adjust the space between the two cymbals to get the "chit, chit, chit" sound you want when the top cymbal crashes into the stationary one at the bottom.

A junkie drummer had swiped the two hi-hat cymbals because they were small enough to sneak out and sell to buy himself some junk. Technically, I was left with no cymbals, but, I hasten to add, the junkie was courteous enough to leave in place of the cymbals two two-pound Folger's coffee can lids! He had even gone to the trouble of poking holes through both lids so he could attach the bottom one to the pole and then connect the clutch to the one at the top.

When I looked closely at what my predecessor had rigged, I discovered that both coffee cans had been opened with a manual can opener. As a result, both lids had a ridge of jagged teeth along their edges. Those teeth were facing up on the bottom cymbal and down on the top one. Listening to my father, I had learned how important it was to crunch the hi-hat on two and four, but early on that first night it was a real challenge for me to make those coffee-can lids chomp together in time with (ironically) the proper bite.

By mid-set I had it down. I got them to hit "chit, chit, chit," crisp and clean. For two nights I made that rude hi-hat work, but there was a price. Hitting the hell out of my left foot to make those lids match up at the right time was the start of the sciatica I suffer so much from today.

Nonetheless, mastering those dilapidated drums was a confidence booster. I proved to myself that I could play on anybody's drum set. Anybody's! That was important because, for years and years after, I did so much subbing that I almost never played my own drums. I got so used to playing other drummers' sets that the only thing I ever had to do was adjust the stool!

Monty

After a month of late-night sessions at Bop City, I left for another gig, but I had my cred with Jimbo so over the next three years I was in and out as his house drummer—sometimes for a night, sometimes steady for a week at a time. It was pure happenstance at Jimbo's, but in the meantime I had become first choice for subbing at a nightclub a few miles south in the Tenderloin, the legendary Blackhawk. By 1950, I was a regular at the Blackhawk, sitting-in on the drums with a local group one night and then backing some nationally known figure in town for a weekend.

The Blackhawk is where I first met bassist, Monty Budwig, who had come up from Los Angeles for a gig. I had never heard of him, but I was struck immediately by how good he was. His time was excellent, I loved his choice of notes, and his fit in the rhythm section captivated me. Once I got to know him, I realized Monty was the kind of man I wanted.

At least twice I had narrowly escaped from the "Fancy Land of the Handsome Men." Meeting Monty, who was very plain-looking, I learned it was the guy who's not so handsome, the guy with soul, who could answer my ad. Monty was real laid back, calm and gentle, so I knew instinctively that he would never hit me. After the hellholes I'd been through with those simple-minded brutes, TD&L and Bob Bennett, Monty was safe and, boy, I needed that quiet reassurance.

I really wanted Monty but he was hard to get because his home life was difficult and he didn't want any more problems. I took it slow at first (echoes of Harry Bossi), just trying to be his friend, which was easy to do because I had so much admiration for him as a musician. That was important to Monty.

I could see he was impressed with how closely I listened to him play. I also made a point of never talking to anyone when he was soloing, which was a page out of my lessons at the Padre Hotel. The irony of using that pearl of wisdom from my father was that from the get-go Dad was against my courtship with Monty. Violently so.

My father's complaint was that Monty didn't have any personality; he sized Monty up as so straight-faced it was hard even to get a smile out of him. It might have helped if my father had known something about Monty's life and what he had gone through; maybe then he would have understood, but I didn't get a chance to tell him. My father's contempt ran so deep that he never gave Monty credit for his gifts as a bass player. I don't remember my father using profanity, but he was so bitter when he learned I was planning to marry Monty that he yelled, "God dammit, you're not going to marry that no-personality jerk!" Then he hit me, a full-out slap that sent me reeling across a room!

I persisted in spite of my father's objection. We courted more than a year and gradually Monty was drawn to me, probably because I would keep my mouth shut and listen to his troubles. Most women would only talk about their own problems; Monty had never met a woman who would listen to his. The silent ones have always interested me. I get along with people who never get along with anybody else. I can feel how much they have bottled up because they haven't been heard.

Monty and I were married on April 13, 1952. I was twenty-two, Monty was twenty-five. The wedding took place at my mother's home in Walnut Creek, and instead of my father I had my stepdad, Bob Musselman, give me away. My father was dumbstruck. He couldn't believe I would defy him. I'd always been an obedient child, but I was furious with him for hitting me! I was so mad that even though we were in the same city I didn't talk to him for a year-and-a-half after that. I wouldn't take his calls even after my daughter was born. "You're denying me my granddaughter!" he protested.

Before we were married, Monty and I talked casually about his troubled home life. From what I could glean, his parents had no idea how good he was, so when it came to Monty's aspirations to be a jazz bass player he was all by himself. Their lack of support had caused him a lot of grief. I wanted to help, but when I tried to dig deeper he pulled the shade down. All I could be sure about was that Monty needed love and I had a lot of love to give, but as a new bride, I really didn't know what I had married into.

I soon found out. God! The first months of our marriage were murder. We were jazz musicians, had no money, and gigs for Monty had dried up in the Bay Area. So, we moved to Los Angeles where, before we met, Monty had established a reputation in local jazz circles. Since we were trying to get on our feet we stayed with his family.

Monty's parents and two younger brothers lived in a typical Hollywood stucco that looked nice on the outside but was small on the inside. After a day or two, once I'd settled in, I couldn't believe how physically cramped it was with six people on top of each other. It was even worse on those days when Monty was out making contacts or at rehearsals. Alone with his parents I felt suffocated emotionally. His father was very German, a grumpy big man who did not speak much. His mother was the opposite: French and Welsh, she was a bizarre mix of ditz and cunning. I didn't get along with either of them; I felt like an outsider and it was hell.

My release from that family came when Monty got an offer to join baritone sax legend, Gerry Mulligan, at the Blackhawk in a group that included trumpet player Chet Baker and pianist Russ Freeman. Things looked brighter as we drove back to the Bay Area, but early into the gig my mood darkened when I learned that Mulligan and Baker were in the junk.

I was less than thrilled with that part of jazz culture, but I took some consolation from knowing for certain that Monty would never get into it. That is until I found out that he was "chipping" heroin! *Chipping* refers to the occasional use of small amounts, or "chips," of heroin or cocaine. Evidently some people can do a little bit of it without getting hooked. So, Monty wasn't an out and out junkie, but he was a user.

When Mulligan's band left the Blackhawk, Monty stayed on as a regular with the house trio but historic world events would soon interrupt that arrangement. 1952 marked the second year since American troops had entered the Korean War and Monty knew his number was coming up with the local draft board. A lot of his friends urged him to find a good military band and join it before he got drafted. He asked around and got the impression that the Air Force base in San Rafael had a hell of a good band. Monty thought that rather than take the chance of being drafted into the infantry he probably should volunteer and have a choice about where he was assigned. Shortly thereafter, we moved to a cute studio apartment toward the beach out in the Avenues in western San Francisco that was convenient to the freeway and the Golden Gate Bridge into San Rafael.

We were pretty happy in our little apartment for about three months as Monty commuted to the Blackhawk and bided his time about the military. He practiced on his bass every day as I sat, listening and knitting. (I was impressed that Monty's bass once belonged to Jimmy Blanton, a key innovator on the instrument.) Plucking those strings put callouses on Monty's fingers, although he had learned how to pull them so the callouses weren't prominent. Since hands with hardened callouses are part of a bassist's instrument we had to be careful. I never even thought about letting him wash a dish because he might soften or even lose his callouses.

Listening to Monty practice taught me a lot about bass sounds, but it was accidental learning; Monty didn't consciously mentor me as a drummer. Quite the opposite, actually. Monty loved my singing but he didn't want me to play drums at all. He didn't think it was ladylike. Although I continued with my vocals, I didn't let Monty's opinions stop me or dent my growing ambitions to be a drummer.

Perhaps it's revealing that despite all my close listening to Monty, the one time we tried to play together we didn't get along time-wise. We got through it, but it wasn't the same groove; Monty put his division in a different spot than where I put my apple pie. Looking back, I think the reason we didn't fit was mental: He was embarrassed by my playing a "male" instrument.

I heard Monty's disapproval loud and clear, but there were times when an opportunity was too good to miss. Like when guys he worked with asked me to play. One evening Monty scheduled a rehearsal in our apartment with local musicians and both he and the drummer were late. Faced with that situation, his bandmates didn't care what Monty thought, they were impatient to go over a chart. So, as it had happened so many times before at Jimbo's, the guys would coax me: "Dottie, here are some brushes, play some rhythm on a magazine until the drummer gets here." I couldn't help but oblige, but, of course, when Monty learned about it he was furious and doubly embarrassed because I had slighted him in front of his buddies. At least it happened in the privacy of our own apartment. I can't begin to imagine his humiliation when a short time later I went public, playing drums at the Blackhawk.

In September 1952, the illustrious tenor-sax stylist, Stan Getz, came as a single to the Blackhawk. I sat in during a sound check shortly after Getz arrived and he offered to hire me for the whole week of his engagement. The only rub for me was that I was seven-and-a-half months pregnant, so before I accepted the gig I wanted to be sure that playing drums for that long wouldn't put my unborn child in jeopardy. "Will I be sitting on my baby's head when I'm playing?" I asked my doctor. "No," he told me, "and keeping active is the best thing for the baby." It turned out well for both of us: I suspect that cooking the great Stan Getz for a week is why I had only four hours of labor delivering my daughter, Deborah, and why to this day her time is great!

As Deborah headed to full term, Monty made the leap of voluntarily joining the military at Hamilton Air Force Base in San Rafael. Before we met, Monty had played with the noted tenor saxist and band leader, Vido Musso, so he had been exposed to a high level of professionalism. Having been told that the Air Force had a "great band" he was heartened and figured it was his best option, but he had been ill-advised. The Air Force had a terrible band. I mean, awful!

Monty's reaction was swift: He wanted out! He wanted out bad, but there was no way he could up and resign. Besides, with me pregnant we needed the medical coverage, so our only option was to stick it out for the long haul. Or, at least that's what we thought at the time.

My water broke in the Avenues just after midnight on November 18, 1952, and Deborah Lee was delivered at 5:10 that morning at the San Rafael Air Force Field Hospital. When they pulled her out I thought, "wow! this little girl has some blend of bloodlines: French, Welsh, German, a quarter Sicilian, and an eighth Native-American and Irish!" A successful birth behind us, we basked in our newfound joys of parenthood. It was short-lived.

Monty was miserable in that unbelievably sad Air Force band, but he didn't go over the edge until his hitch collided with an offer to join a new group, based in Los Angeles and led by one of the most important figures in West Coast jazz: drummer, Shelly Manne. Now desperate to get out, Monty devised his own Section 8: He would flip out and land a "Crazy Man" discharge.

One morning at the base, Monty put his plan into action. He worked himself into such an emotional frenzy that by lunchtime, when he stirred up commotion in the cafeteria by throwing his food tray in the air, he was, to all appearances, deranged. Later that day, after guards had escorted Monty home, he confided to me that his act almost had him convinced: "You know what? I really blew my top and almost went over!" He wanted out so bad that he came dangerously close to seriously hurting himself, but he did it! His scheme worked, he got out, and we paid a price for it.

For a short time after Deborah was born I wasn't singing or drumming; I wasn't doing anything except taking care of her. Monty was out a lot, either chipping on junk or working a gig, playing with anybody so he could keep his chops up. It wasn't long before we were close to broke so I assumed the mantle to provide, protect, and keep us afloat by patching together three part-time jobs.

I started at eight in the morning working the PBX ("Private Branch Exchange") telephone switchboard for a trucking company; afternoons I did typing and filing at a movie studio; and three nights a week I played drums in an all-girl trio at a joint in San Rafael from nine until two the next morning. The all-girl gig was pathetic; three women on a stage high up behind the bar, and my bandmates, a pianist and tenor player, were dreadful. The only thing remotely memorable about that episode is it may have been the first time I sang publicly while playing a full set of drums.

When Monty was home he'd mostly sleep, and even when he was up and around I couldn't depend on him to care for Deborah, to change or feed her. Maybe I've blocked out some good things he did for her because I was irritated by the things he wasn't doing and how that left all the burden on me. At first the solution seemed simple: hire babysitters.

Boy, was that ever a failure! I tried at least four different sitters and none of them took good care of Deborah. Much of the time they didn't even bother to change her diaper so I'd come home to a crying baby with painful rashes. It became a nightmare; there was always something wrong. I had no alternative but to take Deborah to my mother.

Fostering Deborah, even with my parents, was like having a part of my body lopped off. To ease the pain, I rationalized it to myself: "At least I know she's going to be royally taken care of." Little did I realize it would turn out to be a blessing-in-disguise for my parents. Mom and my stepdad hadn't been getting along too well—in fact, they were about to divorce. A big handicap in their relationship was that Bob was behind the eight ball from the get-go: in my mother's eyes, I don't think he could have ever competed with her one true love, Sammy Sampson.

It didn't help that they were childless. My mother was pregnant by Bob four times and had four miscarriages. Their hopes of having a child were gone and the frustration they both felt cast a pall over the marriage, but when I brought Deborah, I brought them their child.

When I saw my infant daughter in my mother's arms I could see immediately that Deborah was the key to a brand new life for both of them, but it killed me. As wretched as I was, though, I felt some relief because I was holding down three jobs and I could no longer adequately care for Deborah. My precious daughter was in a far better environment with my parents than I could provide—Mother and Bob had recently moved from Walnut Creek to Sacramento into a nice little house that had a big back yard for Deborah. Nevertheless, making the best Sophie's choice I could didn't stop the guilt, guilt, guilt, guilt. It was murder for me every week, scrambling to find time to visit—even to find transport since I didn't have a car. But, each time I saw her and saw how happy she was, I relaxed a little.

While all this weighed on me, Monty announced that he wanted us to move back to Los Angeles. Of course, with Deborah at my mother's I was loathe to do it. We argued for days and then I put my foot down: "That's it!" I was tired of bringing in the money while Monty, a proud recipient of a Section 8, wasn't working at all. I had empathy for him for a while, but it got harder and harder until finally our relationship dwindled down and out! I took it as much as I could, but I'm a survivor. I'm not going to wallow in somebody else's mess and get taken down with them. No way! I won't do it. I haven't done it for anybody. Once I catch on, I don't stay long. I take what I want and leave the rest!

I packed my bags and the finality floored Monty. He thought he could talk me out of leaving him because of the baby, but that didn't impress me. I knew he had no interest in being a full-fledged father to Deborah. Monty couldn't extend her that kind of love because he was in love with his bass. All his life, first he was a bass player, *then* he was a human being. I know lots of musicians like that, and I've never thought that was so terribly wrong because I pretty much was that way myself. Except where my daughter was concerned.

Our marriage was over. Monty went to Los Angeles; I stayed in San Francisco. A sad story, but no regrets. I needed to move on. I filed for divorce, and then, with Deborah at my parents' and only one mouth to feed, I quit all those jobs. That gave me more time for music—hanging and listening at clubs and working gigs.

Jerry

I first laid eyes on Jerry Dodgion in late 1952 at Ciro's nightclub in San Francisco. He was in a quartet led by trumpeter, John Coppola, who was a well-known figure in the San Francisco jazz scene of the early 1950s. I was immediately knocked out by Jerry's playing, but we didn't meet until sometime later when I went to work with a trio at a club in San Rafael and he was the alto player on it. I was twenty-three; Jerry told me he was, too, but he was really twenty-one.

The leader of the trio was a drummer. When I joined the band, it became a "Trio Plus" because a singer in those days was never considered a core member of an otherwise instrumental group. Despite hiring me as a vocalist, the drummer had his own ambitions to be a singer, and, since it was his gig, there was no one to stop him from trying to sing as he played drums on some numbers. It was a travesty; he couldn't do it, and to top it off, Jerry hated the drummer's time, the way it wandered around.

Jerry and I were local so he knew my reputation as a swinging drummer and that gave him an idea. He put a bug in the leader's ear about my replacing him at the drums so he could get out front and sing. "Are you sure Dottie plays drums?" he asked, and Jerry assured him, "Oh, yeah, don't worry, you can go up and sing." Jerry got to like my drums so much that he encouraged the drummer to sing all the time!

Little by little, Jerry and I got to know each other. We'd talk at intermissions and on the back seat of the drummer's car each time we made the forty-five-minute commute to and from the San Rafael gig. We discovered that our relationship was very unusual: He didn't want to own me, and I certainly didn't want to be owned; I didn't want any Italian man's thumb on me!

It got so I wasn't afraid to tell him anything, I knew he wouldn't betray me. It was the first real friendship with a man I'd ever had, and I learned so much from him because he was more scholastic than I. We were simpatico on the bandstand, too. Our time fit; we divided in the same place without even thinking about it.

Jerry encouraged me to concentrate on the drums and forget about singing. He was afraid that as a vocalist I wouldn't be taken seriously by other musicians: "They'll either call you a drummer who sings a little or a singer who plays a little drums." Jerry's opinion meant a lot to me because I respected his musicianship; that was the first step in my growing affection for him.

Several weeks into the San Rafael gig sparks began to fly. That is until Monty put a long-distance damper on my romance with Jerry. Monty was offended when I left him, blaming me for our separation, and finding out that I was dating Jerry only bothered him more. Monty knew Jerry, and his first response was to make fun of the way Jerry looked, with his glasses and pony tail. I didn't flatter him with a response.

As time went on and my relationship with Jerry got serious, Monty turned nasty. I don't believe he was jealous that I had fallen in love with someone else because toward the end of our marriage he seemed to quit caring. I think he was furious because he had lost control of what he felt was rightfully his: ME! He figured, I guess, that I owed him something, and wanting to get even with me, he unleashed his big artillery: Monty's mother entered the picture!

She started a campaign to take Deborah away from me under the pretext that I was an unfit mother. Monty's mother wanted my baby and Monty went along with it! Paranoid about losing Deborah, I decided that the last thing I needed was to be caught in a compromised position like having an affair. Jerry and I were in love but we couldn't afford to have sex in case Monty's mother hired a detective to follow us! Celibacy may have been as foreign to us as "champagne music," but for the next several months there was no hanky-panky going on.

It was so cute. Jerry and I sat on the backseat with only our knees touching during those forty-five-minute commutes. That made it even hotter. It was right out of a romance novel—lingering looks of longing across a table. Nothing is more intriguing than when you're forbidden to be together; you fall in love that much harder. Monty didn't have a clue about any of this. He thought Jerry and I were carrying on the whole time we were working in San Rafael!

The madness was headed to a boil when it appeared that Monty's mother planned to take me to court. That was a very difficult time for me, waiting for the axe to drop, and when I'm that unhappy I close down and make the trouble disappear. So, I can't remember if Monty's mother actually filed a petition. Maybe she thought better about getting into a legal tangle because there was no doubt that Deborah was in a good environment with my parents. The final result is all I cared about: Monty and his mother folded and the threat of losing my daughter vanished.

I won an uncontested divorce on September 8, 1954. Poor Monty. To get the divorce I had to make a statement credible enough to establish irreconcilable differences. As reported in the *San Francisco Chronicle*, I testified in City Hall that "a husband ought to be a breadwinner and not simply a baby-sitter."[1] The column continued with another quote from my testimony: "She said that when she finally got him out of the house and on a payroll, he kept all the money for himself, so that she had to hire a baby-sitter and go back to work."[2]

Other San Francisco dailies got wind of the story and the race was on to interview me. It started one afternoon in Sherman and Clay, a very famous music store at the time. I was there looking for a job when a gaggle of reporters caught up with me. Now it's true that Monty's behavior toward me had left a lot to be desired, but I didn't want to slam him in public. He wasn't really a bad person.

So, I was shocked when one of the columns took a big liberty that, as far as I was concerned, misrepresented me by making fun of Monty as if he were a deadbeat. It wasn't a fair story and I was very embarrassed by it. To add insult to injury, a photo caption for the *Call Bulletin* said "Bull Fiddle Went Silent,"[3] calling Monty a bull fiddle player—*bull fiddle* was an old fashioned and by then corny name for an acoustic bass. Fortunately, in all the commotion of being interviewed, I had the presence of mind not to mention the Section 8. Imagine the field day the papers would have had with that!

As part of the divorce agreement I waived alimony but did get custody of Deborah, including a modest monthly sum for child support. That ordeal over, Jerry came back into my life and for the next year we lived and gigged together in the San Francisco area. Sometimes I was the nominal bandleader, like when we played the Blue Lei (with bassist Dean Riley and Mickey Walsh on piano) for four weeks in 1954: "If you like to have the kick of hearing a good jazz group before it gets famous, drop in on the Dottie Grae Quartet now playing at the Blue Lei on Eddy Street."[4] Other times our group was led by Jerry: "Jerry Dodgion and his quartet, featuring Dottie Grae, the lady drummer, have taken over musically at the Blackhawk Club."[5]

I also picked up jobs singing occasionally with David Wheat, who was affectionately known as "Buckwheat." Buckwheat was a guitarist and the bassist for the original Kingston Trio. He'd play flamenco guitar for me, but he also played jazz guitar in big bands and the Chet Baker Trio. As a songwriter, Buckwheat wrote one of my favorite tunes, the jazz standard, "Better than Anything,"[6] with lyricist, Bill Loughborough.

Buckwheat owned a houseboat in Sausalito (Bill Loughborough was two houseboats down), and he was the pot provider for musicians in the area. I'd heard about that houseboat for a long time and one day some of the guys I was working with took me there, and another brand new world opened up.

Buckwheat was the sweetest man. Scuffling musicians were always welcome to take a break, to hang and relax, at Buckwheat's. If you didn't have any pot, have no fear, he was there for you—but there wasn't any hard stuff going on at all. Entering the front door at Buckwheat's, you walked down a hallway the length of the boat past bedrooms on the left, a kitchen on the right where you'd pick up a pot cookie to enjoy as you made your way forward to a living room with a nice rug, soft chairs, and—in the center—a round burned-out fireplace with cactus plants in it.

As a newcomer at Buckwheat's I was intimidated by the company of so many seasoned musicians. In my own head I was still more of a girl singer, not a full-fledged musician, not a drummer yet, really. Buckwheat saw that I was frightened so he watched out for me and wanted me to be comfortable, but he truly made me feel at home when he put me to work.

Even though I didn't smoke joints, he said there was no reason I couldn't learn to make them! He sat me in a little rocker and armed with buds of marijuana, papers, and a shoebox lid, he taught me how to roll a joint to perfection: Roll 'em up halfway, lick them, twist the ends, and make a mouth piece. Almost like a real cigarette. It wasn't easy to do: the joints had to be thin yet full, and I had to roll them loose enough for the cigarette paper to burn evenly. To do it right was an art and I got it down perfectly.

I was the roller; that was my job at Buckwheat's. I'd sit in my chair, roll the joints, and listen as the guys smoked and talked. I didn't talk; I didn't have anything to talk about, nothing to say that would interest them. I was the low one on the totem pole and I was the only chick there so all the more reason to keep my mouth shut and just listen.

They had wonderful stories, it was very grown up. It wasn't lama, lama like when I was the driver for Nick Esposito's band. At Buckwheat's they were into philosophy, astronomy, and the hip poets and novelists at the time. When they talked about music and their gigs it was more intellectual and it wasn't putting anybody down. I loved hearing the stories; those were some of the best times of my life.

Jerry stayed busy working gigs in San Francisco. One of the highlights was when the Vernon Alley Quartet,[7] led by the veteran bassist and with Jerry on alto, backed Billie Holiday for two weeks at the Down Beat on Market Street. Billie would walk on stage, get in the crooks of the piano, open her mouth, and sing her little heart out. She wouldn't talk to the audience, no announcing tunes, nothing. Even today, I wish to hell I could do that.

I remember a funny run-in that Billie had with Helen, the lady who ran the club. Helen was always bitching about the musicians; if there wasn't any business, it was the musicians' fault. So one night, during intermission, Helen was bitching and bitching within earshot of Billie. Billie had been drinking quite a bit and she had her two little Chihuahuas up on the bar. Fed up with the rant, Billie shot a look at Helen and gave the command: "Sic her!" Those little dogs let out a burst of piercing "yips" and Helen pulled back in horror!

Hearing Billie, especially with Jerry behind her, is a wonderful memory, but a week later when the Down Beat brought in the Buddy DeFranco Quartet my life was literally turned around! The bassist, Eugene Wright, was new to me, but I was familiar with the rest of the band from recordings: clarinetist DeFranco; pianist, Kenny Drew (I had played with him at Jimbo's); and drummer, Art Blakey. Still, I wasn't prepared for what I heard in live performance. From the opening measures of their first tune my mouth dropped open. I'd never heard a rhythm section cook like that! I'd never heard anything that could move my whole being with rhythm: furious tempos, choruses flying by, and swinging!

Eugene Wright was a revelation; he was the first bass player I ever heard who could thrill me! I was so knocked out that at intermission I introduced myself and told him how I felt. As Eugene himself recalls, "When I first met her she was just overwhelmed to hear a bass player play like the old 'Senator.'" (Eugene loves to be called by his nickname, "The Senator," a tribute to his bearing as a distinguished statesman of music.) Hearing DeFranco's quartet and meeting Eugene was the turning point; that was the inspiration that really made me commit to the drums! Before Eugene, I had just filled in, just messed around at the drums; but when I heard that group I was hooked. I told Eugene, "I'm going to play the drums!" and he replied, "You bet you are, and don't let anybody stop you."

DeFranco's band was in for the week at the Down Beat Club, and I was there for every show. The second night, after the first set, as Eugene came off the stand and saw me he got a big smile on his face, "There she is, my drummer!" Throughout the week, at intermission and sometimes after the last set, Eugene and I talked music, music, music. I remember asking him about the deep tone of his bass and Eugene told me that he called his sound the "ging-gang," and that it came from accenting one and three.

Earlier bass players accented two and four, which can slow your tempo. Bebop musicians accented one and three which gave tempos a lift, but Eugene didn't get it from the Boppers. He latched on to it during his playing days in Chicago, with greats like tenor saxophonists Ben Webster and Gene Ammons, who had already established this special way of playing. Those were the kinds of conversations we had. He was delighted that I was *that* interested. The stage was set for us getting together and, as he had told me, "Once I find out you can play, lookout!"

When DeFranco's band left town, Jerry and I came to grips with a domestic issue: marriage. We were madly in love, thank you very much, but I didn't want to get married again. Jerry was very understanding about this because, like me, he saw no reason for making our relationship "official" with vows of marriage. We made very intelligent choices and stuck to them throughout the next year of living together. Right up until another unexpected curve changed our plans completely.

Toward the end of 1955, Jerry's mother was dying from terminal breast cancer. Not long before her death, she surprised us by saying, "Before I die I want to see you two married." She was pleading for us to get respectable! Reluctantly, we told her no, but she wouldn't back down: "I'll give you $500 and a Volkswagen!" Jerry and I looked at each other in astonishment, and then, as if it were rehearsed, we shrugged and replied in unison, "What's a piece of paper?"

Before we could second-guess ourselves, Jerry and I, along with two friends to act as witnesses, packed a car and drove to Reno early on October 12th for the nuptials. But despite the gifts and the good feelings I had about honoring the dying request of Jerry's mother, my mind hadn't changed. Deep down I still didn't want to get married!

I almost got my wish because of a national holiday. When we arrived in Reno we were surprised to learn it was Columbus Day. That meant all government offices would be closing very shortly at noon, but we got in just under the wire. My hope for a reprieve foiled, I had to express my defiance with the outfit I sported at the ceremony: a bright orange top and a big orange dirndl skirt, accessorized with an insanely long cigarette holder. Regrettably, my brazen appearance didn't faze the justice of the peace who hitched us in the old county courthouse.

Despite my doubts about the wisdom of it, we were married, but I wouldn't have gone to Reno at all if Jerry hadn't accepted my terms before we left. First, I said, "I'm not a woman to be left alone!" and Jerry promised never to treat me like a "musician's wife"—he wouldn't go on the road and leave me at home. Then I asked him: "What if I fall in love or think I'm in love with somebody else and want to have an affair?" That was very important to me; I was determined to keep my hard-earned freedom in case I had eyes for somebody and wanted to do something about it.

Jerry's reaction was marvelous. If that happened, he said, I was free to go. He assured me that as far as he was concerned, we were both equally free, we were both our own agents. He finished with an unforgettable line: "You can go to bed, Dottie, with anybody you would have dinner with." I thought that was hilarious and loved him all the more for it. And, he was right, of course, because I was very particular. I wouldn't have dinner with just anyone; I won't go unless you can dine me supremely.

We agreed on an open marriage—Jerry knew that was the only way I would go through with it—setting the tone for the next twenty years of marital and musical madness. A few days after the wedding, the prudence of our arrangement got a breezy endorsement when I met the great alto saxophonist, Paul Desmond, at the Blackhawk. "Dottie," he pleaded, "the next time you get divorced, call me first!"

176 Steps

1955 was a terrific year. Jerry and I were married, we moved to a country-style house in a rustic setting, and I went to the "University of Eugene Wright"!

Jerry and I had been living in a little duplex in midtown Berkeley where our neighbors were so close it cramped our style. That all changed when Bud Glenn and his wife, Evelyn—they were the witnesses at our wedding—dropped a godsend of a deal in our laps. Bud was a drummer who grew up with Jerry; he and Evelyn had bought a house in Larkspur, in Marin County, so Bud would have a place to play, and they offered us the downstairs apartment for thirty dollars a month as long as we agreed to fix it up. We didn't think twice.

The house stood atop a hillside secluded in dense forest. To get there we'd pass through a canyon of magnificent redwoods, park at the bottom of the hill, and—on an incline of about forty-five degrees—walk up 176 steps to our apartment. The first thirty steps were constructed from two-by-fours; the remaining one-hundred-and-forty-six were dug directly out of the earth with a plank of wood and two pieces of pipe to keep them straight.

At first, the hike up or down all those steps was invigorating. After a while it got to be a drag on routine tasks like taking the garbage out, and, because we didn't have outside lights, going downhill at night with only a flashlight could be very tricky. Trudging up and down could also be maddening; more than once Jerry got to the car on his way to a gig only to discover he'd left his mouthpiece in the apartment. It took a little time, but eventually we learned to take the aggravation of the steps in stride because in all other respects it was an ideal musicians' house. We were up so high on that hill we could play all day or all night and nobody was the wiser.

Another plus was the Larkspur house had enough space for a music room. We moved Jerry's piano from his mother's house with expert help from pianist, John Marabuto. John made his real living tuning, repairing, and remodeling pianos because jazz didn't pay anything. John took Jerry's spinet completely apart so we could carry it up the hill piece by piece in boxes and then he reassembled the whole piano, as if it were a kit, in a corner of the room that was open and bright with a lot of windows.

Jerry got his piano and then I got my drums. The move to Larkspur gave me my first chance to set up the drum set my father had bought for me from Johnny Berger—I didn't have them set up when I was living with Monty, that's for damn sure! Jerry, on the other hand, loved the way I played and he really encouraged me in my resolve to focus more and more on the drums. And he walked his talk: When I had gigs, Jerry would lug my drums up and down those 176 steps. That was real love as far as I was concerned.

After our Larkspur move, Jerry and I worked separate jobs for a while. He was playing with some of the better Bay Area musicians, like trumpeter, John Coppola, and I was singing at the Blue Orchid. Even though we were both working, the gigs didn't pay that much, so we were pretty much living hand to mouth. I home-cooked my fanny off to save money, and to help with the rent we drew thirty dollars a week from unemployment insurance. Jerry and I weren't drinkers—I didn't taste alcohol until I was 23—but one of the few pleasures we indulged in Larkspur was having a glass of wine. To stay within our penny-pinching budget, we'd get a gallon of Chianti for $.99 over at the Gallo Winery!

Once the music room was ready we started having jam sessions. Sometimes we jammed with touring musicians; when Count Basie's band was in town two of the guys—tenor player, Frank Wess, and trombone player, Benny Powell—would come over. We'd play, I'd cook dinner for them, and then we'd play some more, but visitors from out of town were the exception. More often we jammed and had little rehearsals with local musicians, including trumpet player, Allan Smith; pianist, Mickey Walsh from our Blue Lei days; and, of course, John Marabuto.

Whether our guests were out of town or local, they all made a pit stop halfway up the 176-step hike, where we refueled them with martinis and accompanied them, slow and steady, the rest of the way up. The general rule was "if you wanted to arrive in shape to play you had to take it easy."

Sessions with locals usually included extracurricular activities. After we jammed a while, we might go on the roof where Bud Glenn had a telescope and he'd tell us about the stars. Or we'd take pokes and play parlor games, but mostly—just like at Buckwheat's—we talked about books and ideas. We even had our own book club and I read all the books. "The Prophet," by Kahlil Gibran was my Bible. Thomas Paine's, "The Age of Reason," was sobering. Paine pokes holes through the Christian Bible, revealing what to me is hypocrisy in the highest realm.

I was attracted to Paine's arguments because of my time at the convent and my memory of a drunk priest at confession. Thomas Paine helped me justify why I didn't want to return to the fold; his arguments confirmed for me that the Church isn't the supreme authority like it was made to appear when I was growing up. Instead of Catholic dogma, I believe in karma. There has to be karma. I told my daughter not to lie because negative karma means she'll have to come back for another life.

Then there are my guardian angels. Shortly after we took the Larkspur house they raised my game when, amazingly, the Senator called; he was back in town and wanted to play the blues! Jerry and I picked Eugene up at his hotel next to the Blackhawk and took him to Dee and John Marabuto's house in El Cerrito, ready to jam and eat good food. We went there every day for practically two weeks and, as Eugene described it, "We met and became a family. This was all family style."

After those early sessions at Dee's place, and for the next several years, our get-togethers with Eugene alternated between the Marabutos and our house in Larkspur. Eugene remembers that "whenever I was in town, we'd spend most of the time at either one of the houses. . . . Every time we'd meet, we'd play."

Our close-knit "family" circle—Eugene, John, Jerry, and me—played most of the sessions. Now and then we'd have guests, like the Basie band members I mentioned earlier. One visit caught us completely off guard. We were playing "Pennies from Heaven" in John's living room when, midway through the tune, the foghorn sound of a baritone sax boomed like the voice of God. We turned to see Pepper Adams strolling toward us, playing in his slippers and looking like he had just climbed out of bed! Turns out Pepper, who was in town with Stan Kenton, was staying with John and Dee and our sweet sounds had awakened him. That was the first time Jerry and I met this great bari player; about ten years later, Jerry and Pepper were together on the Thad Jones–Mel Lewis Orchestra.

Over a five-year span, from 1955 until 1961 when Jerry and I left for New York City, musical get-togethers with Eugene were a fixture in our lives. Those jam sessions were fun for all of us in the "Family," but for me they were so much more. Eugene was my mentor, the most important teacher I ever had. What he taught me encompassed everything I ever thought I would want to do in music.

Times when everyone else was late, Eugene and I would play by ourselves, and that was the most fun in the world. Without a horn or piano getting in my way I could really understand where he wanted me to place the notes. For his part, Eugene was overwhelmed that I played in the same spot where he divided. He'd shake his head, like, "Yes! Just keep playing!" There was a smile on both our faces, I mean, all the time.

Here's Eugene's take on those early sessions: "I'd enjoy playing with her because she likes to swing. . . . Then we get to talking and I said, 'you know, you're blessed.' She said 'what do you mean?' 'Well, your father was a drummer, right? He evidently left a lot of it on you.' . . . That was the difference between other people that I've played with that were very good. She had that little extra extra, which comes from her father's genes . . . that she had a chance to listen to her father practice and play ever since she was a young girl. . . . It was built into her to be a good drummer. . . . She had a head start on her education."

I remember how Eugene would cheer me on as we played: "Come on, Dot, yeah, Dot, yeah! You got it, Dot. You really have it! Whoa, cookin'! Wow!" When we'd break he'd put his bass down, wipe his forehead with his handkerchief, and say to me: "Don't let anybody talk you out of playing drums. Don't let anybody tell you, Dot, that you haven't got it. I mean, it's there!"

After playing intermittently for months at the Marabuto's or at Larkspur, Eugene and I occasionally picked up a casual for a single weekend. One thing that really irked Eugene was how musicians who wouldn't call me for jobs would show up at our gigs wanting to play. "They all come in every night on our last set and want to sit in," he recalled. "But the thing that got to me is none of them would ever call her for a gig; she'd be there and be available and a certain guy would say, 'Yeah, well, Dottie, we got a gig, I'll be in touch,' but he never called her. . . . Why would they turn her down other than the fact she's a girl drummer? . . . They never really accepted her as part of the musicians and a drummer on top of it. . . . They had that attitude that, 'well, she's just Dottie Dodgion, she's a girl drummer, we can go on by and sit in with her.' . . . And the ones with the . . . attitudes, you don't catch it until you get them in conversation. . . . 'Yeah, well, she's good, yeah, she's alright.'" "No, no, she's not alright, my friend, 'cause if she was *alright* I probably wouldn't have met her and I probably wouldn't be playing with her. She's a master drummer and we can do what we have to do anytime."

As our relationship matured, Eugene's counsel looked beyond the small pond of California jazz to prepare me for the sexism I might face in the "Big Apple," just in case I ever got there. Here's one piece of his advice that stuck with me: "Now, when you first get to New York and the musicians all find out that you play the drums they'll pat you on the head and say, 'Isn't that cute?' But wait until you start taking their jobs away, they won't think it's so cute."

That's just what happened; I got to be a first-call sub in New York and I did take some of their gigs!

Eugene's Lessons

My professional relationship with Eugene Wright taught me the most wonderful things about music, things I'd never known or felt before.

Above all, Eugene stressed the importance of the overall sound of a performance. When somebody kicks off a tune with a confident "one, two, three, four," it unifies the band with energy right from the start. The overall sound is what happens when the band settles into the tempo that was counted off and everybody is together at the same time on "one."

Well, not precisely at the same time. Eugene coached me on the nuances of playing in a rhythm section, including some intangible insides on how to fit with the piano and the bass. He told me that in a rhythm section, the piano, bass, and drums don't play in exactly the same spot; they wouldn't be trying to hit a groove all together all at once in a single line. Instead, they each occupy a different "level" in relation to the others. To illustrate this, Eugene took my hands to show me that a rhythm section fit is three-dimensional; it's like the different points you feel when you interlock your fingers.

So, just like there's no perfection in breathing or walking, there's no perfection in playing. Although it may seem that everyone is playing the same note at the same time, each member of the rhythm section will have a slightly different feel about where the beat is and that enables the music to breathe. That "broadness" of interpretation of the beat should still come off as sounding natural because the differences are really so minute, the size of a "gnat's ass." When everybody finds that groove, playing somewhere within the tempo—that's the broadness again, the breathing—then the band will have a marvelous time swinging!

In a rhythm section, when all three musicians are close together in their interpretation or division of the time—what I call their "triplets apple pie"[1]— it's complete Nirvana. To stay there consistently, not rushing and dragging or going in and out of the "pocket,"[2] I mean it's just a thrill! Eugene showed me how to get there and to really feel it, and because he showed me that, when I went to New York I knew how to do it with the big boys who knew how to do it, too. Nobody ever dissected it or thought about it; if you start thinking about it you can really mess yourself up! Fortunately, it's intuitive with me, but if I ever feel like I'm starting to rush the tempo a little bit, I go back to concentrating on where I'm playing beat one with my bass drum and that settles me down every time. You get straight with where the time is and then everything else fits with that. It's the most natural thing, like when you're sitting and talking to somebody or you're waiting for a bus and you tap your foot.

Eugene's lessons about working a rhythm section started me down a path to my own secret in New York, and that was to play soft and fit within the volume of a band instead of being heard first. I know that one reason I got to work a lot in New York is because most drummers play loud—they have to "lay it down," as they say. Yes, the drummer has to lay down the tempo, but often for drummers of a particular gender persuasion, that means power and volume. To the contrary, I've found that a rhythm section works together best when I moderate my power. When somebody kicks it off, I give that first note life; I make that first snap of my stroke swing by giving it a "hint" of an edge on top of beats one and three. I listen to the overall sound and then I play right in the middle or just under the rest of the band so I never get in their way. I don't change their conception; I make them feel comfortable with it: I'm a supportive player.

As a supportive drummer my role is to play a tempo and time feel underneath that makes the frontline want to go to heaven. For example, I lay down "four" on the bottom, but I make sure not to drag the bottom of my four.[3] As Eugene would put it, "You know it's so wonderful to be swinging a horn player out of this world when they don't even know it!"

Being a supportive drummer can also mean fine-tuning within the legal right of where the time is laying. If a leader kicks off a tempo that gets kind of "harum-scarum," I go as fast as the tempo was set and then sit on that swing with my hi-hat[4] so nobody rushes and everybody blends. It's a leveling-off period so the band can settle solidly into the tempo that was kicked off.

It's hard for most drummers, and most bass players, too, to know when to sit down on the tempo because although the guys in a band will have the tempo in their heads, sometimes it changes once they get past the first four bars. When we're playing in 4/4 time,[5] the count off is 1–2–3–4. Then what usually happens is the "one" is okay but by the third note they've already rushed it and they don't give "four" its full value. They've shortened it just that much so the tempo is speeded up. Then there's the problem of somebody going over the bar line. Using the same example, when a band plays in 4/4 time a bar is 1–2–3–4, but if someone plays five pulses in a measure—1–2–3–4–5—they've already gone into the next bar and turned the time around. That player will never catch up unless he can let go, unless he stops playing and listens to the rhythm section. But they never do that!

There were times when, after somebody turned the time around, the leader would yell over to me: "Just go with him." But I'd make it clear: "Not me. No sir!" So, I'd wind up fighting whoever turned the time and the group would sound like a train wreck. I mean, what would you expect with one person playing one tempo and me playing another? I never gave in when that happened even though it's hell to play like that. A lot of times my way of handling it was to lay out, to quit playing for several measures, and let the rest of the band have the train wreck all to themselves. Then when there was an open spot I'd jump in and set the time right so they'd all have something to hang on to. I'm not heartless, I'm a musician! It isn't a matter of winning, it's where the time is. Make no mistake, turning the time around was the sin of all sins in New York. Man, if you turned the time around even once, you were out of there. They could never trust you again.

Eugene's guidance about playing in a rhythm section included pointers about the placement of the beat. One pointer was about tipping, which means to play ahead of the beat to achieve a feeling of forward motion in the music, similar to the sensation of physically tipping over if you lean too far forward.[6] Piano players can be very different in the way they place the beat. In response, I adjust my apple pie on the ride cymbal, shifting gears on my triplets to change my division to match the pianist's interpretation. When we'd work with a piano player who would drag—he'd lean on four more than one and play way behind—Eugene would say, "We gotta play on top of him." See, piano players who play way behind don't always have an edge, so that would be my cue; I'd play the edge and the edge came from tipping.

Tipping on top in this case meant leaning on one, hitting one with a little more energy but without rushing the time.

Then there were pianists who played on top and never held sustained notes and waited. They liked to play up tunes and fast, almost rushing the tempo, trying to make it exciting by playing a note on top of another note practically before the first note got there. In other words, they were already tipping. When that happened Eugene would say, "Okay, Dot, let's lay back and sit on him," referring to my stroke, my division on the cymbal, and his stroke on the bass. It was a wider sound that we'd get out of the division. It was like we were holding the reins, and it meant that Eugene wouldn't pull the strings so hard and I'd broaden my triplets by stretching out my cymbal beat a little bit and playing softer. We'd widen out a little bit because the piano player was already playing tight, and if we played tight with him then there'd be no spacing and no swinging. To swing, we'd widen out.

Most piano players leading a trio want a rhythm section but they don't want them to be heard. They want to be heard. They want to take credit for the whole thing like they did it all by themselves. It's a conceit but it's the way of the beast; after all pianists don't need anybody. They have the melody, the bass, and the treble—they're the whole orchestra. Since a lot of piano players feel that way, you've got to be smart and know your place. That never bothered me. I understood the pecking order.

I accepted that the pianist, as the featured player, usually decided where the time was, and the bass and the drums molded to fit him; it was up to them to make subtle accommodations in their apple-pie division of the beat. It's that "gnat's ass" adjustment again and it's called "fitting," rhythm-section fitting. Then, to keep the time consistent, Eugene used to tell me, "If you can get two on the bandstand to fit, who agree where the time is, the third one's got to go with you." He called it "locking in." When we worked trios together and the tempo was kicked off, Eugene and I would start swinging—not to take anything away from the pianist—and we were steady enough to lock in and play in a comfortable spot, keeping that initial tempo very even underneath so that the piano player got relaxed and would play easier.

Eugene also gave me important advice about bandstand conduct. First, there are no "oops" up there. "Oops" means to make a mistake, like rushing or dragging the tempo. There are no second chances; you lay it down where it's supposed to be the first time or forget it. On the matter of concentration, Eugene told me that when your foot hits that stand you focus solely on playing, on listening, and on giving each bar and each note its full value. Everything else has to disappear. I don't care if you had a fight with your old lady, if your day has been hell, or if some little gal sashays across the room—whatever your problems or distractions, you're playing music. It has nothing to do with your personal life, so you leave it off the bandstand.

The irony is that by releasing your ego on the stand you escape your old lady, or whatever your problems might be. People have had tragedies, someone close has died, and the work has been their salvation. They gave all their sorrow to the music.

* * *

Closing this record of my lessons with Eugene are a few of his memories of our time together:

"The one thing people don't understand is Dottie Dodgion and the Senator were in love, musically."

"When we first started playing over in Larkspur, I said, 'You see, Dottie, see how much fun we're having, it's like putting the spice into your Italian food.' . . . She also puts her Italian sauce in it when she's playing. . . . Then another time we'll be playing somewhere and I'd say, 'Dot, the pot's getting a little bit chilly'—meaning let's don't be playing at it too long, it's gonna be cold, so let's do this thing and get outta here. Then another time I said, 'You know, we had a strawberry time,' because I refer to food that people eat and people will like. . . . And then, before the gig is over, I say, 'Dottie, let's play the blues'. . . . Bam! We start marching . . . and I said, 'Now, you see, we put some greens on them that they didn't know about.' Everything you play has color in it . . . that means you play dynamics, you play all kind of phrases that mean something and people hear it, sometime they catch it, sometimes they don't."

"One thing I'll never forget, she said, 'You know, we were playing that tune and I remember the first thing you told me was: find out their spot. And ever since then, when I'm playing and I feel that it ain't quite right, I start paying attention to the guys up in front and I automatically know right after that what to do.' I said, 'that's what it's all about. It's called playing together.'"

"I would hip her to all those things over a period of many years, but the key to Dottie and myself and what Dottie can do, was she already had it in her to do it but never had the opportunity to do it. That's all it was."

"I said, ' Dottie, you want to not play your bass drum that hard. Play it so it blends in with my bass fiddle.' She said, 'Oh, yes, that's what I was trying to do, but I didn't know exactly what to do.' I said, 'Learn the temperament[7] . . . and learn to be able to hear my bass all the time. . . . When I get a little stronger, you get a little stronger. When you get a little stronger and I feel you got a top I'll ease up and play it behind you. . . . Back and forth.' Whatever we're playing she might be the boss of that tempo, and if she's the boss of that tempo we'll get down the line and when she gets to set it down and really playing the things she wants to play, then I'll listen to her and I'll take my bass and complement her."

"She would listen to everything I'd be doing, at the same time playing her stuff. Very few drummers will do that . . . that's because a lot of people don't know how to play together. They can play and sound good and do all the hip things—I ain't talking about that. . . . Dottie and I were like a rhythm section's supposed to be—like with Joe Morello with Dave [Brubeck]—we played together."

"I said, 'the first thing you want to do is you don't ever want to allow yourself the gift to not do what you feel should be done at that time.' Everybody does that, too, in life not just in music. What that meant really is that if the piano player didn't know how to really get this thing going and she'll say, 'Well, then I'll just finish the gig,' but she would kind of lay back. And every time she'd talk about something like that I'd say, 'Listen, don't you ever give up what you got. If the other people are not that great a player, you get up on your drums and play and swing them, make them play. Don't just go up there and play half-heartedly and say, Well, they ain't doing nothing."

"I used to tell her, 'Dottie, learn to play with the worst ones as well as the good ones.' . . . If you can't play with a person who can't hardly play then you ain't got yourself together. Your take is, when you find someone like that, play what you know it's supposed to be."

"And what she's saying about being her mentor, she's right about that. . . . Man, Dottie . . . learned a lot of stuff from me, but it was because I had the edge. I was a hundred years old, she was 4 or 5 years old. . . . Every time we'd meet I had something to give to her, she had something she wanted to learn from me. . . . Anything that I wanted her to know I passed on to her. . . . So she'd pay attention, pay attention. . . . Anything I would tell her or suggest to her she would do it and come back doing it better than what I do."

"She went through a lot. . . . I'm very proud of her."

First Time in Vegas

My marriage to Jerry in October and the start of my mentoring relationship with Eugene were defining moments for me in 1955, but other things happened earlier in the year that, in a roundabout way, set in motion a series of turning points in my life between 1957 and my New York debut in 1961. Some of the seeds for those changes were planted even farther back, in 1953.

That was the year the beloved bandleader and composer/arranger, Gerald Wilson, moved from Los Angeles to start a band in San Francisco and Jerry was called to play in it. Jerry started as second alto, sitting next to lead alto, Jerome Richardson, who eventually played a key role in our move to New York. Jerry stayed with the band for its full two-year run in the Bay Area, and when Gerald disbanded and moved back to Los Angeles, he recommended Jerry to alto saxophone giant, Benny Carter. That in turn led to our first trip to Las Vegas.

In May 1955, the Benny Carter Orchestra was booked to play opposite Count Basie's Band for the grand opening of the Moulin Rouge Hotel. The band started rehearsals in late May and played the entire summer. I went down to Vegas about the middle of the gig.

The Moulin Rouge, the first desegregated hotel-casino in Las Vegas, was located across the railroad tracks on the west side, in an area known as the "Dust Bowl," where the Black population lived as a segregated community. This historic, interracial landmark closed six months later in November 1955.

The racial divide in Vegas at that time was difficult to miss, especially for us musicians working in an integrated jazz world. Sometimes we'd good-naturedly kid about it. I remember one night we were in a car heading to the hotel with two African American band members from Basie's band, Frank Foster and Frank Wess. To get to West Las Vegas we had to drive through an underpass. Frank Foster, who had the nickname, "Foss," was real light-skinned and Frank Wess was dark. As we drove beneath the underpass and saw a sign that read, "No passing," Frank Wess blurted, "That means you, too, Foss," teasing Foster about passing for white.

I was privileged that summer in Vegas to befriend one of the most conspicuous interracial couples of that era: Louis Bellson and his wife, Pearl Bailey, vocalist and star of stage and screen. When we met, Louie and Pearl were working one of the hotels; he played behind Pearl and was her musical director. Louie was sooo handsome, a regular Cary Grant, and I saw how jealous Pearl got when she was singing onstage and girls in the side boxes of the theater were all aglow looking at him. I remember one time when, between numbers, Pearl turned around to the sides and with her hands on her hips gave those ladies a look and said right out loud on the stage: "Don't any of you little darlings think that you're going to hit on my old man. He's my old man, you understand?" The audience roared, but she meant it. If she caught you looking at her husband you were dead. I was scared to death of her.

Shortly after my arrival in Vegas I met Terry Pollard, a fantastic lady pianist and vibes player from Detroit. Terry was in town playing on the Strip with fellow vibist Terry Gibbs's band, and her husband, tenor saxophonist Ray Black, was a bandmate of Jerry's on Benny Carter's band. (Wardell Gray, an important swing-to-bop transitional figure, was in the Carter band for the Moulin Rouge rehearsals but died shortly thereafter, on May 25, 1955. At Jerry Dodgion's suggestion, Benny Carter hired Terry Pollard's spouse, Ray Black, as Gray's replacement.)

With our husbands so busy, Terry and I would meet after hours in the lobby of the Moulin Rouge and she'd say, "C'mon, we're not going to lay around here all night. Let's play someplace!" Off we'd go to sit-in at clubs along Jackson Street on the west side—there were three or four little jazz joints in that district. It was just the two of us, Terry and me, both about the same size, one Black and one white, and I must admit that initially I felt uncertain about going out together because Terry was a known quantity in those clubs and I most certainly was not. When I expressed my misgivings, Terry assured me: "You'll be alright with me, Dottie," and sure enough, I was.

Our first night out, in the first club we found, Terry announced to the house musicians that we wanted to play. Looking a bit skeptical, one of the guys asked, "Hey, Terry, who's this little white thing you brought in?" Terry retorted, "Never you mind, she's a drummer and wait 'til you hear her play!" With that, we climbed on the stand and cooked, just cooked to death. The house band applauded and we played all night long!

A few nights later, Terry told me that the great tenor sax stylist, Harold Land, was working one of the Jackson Street clubs. "Let's go hear Harold," she said. Well, as soon as we walked in and heard Harold Land playing my heart skipped beats. He moved me musically so much I was just in awe. At intermission, Terry introduced me to Harold and there was an immediate connection. He excited me, and not only musically this time. There was something so magical between us that I panicked. I got panicked that I was attracted to him like that, and he knew it, because before he went back to the stand, Harold said "Stick around" to Terry, all the while looking at me and smiling. That got me even more flustered. I mean, I had never even thought of another man because I was so happy with Jerry.

The second set was just underway when I told Terry "I have to go!" Her loud "What?!" rang in my ears as I dashed out the club. I ran to the parking lot and jumped in my car, but before the engine turned over Harold caught up and sat right beside me. "Don't run," he pleaded. "No, No, No, No," I protested, "I'm deeply in love with someone else," but Harold wouldn't be deterred. "Don't fight it," I heard him say as he leaned over and kissed me!

Oh my God, I couldn't believe I was kissed! Now, it was only a kiss, but I had never felt so guilty or been so shaken up. I hadn't kissed anyone else in the three years Jerry and I had been together. Nobody had even been interesting to me. That's why Harold's kiss shook the very ground I walked on. It was so passionate and I collapsed so easily it scared the hell out of me. My God! He might as well have fucked me right there! "Harold, you have to get out of this car!" I shouted. "Don't run from me," he begged, as he leapt onto the curb and I pulled away muttering like some mad woman: "No, No, No, No!"

I cried all the way back to the motel. "What's the matter?" Jerry asked. "Oh, Jerry, Harold Land kissed me and I'm sorry." I knew I really hadn't done anything wrong, but I needed to confess to Jerry that I'd had those sensual feelings and how ashamed I felt about betraying our relationship.

I needn't have worried; Jerry consoled me with an embrace and tried to help me get the whole thing in perspective. In a soothing voice he counseled me to go back to the club to confront my feelings: "You've got to face it, to see what it is. You don't run from these things, Dottie, because if you do, they will seem bigger than what they are." Jerry proved once again that he was my best friend. I finally calmed down, but I wouldn't go back to that club. I was too afraid.

When Benny Carter closed at the Moulin Rouge, Jerry and I returned to the Bay Area, got married in Reno, and resumed our local gigs separately or in each others' trios and quartets ("The Dottie Grae Trio at Crims Is a Wow," *Oakland Tribune*).[1] One of the turning points I referred to at the beginning of this Scene occurred two years later. It was 1957 and we had a summer gig at a chalet-type hotel in the mountains east of San Francisco. We worked Monday through Saturday, and on our day off Jerry would play in a jam session in San Mateo. At one of those sessions, Jerry remembers that he was playing a solo on a slow blues with his eyes closed and when he got to the end of his chorus he heard another alto start to play! To his great surprise it was rising jazz star, Charlie Mariano.

Mariano, who was at the time playing in drummer Shelly Manne's band in Los Angeles, came over from a gig at the Black Hawk. A few weeks later, Jerry got another surprise: a call for a December record date in Los Angeles with Mariano and a choice lineup of musicians that included Monty Budwig on bass! Jerry played both alto and flute on the date,[2] and he remembers that during playback of some of the tunes, he saw the well-known West Coast trumpet player and arranger, Shorty Rogers, walk into the control room to listen. Jerry couldn't have guessed the impact that brief control-room visit would have on the arc of his career.

We collected Deborah from my parents in Sacramento on our trip south for the recording date. Soon after arriving in Los Angeles, word came down from my father that we had to see his parents. We did him one better and stayed with them overnight while Jerry was busy with the Mariano recording. Our visit was Deborah's introduction to her grandparents, and it had its bumpy moments, especially with her great-grandmother, who struggled so much with English that Deborah had trouble understanding her. From the get-go, my grandmother was alien to Deborah, and as the day progressed, her ornery behavior, yelling at everybody, and her cronelike appearance, stooped and gap-toothed with a hook nose, conspired to frighten always fairly dainty Deborah.

Which reminds me of the second and only other time I was at my grandparents' place with young Deborah in tow. The occasion was their 75th wedding anniversary and it was a big deal. President Ronald Reagan wrote my grandparents a congratulatory letter for staying married for three-quarters of a century and the family organized a big celebration. As part of the evening's festivities, drums were set up in the living room for me to play. Deborah was upstairs when I started but the sound rumbling through the house attracted her down. She had never seen me at the drums before, and as soon as she saw what looked like her Mother flailing about hitting some objects with sticks and she heard what, to her, must have seemed like thunder, she screamed and burst out crying! "Oh, great," I said to myself, "I scared my own kid!" If ever before I had suspicions that being a girl drummer was weird, Deborah's reaction settled it!

It was hard for me to return Deborah on our trip back to the Bay Area. My guilt about leaving her with my mother cast a giant shadow in my life. I'd try to fill the void by visiting every time Jerry and I were close by—usually about once or twice a year—and I'd send her things from far-away places, like Carnaby Street in London. My conscience was relieved to some extent because Deborah took our separation like a trooper. The way she looked at it, she had a "Mommy One" and a "Mommy Two," and she cared equally for both of us but for different reasons. Jerry and I represented adventure; with us you never knew what was going to happen and Deborah loved that. My mother was the safety net.

A few years later, when Deborah was about nine, she made a rare holiday visit to Jerry and me in New York City, and like her mother on the bus to Berkeley at the same age, Deborah wasn't afraid to travel alone. After the holidays, I took Deborah to the airport for her return flight to Sacramento. Waiting at the gate, I bent down to kiss her and big tears welled in my eyes. Deborah, more composed than I, said: "Now you can't cry, Momma, because I get to come here and go to great places and then I go back to my other home where I'm loved. So, I have two Mommies and two great places to go to."

She's nine and she's straightening me out!

Followed by Myself in the Moonlight

A few months after we were back from Los Angeles, Jerry got a phone call that changed our lives forever.

Red Norvo, noted band leader and swing vibist, asked Jerry to join his quintet for a job in the lounge of the Sands Hotel in Las Vegas. After Jerry accepted he wondered, "Excuse me, Red, I know we've never met, how come you're calling me?" Red told him that he got the tip to call Jerry from his brother-in-law. "Who's your brother-in-law?" Jerry asked. "Shorty Rogers," Red replied. Red had called Shorty, looking for an alto player who doubled on flute and Shorty just happened to remember hearing Jerry at the Mariano recording date.[1] As Jerry often says, he's a lucky guy.

Jerry started work with Red Norvo in March 1958, in a band that included guitarist, Jimmy Wyble; drummer, Karl Kiffe; and bassist, Red Wooten. Frank Sinatra got the gig for the quintet in the Sands Hotel lounge. Sinatra and Norvo knew each other from years before, and being under Sinatra's wing in Vegas was a gift for the group since they were never out of work in the three years Jerry was with Red.

After Jerry left for Vegas, I stayed behind to pack up Larkspur and then joined him in April. The engagement at the Sands was originally scheduled for six weeks, but the group kept getting held over so the six-week job extended to six months. Long enough for me to develop Vegas roots and start getting calls for work. One of those jobs was so bad I wish I could forget it.

I was recruited for a terrible slapstick outfit from Los Angeles that was booked into the Flamingo Hotel, and the whole scene was demeaning. We wore big, funny hats and ridiculous shoes and I had to really set the time hard otherwise the guys in the band would get lost! The only blessing was that our "Funny Hats Band," as I called it, did shows at nine and eleven in the Flamingo lounge, opposite Sarah Vaughan! On second thought, maybe it was a mixed blessing. Both of our acts worked on a turntable bandstand, so when Sarah finished her show and circled behind the curtain, our bush-league group appeared from the other side like the next serving on a Lazy Susan. Imagine, we literally had to follow the great Sarah Vaughan!

One night not long into the job, we were doing our second show when I saw that Sarah was back in the room and sitting at the bar. I watched her from the bandstand, the way she self-consciously played with a drink she held between her hands, and how she kept her head down as if she were either concentrating or hoping to be invisible. Her attitude was a symptom of that time in Vegas because back then a Black person being admitted into a Las Vegas lounge was almost unheard of—I was told that even Sammy Davis Jr. had to go through the kitchen!

Sarah was one of the first African Americans I'd seen who was allowed to sit inside the lounge at the bar, and I think she knew it. So, there she was, big as life, already half loaded and not saying a word. Except when I'd hit a rim shot. With the crack of my stick she'd immediately look up and yell, "Yeah! Dottie!" (I guess she must have learned who I was from some of the guys in the band.)

When the Funny Hats finished its last set that night, Sarah was still all by herself at the bar so I approached her. We started talking and pretty quick it was clear that we both needed company—Sarah, because she was lonely; me, because I was so embarrassed by that band. In a sense, we were thrown together, there was no one else around that late at night. Sarah Vaughan and me! I just happened to be at the right place at the right time. Like a lot of things in my life, I can't say I had very much to do with it.

Each night after our shows ended, we would go back to her hotel room, gossip about musicians, and have serious musical talks. I had all of Sarah's records and I remember asking her why she did some tunes that I thought were beneath her. "How come you'd do a tune like that, Sarah? I mean— God!—you're Sarah Vaughan!" "Oh, you think I get to pick my tunes?" she asked. "Not on your life, baby! On my records I have to do eight tunes they pick for me and I get one." The record company people would make her do covers of pop hits of the day.

Hanging with Sarah, I got to know her bass player, Gus Mancuso. Aside from our ties to Sarah, Gus and I had the Mary Kaye Trio in common (he joined them in 1957). During Sarah's Flamingo gig, Gus and I split away and did some sessions together on the Strip. After that short window, we didn't cross paths again until a couple years later when I was working the Vegas hotels and Gus, on a break from touring with Sarah, had two jobs on the Strip making around a thousand dollars a week. Since Sarah paid him only seven hundred he decided to stay in Vegas and not go back on the road with her. A short time later, when Sarah called Gus from Los Angeles, she told him she had a new car and was planning to drive up to see him. Gus recalled telling her "Good, Sass, because I have something to talk to you about."

Gus asked to use my apartment to meet with Sarah, so I gave him my key and went to work so they had the place to themselves. Gus dropped hints that Sarah should give him a raise, but when she didn't get the message he told her, "Sass, I'm not going to be able to go back out with you." "I knew you were going to pull something on me," Sarah said. Furious, she told Gus to "come with me."

Gus followed her outside where the nighttime desert gusts were blowing maybe thirty miles an hour. Sarah opened the trunk of her car, he remembered, "and there were three books—the piano book, the bass book, and the drum book. She took them and she just threw them out in the street, she got in the car and drove off." Throwing away all those charts, written by leading musicians of the day, could have been a catastrophe for Sarah. I got home a short time later and for two hours Gus and I used flashlights to scour the neighborhood streets and yards. We found most of the charts and reassembled them in my apartment. Gus remembered that Sarah called a week later: "Hi, Gus. Are you mad?" And he told her "Sarah, you just about threw away thousands of dollars' worth of charts." "Well, I just got upset," she replied.

When Red Norvo's quintet finished the six-month job at the Sands, they went on a two-month tour to the East Coast. That was Jerry's first road trip with a major jazz group and I went along in our Volkswagen with my drums packed on the back seat. The Quintet caravanned across North America with gigs in Detroit, Toronto, and upstate New York. It was fun as hell being on the road that time. Jerry and I were having a ball being married and I'd make a home out of every motel stop with my bean pot, hotplate, and little bag of spices. It also helped that we were tight, like a little family really, with guitarist Jimmy Wyble and his wife, Lily. Many nights Lily and I hung out at the motel and when our husbands came home from the gig we'd listen to them bitch about what Red did to Jimmy.

We'd hear how Red had bawled out Jimmy all night for nothing at all; he'd do it just because he felt like it. Granted, it was complicated. As I understood it, Red had been the one who put Jimmy into AA and saved his life, so Jimmy felt indebted to him, but there was also an abusive side to Red. Anytime he didn't like something he'd use Jimmy as a scapegoat, and Jimmy was so weak that he'd take Red's verbal abuse personally and hang on to it. Jerry was indignant for Jimmy but neither of them would say anything back to Red. Finally, Lily and I told the boys that we were tired of hearing about Red. We didn't say it mean, but we gave them an ultimatum: "If you don't like it, quit." Their eyes got wide but neither had balls enough to do that.

Our last gigs were in Rochester and Buffalo. The band was just finishing up the Buffalo job when Norvo got a call to do the Dinah Shore show in Los Angeles, which was great, but they needed us to be there in three days! Jerry and I hurriedly packed up the VW and shortly after pointing the car west we ran smack into a blizzard that lasted all the way to St. Louis. The snow was—God!—at least ten feet in some places, but because VW tires were turned inward we didn't slip and slide a lot. Plus, whenever we could, we made good time by following the grooves made by semis ahead of us.

The VW started sputtering just outside St. Louis. We limped into the nearest station and learned that our gas line was freezing! A smart mechanic, bless his heart, saved our bacon by putting dry gas in the fuel line to remove water from the gasoline. Good to go, we drove nonstop to Arizona, found a motel for a few hours of sleep, and then made it to Los Angeles in time for the rehearsal.

While the show was being taped (it aired December 14, 1958), we crashed for a few days at the home of one of Jerry's friends, jazz flautist and alto player, Paul Horn, and his wife, Yvonne Jourdan. Immediately after the Shore recording, Red landed a three-month job for the quintet in Pasadena, so Jerry and I left Paul and Yvonne and settled into an apartment in Hollywood. That was a nice stretch of calm in our lives. Little did we expect the whirlwind of change in Jerry's career that began shortly before the Pasadena job was finished. The quintet worked a local benefit with Frank Sinatra and then started rehearsals at Sinatra's home to prepare for an Australian tour. (At about the same time, drummer, Karl Kiffe, left the group and on Jerry's recommendation Red hired my Nick Esposito bandmate, John Markham, as his replacement.)

The day before the band left for Melbourne in late March 1959, I told Jerry I was pregnant. I wanted to have the child; I thought he might feel the same way. After all, Jerry had made Deborah feel very loved. On the other hand, our visits with Deborah were always short; she didn't stick around long enough to interrupt any of Jerry's plans or, for that matter, any of mine. So, in a very real sense I was prepared for Jerry's response that "I had to take care of it." He was just being sensible. After all, we were musicians first and human beings second, and, as a musician, Jerry had too much at stake. He had worked so hard to get accepted into the first string. You give your whole life to it and then to not be able to follow through because of your obligation to something else is plain lousy. I accepted the decision and actually felt grateful for it because I couldn't even take care of my first child.

Since Jerry was leaving in a few hours for his flight overseas, we needed to decide, and quickly, how to end the pregnancy. We were still talking about it that night when we went to a party at Paul Horn's house. One of the guests was a B-List actress who had befriended many of the L.A. musicians. After Jerry introduced me to her I realized she'd overheard some of our conversation because she whispered to him, "I know somebody you can take her to, you know, across the border." Jerry told her, "I leave tomorrow." "I'll take her," was the terse reply.

She took me at night across the border to Tijuana. She was sympathetic, but movie star or not, she was a stranger. With Jerry gone I felt completely alone. As we made our way to the abortionist, I had the most eerie feeling, as if I were outside my body following myself in the moonlight.

It was terrible. This butcher had a long pole that looked like a mining drill, with little screws on it that went around and around. The pain was excruciating! My actress-escort sat outside and waited. She said she heard my screams. When it was finished I got back in her car and escaped into myself. I laid low for a few days worried about complications, but I didn't have any. I was lucky in that sense.

The It Club

Jerry left me alone in Los Angeles, my "Death Valley," the town I hated. The upside was that the overseas tour was brief (March 31 to April 4, 1959), so I expected him back in no time. It didn't happen that way.

After Red's quintet finished the week-long engagement backing Sinatra in Australia, they had a hotel gig in Miami and didn't return to Vegas until May. Left on my lonesome I got frustrated; despite what Jerry promised before we were married, I was becoming a musician's wife! That would not have happened if I had made the Australian tour with Jerry, but Sinatra had a rule against wives on the airplane (the only exception was Ava Gardner). What could I have done? Should I have told Jerry, "You can't go with Frank because you promised?" Well, I had to give that promise up or be an asshole myself because we also had agreed that music would always come first in our lives. It was a "Catch-22," but finally the waiting game got to me—I was a musician, not a housewife—and I had to take matters into my own hands.

I needed a gig and a new pad. Although Jerry sent me money and I was drawing unemployment, the rent on the Hollywood apartment was too much for me to cover. After I moved out I had no place to live, so I moved back in with Paul and Yvonne and went looking for work. The Los Angeles Musicians' Union, Local 47, was my first stop but I came up empty. As I left the Union, walking down the flight of pyramid steps that fronted the building, my heart dropped into my stomach. Walking up the steps was Harold Land!

Harold didn't see me right away, so I walked real fast with my head down. That was useless. After four years, it took just one glance before he recognized me and hollered the same line: "Don't run, please Baby, don't run! Have a cup of coffee with me." "Sorry, I'm in a rush," I yelled, but that didn't stop him. Just like in Vegas he started chasing me. Breathless, I got to the curb and a beautiful Porsche convertible pulled up beside me. Grinning at the wheel was Louie Bellson! "Hey, Dottie, want a ride?"

Desperate to find an apartment in line with my pocketbook I started looking in Watts, the Black ghetto in South Los Angeles. Nights I went alone to the rough and tumble It Club, located deep in the heart of the L.A. jazz world. Trying to be incognito, I sat in a corner dressed in black with my hair cut real short so no one would know I was a girl.

Despite my efforts to lay low, I was conspicuous in that African American haven and before long I was hanging out with a lot of the musicians. One of them was Eric Dolphy. An icon of avant-garde jazz today, back then he was still early on the scene. When the guys learned that I needed an apartment, Eric volunteered, "I know one about six blocks from me."

When I moved to Watts I was the only whitey around so it really helped that Eric was there to introduce me. He told all the locals, "She's a musician and needs a place to stay," and in short order my neighbors welcomed and kept watch over me. It was really wild; I was more protected in Watts than in most white communities where I've lived! It was because I was a musician, I'm sure of that. Once the Black cats accepted me—a white woman—as a musician, then my neighbors knew I was okay. They knew I was there for the music.

Eric Dolphy was a beautiful man. A quiet person, not one to gab about nothing. After he learned I was a drummer, I went to Eric's a lot; he'd invite me to his music studio in a little house behind his folks' place. Sometimes we'd jam; other times we'd go over a piece of music he was studying. Eric had a podium and a baton in his studio, similar to what I imagine a symphony conductor would have. On the podium there was usually a huge sheet of music paper where he'd transcribed a section of some classical piece. When I'd come by, he'd cue up a record to the part of the score he'd transcribed and have me read along with him as he waved the baton to direct the music.

Reading scores with Eric gave me some basic training: For the first time, I was able to see what I was hearing. With his help, I could count the bars and learn the value of each note. Before I met Eric, I knew a little bit about reading from the brief studying I had done with other drummers, like John Markham. I had studied drum patterns but not necessarily the notes, like half notes, quarter notes, and eighth notes, and how many beats to hold them.

Working with Eric, I made the connection between what the note was on the score in relation to what I was hearing in my mind and it really helped my confidence.

Around the time I settled into my apartment, the Harold Land Quartet was playing at the It Club. That posed a dilemma; I still worshipped Harold's playing and was eager to hear his band, but our awkward history made me hesitant to see him. Finally, the temptation was too great. I stiffened my courage and went to the club, and, oh, my God, what a band! Harold had the brilliant pianist/composer, Elmo Hope; "walking" bassist, Leroy Vinnegar; and the driving West Coast drummer, Frank Butler.

Harold spotted me during the second set. The emotion in his playing had moved me so much I had tears in my eyes when he came over to my table. "What's the matter?" he asked. "Oh, Harold, that was so beautiful and so sad," I told him. My comment really touched Harold and in that moment the tension between us melted. In effect, Harold and I were reintroduced, and this time it was all about the music. We became very close friends after that.

Eventually, I learned that Harold and Eric Dolphy were also tight, a piece of serendipity that worked in my favor. Harold hadn't been aware that I was a drummer—our encounter four years earlier wouldn't have given him any indication of that—but Eric knew and he was my champion. He told Harold, "Boy, she can really play," and not long after that, Frank Butler was sidelined and I got an opportunity I never dreamed would happen.

Frank Butler was a junkie. He hocked everything including his drums, and sometimes he stole other people's drums, to pay for his habit. So, I was worried one night when Harold came over to my apartment and said, "Dottie, I know Frank would sell his mother, but we've got a heavy gig tonight and I need to borrow your drums for him." "Are you kidding? I'll never see them again!" Harold assured me that wouldn't happen, and at the end of the gig Harold returned them safe and sound. He also brought Frank!

Frank didn't try to ply me for drugs money that night, so his visit, tagging along with Harold, was harmless. Or so I thought. Opening my apartment door to Frank evidently gave him ideas because, sure enough, a few days later he was back. "Harold sent me to give you some lessons," he announced. I was skeptical at first, then thinking it might be a good idea, I said, "Okay, great."

Silly me. What Frank really wanted was to chase me around the house. Like the Keystone Cops, the two of us zig-zagged through rooms, circled furniture, as I toppled chairs to keep him at bay. I had to laugh when he shouted, "I never kissed a drummer," followed by the pledge, "Oh, Baby, I won't tell Harold." "I will!" I shouted back. We were both exhausted by the time he gave up and left.

Not long after, my persistence on the scene paid off. I was seated in my usual back corner at the It Club waiting for the band to start when Harold rushed over to me. "Frank has gotten himself busted! Will you come up and fill in for him tonight?" He didn't have to ask twice. Later I learned that Frank Butler had been sent up to the "Farm," a minimum security California prison in the country where the inmates worked outside. Frank was in and out of the Farm; he didn't mind going because if he was out of junk he could always get a connection there. In truth, Frank could get more junk at the Farm than he could on the street!

Frank Butler had so much talent—what a shame he preferred junk to music. Harold wasn't going to permanently replace him because he knew all the charts, he could read and he wrote things. However, since Frank was forever breaking the law to get sent back, after my first night subbing Harold asked me to rehearse with them in Elmo Hope's garage. I played simple time, that's what they wanted. I didn't have to play drum solos—I don't like to play drum solos—and I didn't have to read. It was my ears again, they trusted my ears. After my first rehearsal, Elmo said, "Yeah, baby, yeah!"

Whenever Frank was off on a binge, Harold would hire me at the It Club. Sometimes it was brief: If Frank was gone too long shooting up at intermission I'd play a tune until he got back. I'd play full sets on a string of nights if he was back at the Farm. The band took a chance using me, because a lot of Blacks in the audience didn't understand why this little white girl drummer was up there. They would have preferred an all-Black band, and all male at that, but the musicians were unfazed. They were wonderful to me and some of them began stopping by my place to get together and talk. It started out casual, but word got around I guess, because pretty soon Harold asked me if some of the guys could use my apartment as a regular place to hang out. "Sure, anytime," I told him.

I knew there was no other place where they could all get together, no restaurant where they could sit back, smoke a joint, and have a drink. They couldn't all meet at the Union, and their houses were off limits because of wives or kids. The guys gravitated to my kitchen, which was about fifteen-foot-square with a table and a stove. They might show up every day for three days, or it could be once or twice a week. The cast of characters was fairly steady: Elmo would bring jazz composer/arranger, Gerald Wilson, and I'd squeeze in about five or six cats that Harold knew. I'd make a pot of coffee; they'd talk over charts and reminisce and I was absolutely in awe that some of the greatest musicians in the world were sitting in my kitchen exchanging musical stories!

I had a lot of fun playing with Elmo, Harold, and Leroy. They pushed me way beyond my expectations, but it wasn't steady work with those cats. I mean, you didn't keep a gig week after week at the It Club. They had different names coming through. When work with Harold dried up, there wasn't much else happening for me so I was anxious to leave Los Angeles. Sure, I had gotten into a wonderful clique of musicians, but without work what good was it? I just wasn't making enough money. On top of that, I had to fend off Harold whose attentions had begun to revert—God, he had a wife at home and I had a husband on the road!

Out of the blue my angels left another calling card: Gus Mancuso phoned from Vegas and said flat out, "I've got a gig at the Thunderbird. You want a job?" I gave notice to my landlady and bolted without saying goodbyes. Years later, I ran into Harold and he told me how some of the musicians felt abandoned when I left—"Where's our kitchen, where is the gang going to meet?"—and how disheartened he was at the time: "You didn't even let me know you were leaving." "I didn't dare stick around," I told him.

I knew when enough was enough.

Thunderbird

It was late summer, 1959. I was back in Vegas and back with Jerry.

Vegas would be home base until Jerry and I left for New York in early 1961. We became residents of the city and rented a small house; buying a house would never have occurred to us because musicians knew that if you bought a house you'd get a divorce for sure. Not that we had thought about splitting up, but there were cracks in our marriage because Jerry was on the road for such long periods of time.

After Red Norvo and his band returned to Vegas, Benny Goodman hired the whole quintet (folding it into his band, making it a ten-piece outfit) for the first of four tours over the next two years. In between the road trips with Goodman, Norvo's band continued to back Sinatra on his personal appearances. Jerry was doing a lot of traveling and our lengthy separations were taking their toll. I told Jerry he was asking too much of me, reminding him that I hadn't wanted to get married in the first place! Besides, I warned him, I was a woman who needed sex.

One of the reasons Gus called me about the job at the Thunderbird was that he had Carl Fontana in his band, a trombonist who was known the world over as having one of the fastest slides in the business. Accurate and in tune, Fontana played so quickly for so many choruses that a lot of his drummers got worn out. Gus told me I was the only drummer he knew who could keep up with Carl. Despite Gus's confidence in me, I feared I couldn't make those tempos either.

My fears faded the first time we played together. Carl loved my time, he loved that I never got in his way, he loved that I never dropped a beat, and,

I'm proud to say, he loved that he didn't have to worry about me keeping up because, like him, I could play fast! From then on Carl Fontana was in my corner, and working with him put a feather in my hi-hat because very few drummers can keep that steady of a beat with that intensity and last. That's the way I've always played: from the first note I think of nothing else but the next note. It takes a lot of concentration, but I love it.

I worked the evening shows with Gus at the Thunderbird Hotel. He also got me my first Vegas after-hours joint to play, the Black Magic, one block down from the Strip. That gig, from two to six in the morning, was with veteran jazz/blues singer and pianist Gladys Palmer.[1] It was just the two of us and boy we really fit! At that time, Gladys was in her early fifties, and though she was limited to the keys of C and F, she was a swinging piano player with a mean, stride-like left hand. She was also one of the sweetest women I ever met, not to mention a genuine character.

One of my favorite stories about Gladys is when she got busted for smoking a joint in Vegas. Nevada law at that time was severe: Get caught with just one joint and they sent you down for as much as ten years. That didn't intimidate Gladys. Standing in front of the judge she explained that her Granny had raised her with a bunch of other siblings. Granny would smoke pot through a corncob pipe, and whenever the kids made too much noise she'd blow smoke in their faces to calm them down. Gladys told the judge that "God grew that grass on this earth for a purpose; some scientist didn't go into some laboratory and make it." Gladys won her case and never did jail time because God grew pot and she had a right to smoke it!

I got to know Gus Mancuso a lot better my second time in Vegas; he was an all-round versatile musician who played piano, vibes, bass, and trombone. Thrown together on the Thunderbird job and working jams along the Strip month after month, most of my waking hours were spent with Gus. We were two people who loved the music and could really swing and that's why it got so deep with us. That's how the love affair started. There really was nothing to stop us: Gussie had a girlfriend but he was between marriages, and I felt free to take up with him because Jerry and I had an open relationship.

Gussie captured my heart and moved in with me. He brought his vibes and bass, and with the piano Jerry and I had set up, Gus and I could be a whole band! We were a well-oiled professional team and that meant I wasn't a musician's housewife. I thought Gussie was what I wanted, long term. We'd make love and then we'd get up and play; then we'd go back to bed, make love, and get up again to play. Why should I have turned that down?

We spent a lot of our free time hanging out with the Mary Kaye Trio. Gus and Frank liked to play basketball and sometimes I'd play with them—Frank dubbed us "Dottie and the High Steppers"—and whenever the trio had to make an extended road trip and I wasn't working, I'd join them to get out of Vegas for a while. One time I was getting ready to go with them for three weeks to Amarillo when Jerry returned from the road. It was an awkward reunion for me. Although I was happy to see Jerry, I wanted to be honest with him so I said straight out, "I've fallen in love with Gus and I don't know what to do about that and about the trip to Texas we're supposed to be taking." "Go ahead with Gus," he replied. That took me by surprise; Jerry was so open and understanding, so free of attitude, that he had me in the palm of his hand.

Jerry was so obliging he took over the arrangements: "Dottie, when you go to Amarillo, I'll stay here and take care of the house." Turning to Gus he said, "I'll console your girlfriend, I'll take her out." "You're something else!" I said with love in my eyes, but Gus was brought up short. "What? My girlfriend? Are you kidding me?" Jerry reassured him, "No, no, I'll take her out, I'll make things okay. You guys go ahead."

I remember the night we left. Jerry was standing outside waving and smiling as we pulled out of the driveway. I also recall the pang of doubt I felt, wondering for a moment if maybe Jerry's smile was "plastered on," that maybe he was putting on a brave front because my leaving with Gus was killing his ego. My intuition told me that Jerry was more vulnerable than I thought and I felt a tug to be with him.

I felt so uneasy about Jerry that I called him every day the first week. The second week I turned our daily chats into bitching sessions. I was disillusioned because once again I had been reduced to playing a musician's wife; while Gus was off at the club, I was cooped up waiting for him in an Amarillo hotel room. Worse yet, when he did show up he'd be sloppy from drinking. "It's not for me, Jerry," I complained.

By the end of the tour, the contrast between Gus and Jerry was stark. Throughout my absence, Jerry had acted like the exceptional man I always thought he could be. I put him up on a pedestal, and it's no wonder. He said some very wise things, like "If you really love somebody, you can let them go when it's necessary." After the road trip ended, I left Gus and went back to Jerry and things were better than ever between us.

My affair with Gus ended at the same time as the Thunderbird gig, but I kept busy with Gladys at the Black Magic and occasional jobs at other Vegas clubs and casinos. Jerry continued to tour, but whenever Norvo's band was back at the Sands, we'd spend some of his down time catching performances by popular big bands like Harry James, Tommy Dorsey, Count Basie that headlined hotels on the Strip.

One occasion in particular has stayed fresh in my memory. Frank Wess and Benny Powell, buddies from my Larkspur days, were in town with Basie, and after they got off Jerry and I went with them to see Lionel Hampton at the Flamingo. At intermission, Hamp came over to our table to visit with Frank and Benny. Suddenly he did a double take: "Who's this pretty little thing?" A grinning Frank gave me the perfect introduction: "This is Dottie Dodgion, she's a swinging drummer!" "Is that right?" Hamp said, shooting me a quizzical look. I smiled, kept my mouth shut, and heard four delicious words come out of Hamp's mouth: "Want to sit in?" In unison, Frank and I shook our heads up and down, "Yes, yes, yes, yes!" while from the corner of my eye I caught Jerry's head turning from side to side, "no, no, no, no!"

That was the first time I had a chance to play with a big band, and to be fair, Jerry wasn't telling me not to do it, he was red-flagging me—telling me that because I didn't read he didn't think I could pull it off. But I knew I could do it. I knew Hamp's records backward and forward. I didn't need to read a chart! Besides, Hamp's arrangements were so pared down and swinging, anything I didn't know I could pick up in a minute. I'm not being chesty about it; stuff like that came naturally to me. I was ready and more than willing to capitalize on Eugene's sage advice: "Jump in where the water is deepest. Otherwise how will you know if you can swim?"

I sat in for one tune, "Flying Home." It was long and it was fast and we cooked! Hamp took the first five choruses on vibes, turning around several times to smile at me. Tenor, trumpet, and piano took two each, followed by a chorus of Hamp and me trading fours and eights. Oh! Hamp was so happy, he was having a ball! He soloed on the last chorus and we took it out. Later that evening, Hamp walked over to me and with his wife, Gladys, nearby he said: "That was great, baby. You want to go on the road?" Before I opened my mouth, a categorical "uh-uh!" came from Mrs. Hampton's direction and that was the end of that.

In the summer of 1960, Jerry and I left Vegas for separate gigs at Lake Tahoe. I worked with organist Ron Rose at the Top of the Wheel room at Harvey's Casino Resort on the South Shore, and Norvo's quintet was at the Cal-Neva Lodge on the North Shore. They were backing Frank Sinatra for the very last time, so when my gig at Harvey's finished I drove thirty miles to the lodge to enjoy several of the final performances.

When Sinatra performed there were never any seats in the audience, so I had to watch from backstage. Since I was just another musician's wife and had no business backstage, I had to be inconspicuous whenever Frank was around. His dressing room was stage right and I noticed that he never went stage left when he walked from his dressing room to go on. So, after sneaking in, I went stage left, clear to the other side, where I would stand in the back in a corner, unnoticed by stagehands and the audience. Safe in my backstage "hideout," I could concentrate undisturbed on his singing and—oh, God!— he just blew me away! I'd watch until he started his closing speech and then I'd scatter.

As far as I knew, Frank had no idea I was secretly watching him from backstage. What I didn't know was that after a couple of nights he had picked up on my movements. The following evening while I was standing in my spot waiting for the show to start, Frank appeared right beside me in that stage-left corner! My heart fell to my stomach! He looked directly at me, eyes screaming a brilliant blue. Straightening his tie, he beamed that famous smile and purred, "Hi Sugar." Oh, God! I melted! It was brief and good-natured and no harm done; he played it for a laugh because I had tried so desperately to stay hidden.

Norvo's group made regular tours back East and every time they went through New York City, Jerry would touch base with his former bandmate, Jerome Richardson. As Jerry tells it: "I'd call and say hello and he'd invite me over and play all the records he'd just been making—he was very busy, recording all the time—and he was constantly encouraging me to move to New York. He's much bigger than me, he's taller and bigger, and I remember him sticking his finger in my face, 'You've got to move here!'"

Toward the end of 1960, Jerry and I agreed to make the leap, that we'd test living in New York for five years. We decided to dovetail our move with a job the Goodman band had in March, 1961, at Basin Street East. To hedge our bet, Jerry didn't tell Red that once the Basin Street gig was over he would be staying in the city.

After Jerry's Cal-Neva Lodge gig with Red ended, we returned to Vegas. Jerry joined Benny Goodman at the Dunes and I was back at the Thunderbird with Mancuso. The night before we left for New York and Basin Street, I finished up my gig with Gus and went over to the Dunes to catch the last set of Benny's band. When the show finished and the audience split, the musicians were milling around as the stage crew started clearing the bandstand. They hoisted the drums onto a wheeled platform and started rolling it backstage when tenor man Flip Phillips stopped them and said to a few of the guys, "Hey, let's jam a little."

Pretty soon most of Benny's band had climbed on the platform and joined in: bass, bone, trumpet, two sax players, but no drummer. They hated Benny's drummer; he didn't swing for them. I listened off to the side for a couple tunes until one of them spotted me and yelled, "Dottie, want to play one?" "Yeah, you bet," I said and got behind the drums. We started with a really fast one and right when we hit a groove Benny wandered over and asked, "Can I sit in?" "Sure, Benny," we said, and he kicked off "Seven Come Eleven" at an even faster tempo. Our impromptu group just cooked and that was the first time Benny ever heard me play!

We quit a few tunes later and I walked away elated. My chops were up and I was ready for New York.

PART II

THE NEW YORK AND EAST COAST YEARS

14 Drummers

My life hit a reset button in 1961. That was the start of the happiest run of my professional career, playing in the jazz big leagues of New York City.

Our flight from Vegas arrived early on a cold March morning. Jerry and I took a taxi downtown to the apartment on Jones Street in the Village that he had subleased from Maria Marshall who was a singer in Benny's band. It was a one-room flat, but at $150 a month and furnished it was a bargain.

The welcoming committee on Jones Street left something to be desired. As the taxi pulled away we saw rats, lots of rats, prowling the street and scavenging the trash piled up near our front door. One in particular caught my eye; at least a foot long and fat, it was perched on a garbage can a few feet from where Jerry and I stood transfixed, holding our suitcases. Like I was a magnet, that big fat rodent hopped off the lid and scampered in my direction to greet me. Oh, my God! Instead of enjoying the curbside view of our beautiful brownstone, I was flooded with memories of the rat in the Berkeley shed more than two decades before. A few moments later the rat turned tail and I was left muttering, "So this is New York, huh?" Maybe we shouldn't have been surprised by our rude introduction to the Big Apple; after all, our new street address was number 13.

We lived at that address for almost four years, the same amount of time it took Jerry to break into the clique of the New York recording studios. Our one-roomer was under a flight of stairs at the end of a tiled hallway on the bottom floor. We had a bed, a table, and a kitchen sink with a long drain board. The bathtub was under the board and our private toilet was in a little room across the hall. The cramped quarters felt more like home once Jerry cleared out a corner nook and made me a make-up room complete with a vanity stand, a place to hang my clothes, and a curtain for privacy.

Our bags unpacked, we took a cab uptown to Basin Street East on Lexington Avenue where Jerry had a one-o'clock rehearsal with the Goodman band. I dropped Jerry off, strolled 5th Avenue and got back to the club at the end of the rehearsal. As I walked in, the guys were still on the stand and Benny was leaning against the piano with his feet crossed, deep in thought. So I was surprised when I heard him ask, "Dottie, do you have your shoes?" "Sure," I replied—as usual, I had Kung-Fu flats in my purse—and he told me to come up. Since the rehearsal was over I assumed we were going to have another jam, and I was knocked out that Benny wanted to do that.

When I climbed on the stand, Benny stared at me and made an obvious show of closing the band book. It was a challenge because he knew I couldn't read. What he didn't know was that Daddy had weaned me on Benny's charts, the 1937 charts that he was still playing—but then, he was still wearing buttons on his fly, for cryin' out loud!

I didn't need his charts. I knew all the fill-ins, all the licks and breaks, by heart. So, when he kicked off a fast-tempo sextet number, and I played it perfectly, Benny must have thought I was some sort of genius! After the small-group opener, we did a few numbers with the ten-piece band.[1] Since I was still under the impression that we were jamming, when the last tune ended and Benny said, "you're hired, you start tonight!" I was speechless.

Tenor man, Zoot Sims, who was on the band, walked up as I stood frozen on the spot, gave me a pat on the back, and said, "Wow, that's big, Dot." My jaw hit the floor when Zoot explained how Benny had auditioned 14 drummers before me and didn't like any of them! (In my excitement I took what Zoot told me at face value. Later I figured that was Zoot's sense of humor, his offbeat way of telling me how amazing it was that Benny, who had been looking for a new drummer during that afternoon rehearsal, had no success until out of the blue I sauntered in from buying a raincoat and answered his ad.)

That first day had been crazy and exhilarating, from hitting the plane for our red-eye to the rush of big-city cacophony as we taxied from one end of Manhattan to the other. I was already thrilled about arriving in New York, so sitting-in with Benny's band and then getting his big-time endorsement shot such high emotion through me I almost collapsed. I didn't know what I was capable of at the time, but I never dreamed that my first day in New

York I'd be playing with Benny Goodman! At Basin Street East, no less! I never doubted it was a lucky break, but I never thought I didn't deserve it, and I was proud of myself for not being insecure.

Time-wise, Benny and I fit like a glove. Because I had listened to him all those years, I knew him inside out. Other drummers didn't know Benny's time or how he would phrase, but I'd been to school for it, you might say, since I was 9 years old. Benny thought I was a girl wonder. Or just a wonder. He didn't know I was a girl.

Later, as we were shuttling back across town in a cab, Jerry said, "Geez, Dottie, there's no place else to go but down." Maybe he meant that to be funny, but I didn't appreciate the humor. It did nothing to help my confidence. I understood that it was a shock to him; I knew he was thinking, "What are you doing, going to work with Benny Goodman the very first day you get to New York?" After all, I had always been the student and he was the teacher, plus I didn't read, so how could I possibly land this opportunity?

I can laugh about it now, but at the time I stifled those thoughts because I didn't want to be better than him. I liked being subservient in that sense; I liked that he was the man and he would protect me and never be jealous of me. I think I was wrong about that, but I didn't take time to sort it out because my very first day in New York I was hired as the drummer in Benny Goodman's band! For the first time in my professional life I definitely felt like a pioneer.

We opened a three-week engagement at Basin Street East on Thursday, March 9th,[2] and all I can say is: "What a night!" I got to the gig about 45 minutes early. Zoot had already arrived and picking up that I was a little nervous, he said, "C'mon, Dot, let's go around the corner to the Irish bar and have a taste before we hit." Man, I threw down three shots of Dewar's and didn't feel a thing. We went back, played the first set and I worked off those shots. At intermission, seeing I was still uneasy, Zoot said, "Let's go around the corner again." Zoot was so laid back; we sat at the bar talking about anything else but the gig. He didn't have to hold my hand and give me a pep talk. He knew I just needed a friend and that helped me get through the last set.

Musically that first night went great; John S. Wilson, music critic for the *New York Times*, described me as "a chic and remarkably capable drummer."[3] The only trouble I had was due to the clothes I wore. They caused a stir, but I had warned Benny about it ahead of time. Earlier that day, right after he hired me, Benny yelled over to the band manager, Jay Feingold, "Go get her a blazer and skirt." I yelled right back at him, "Benny, I can't wear a skirt!"

Benny was adamant, "No pants, No, No, No!" So, Feingold got me the skirt. Well, that night I was embarrassed but it wasn't as bad as it could have been; the horns in the front line helped to cover me so I was only really exposed on each side. Frustrated, I had to get my point across to Benny so that night I got a photographer to take a shot of me at the drums with my thighs fully exposed. The next day, when Benny saw the picture he exclaimed, "Get her culottes!"

Basin Street East was a huge club and when you're on stage the lights hit your eyes and you can't see the audience. That was okay with me because I didn't want to see or think about the audience anyway. Whenever I played, wherever it was, I always wanted my concentration to be centered from the moment I stepped on a stage and got behind my drums. I was so determined not to let anything get in the way of the music, I played with my eyes closed. Until Frank Wess, the tenor player with Count Basie's band, straightened me out.

"Dottie," he said, "you've got to keep your eyes open and on the leader." "Yeah," I told him, "but it's distracting when someone in the audience is looking at me funny, and their eyes go up and they wrinkle their nose in distaste as if to say, 'How freaky, a girl drummer.'" Frank's answer was on target: "Instead of closing your eyes, Dottie, what you do is look at the top of their heads and, believe me, they'll think you're looking right at them." That really helped me wash those distractions away and keep steady on my job, which was to play the drums and swing that band.

One distraction I hadn't planned on was Benny Goodman. You never knew what to expect from Benny on the stand, how his mind would work. He was the "King" and he wanted to be the King always; his ego was huge. Before I got too deep in the gig with Benny, my old friend, drummer John Markham, who had played with Benny a couple of years, warned me to be careful of Benny's "ray."

The ray was a devastating glare Benny would fix on a musician if he was unhappy about something. For example, John told me how it would gall Benny when somebody in the band was taking a hard swinging solo and it wasn't him! Jealous, Benny would try to kill the excitement by leveling his ray at the drummer to get his attention and then motion him down, "Shhhh, get softer, get softer." Forewarned that Benny could easily disrupt a drummer, I devised a plan. When the band was really cooking and I could feel that Benny was aiming to give me the look, I'd keep playing the time on the bass drum and hi-hat while I got busy "fixing my drums"—adjusting a drum pedal, tightening the heads, whatever I could do to avoid eye contact with the ray and keep on swinging until I got off.

We did hour-and-a-half shows at Basin Street. I was pretty excited, but at the same time it was a heavy load: We had vocalists Jimmy Rushing ("Mr. Five By Five" as he was affectionately known)[4] and Maria Marshall, and a ten-piece band plus Benny's sextet, all playing bright tempos. I got exhausted each night, but I wouldn't miss a beat because that would have been the end of me. I had to play it picture-perfect down, but God, by the end of the show when we got to "Sing Sing Sing" my hands were limp like mops. When it came to my solo on "Sing, Sing, Sing," I couldn't do any long rolls and paradiddles—I wasn't that flexible. Iconic Goodman drummer, Gene Krupa, had played the hell out of "Sing, Sing, Sing"; he liked to throw up his sticks and the audience would cheer. There's no denying that many drummers love getting the spotlight, but I never had that attitude. That's why I sometimes say I'm not a "real" drummer!

Fundamentally, I'm a rhythm player, I get my kicks playing rhythm. Whenever I did take a solo my approach came from being a singer: I'd hear the melody inside my head so the rhythms I laid down always followed the song form of whatever tune I played. So, with "Sing, Sing, Sing," instead of fancy stick work, I played the melody on my tom tom. It seemed to work. I had musicians in Goodman's band tell me, "I knew where you were every second of your solo." I took that as a compliment.

Everything was going along fine until about ten days into our engagement. At the end of the show, Benny didn't announce me to the crowd. Benny was very forgetful, he'd forget to recognize guys all the time, but when he failed to introduce me, the only woman player on the band sitting in plain sight on the drummer's throne, people in the audience yelled, "the drummer, the drummer!" Benny, momentarily dazed, muttered, "huh?" and then recovered with, "Oh, yeah, Dottie Dodgion!" Well, that brought the house down and I got a standing ovation! I was feeling pretty good about myself until I walked off the stand and passed Jay, the manager. "Bye," he whispered in my ear. I knew immediately what he meant: Nobody gets a bigger hand than the King, and sure enough, the next day Jay phoned to tell me, "You're fired."

Two weeks notice was the rule, but of course Benny could do anything he wanted. The King was the King and I got the heat. It got me down, but a few days later my spirits were lifted when roses arrived from Gene Krupa with a note that said, "Just remember, Baby, he's fired the best!" Looking back, maybe it was fated to happen because not long after my departure Benny did an afternoon date at the 92nd Street YMCA, playing a piece composed for him by Morton Gould, and I could never have read those charts!

Because I played with Benny Goodman I expected nonstop calls for gigs, but the jazz-world afterglow was short lived. Yes, I'd rung the bell, but there were so many important musicians in New York doing impressive things that my small victory quickly slipped from view and I was just a footnote again. Instead of mainline music jobs, I got opportunities associated with my limited "celebrity," like when, not long after I was off the Goodman band, I got a call to be a contestant on the popular CBS television game show, "What's My Line?" I agreed without realizing how easily the invitation could turn into an endurance test.

I went to the CBS studios on two consecutive weeks only to sit in the green room for the entire program. The third time was the charm, although it was still a squeaker. I was the fourth and last guest on the broadcast that aired April 16, 1961. Contestants before me included a circus strongman, a base-ball glove designer, and mystery guests, actors Gordon and Sheila MacRae. Celebrity panelists that night were journalist, Dorothy Kilgallen; publisher, Bennett Cerf; actress, Arlene Francis; and her actor husband, Martin Gabel. Time ran out before the panel could guess my occupation so by default I got the top prize of $50![5]

I had been on television earlier that spring when Jerry rejoined Red Norvo's quintet for a guest spot on the "Today Show with Dave Garroway."[6] Looking back, it strikes me as odd that I was on drums for that broadcast. Neither Jerry nor I can remember what happened to Red's regular drummer, Karl Kiffe, but it seems most likely that his absence was last minute and I was chosen as a quick replacement.

On the heels of those televised appearances, I started getting offers from agents who, if I hadn't balked at their schemes, would've tried to make me a "girl wonder" of the advertising world. The strangest offer was pitching Ex-Lax in a television commercial for $2500! How degrading! I grumbled to the agent, "I've worked my whole life to get respect as a woman drummer and you think I'm going to sell my soul for $2500?!" It wasn't until I was ap-proached by William Morris Jr., president of one of the powerhouse talent agencies of the era, the William Morris Agency, that it finally seemed I was being recognized for my work as a musician. Dream on.

When I arrived for the appointment, William Morris Jr. was busy on the phone, so his secretary put me in the next room with assurances he wouldn't be long. As I settled into a plush leather chair I noticed that Morris's office door was ajar. I saw him behind his desk and couldn't help but overhear him: He had one of his clients, jazz pianist Dorothy Donegan, on one line and somebody else on a second phone. At first I was amused as he juggled the two conversations. Talking to Dorothy he insisted, "Oh, no, I can't get $1500 for you, Dorothy. No way they're going to go for that." Then, telling Dorothy to "Wait a minute, wait a minute," he switched to the other phone. "You can't have her for less than $2500," he argued.

Boy, that made me leery about talking to him, but I got a reprieve because Morris was tied up longer than expected and one of his deputies was sent to deal with me. "Tell you what, we'll give you $700 a month for seven years" was the upshot of what he offered after a brief and mindless interview. It was clear I was somebody they'd just found out about. I wasn't there because they thought I was a great musician; I was there because I was the first woman to play drums in Benny Goodman's band, and they wanted to sign me before somebody else did, just in case I might have some publicity value. I told the guy that I'd think about it, but as I walked out onto the street I said to myself: "What? Tie me up for seven years at such low pay? That's outrageous!" That experience put a fine point for me on why musicians hate agents.

We were broke, but Jerry, God love him, he understood perfectly that none of the agents really knew how to sell me. I had several opportunities to capitalize and gain some measure of fame and fortune, but I'm proud to say I resisted any sort of commercialism. My life has been all jazz all the time because, as my father told me, "If you go for the money, you'll never get to play your heart." I stood firm on my principles, did the odd gig, and drew unemployment. This was completely in line with the ethos of New York City jazz: You played for nothing most of the time because the money wasn't the thing. It was the music that mattered, and it was who you got to play with that built your resume.

Mount Airy Lodge

Jerry was the main breadwinner our first year in New York. While he was working I made the rounds of clubs, playing occasional, mostly forgettable jobs, but in spite of my diet of humdrum gigs, I stayed upbeat. Jerry and I were on an adventure. We were looking to play with the best guys in the city and we knew we'd have to pay our dues to get accepted because there weren't that many empty slots in New York and an awful lot of good musicians waiting to fill them.

The city always seemed more hospitable when I was with Eugene Wright. Eugene was on the road a lot, but whenever he was in town Jerry and I would go over to his apartment, usually once a week, to visit and jam. We did that until around 1968. Having sessions with my mentor in the Big Apple was a great comfort (we even played some club gigs together); the icing on the cake was when Eugene got me a great deal on one of Joe Morello's drum sets.

Joe, who held the drum chair in the classic Dave Brubeck Quartet, had five complimentary sets specially made for him sitting idle in his house. When Eugene heard about those extra sets he went to bat for me, telling Joe that I'd had an old Slingerland drum set for years and it was time I had a new one. "Okay," Joe said, "If she can pay the taxes to ship them, they're hers." I scraped the funds together and, thanks to Eugene, I got a $2,000 drum set with a custom-made Joe Morello snare for just $260.00. I still have that set today, all yellow and old as Methuselah—I kind of identify with it!

My entry into the exclusive New York jazz community finally got into gear when I discovered the Half Note, a storied Manhattan nightclub. It became a hangout for me; I went there at least three to four times a week. The Half

Note was also unofficial headquarters for the mainstream saxophone duo of Zoot Sims and Al Cohn. Zoot knew me and that I could play from our time together on Benny Goodman's band and he introduced me to Al.

I'd arrive at the Half Note with the look I'd adopted in Los Angeles, hair short, wearing black, because if you were glamorous you were not a jazz person. Before I was established in New York, I was too insecure to even smile; if you smiled you weren't jazz. It took me a long time to really relax a smile while I was playing. Too afraid that I'd be "show biz." Inside the Half Note I'd disappear into a back corner and wait, hoping for Zoot or Al to ask me to play. I think I was one of a few musicians, or maybe the only one, who regularly sat on the sidelines in a jazz club ready to pinch hit.

The first time I sat in with Zoot and Al it was déjà vu the It Club: their regular drummer, Mousey Alexander, was out "smoking a bowl,"[1] but he took too long and so the guys called me up to sub. A lot of times that's how I got to sit in, and not only with Zoot and Al. Pianist Duke Pearson and others who played the Half Note always had the best musicians in their bands, but if a drummer took sick, was late, had habits, or lived in New Jersey and couldn't get across the bridge, I was there and, by God! it always paid off. That's why it was my hangout.

Lots of musicians came into the Half Note to hang and drink but Zoot and Al didn't ask too many of them to sit in. Zoot and Al didn't want to jam when they were on the stand; they wanted to play the charts that were written for them. Even big-name musicians were seldom asked, striking at times a sour note that could rub off on me.

Like the night I was subbing on the drums while at the bar stood tenor sax giant, Johnny Griffin, waiting for an invitation to play. When I got off, Johnny vented his frustration by ridiculing me: "Boy, if you were my old lady I wouldn't allow you to go out by yourself and be playing with the guys." "That's why I would never be your old lady!" I shot back. He laughed and things cooled down, but, in a way, Johnny had fed me a pick-up line. He was fishing because he was so shocked. Johnny was an old-fashioned Black man. In his era, if a woman hung out by herself she was available to everybody. Especially a cute little thing like me who was hugged by all the guys. And there were a lot of white women who strictly liked Black men so he put me in that category. I think he kind of knew better, but he shot his arrow just to see where it would land.

I found it ironic that during the same period the feminists wanted me!

Someone from the movement came into the Half Note one night and asked me for an interview. Thinking that I was perfect, that "my old man put me down," she wanted to use my story to show how unfair it was that women musicians didn't have enough time to play because they had to clean the house. But I said, "You better get someone else because that doesn't apply to me. My old man helps me do the dishes so I can practice." "Well, I don't want you!" she said. "I don't want to hear about a happy girl." They were out to get the guys, and truth be told, I did know a lot of lady musicians with husbands who sneered at their playing: "Forget your hobby, Baby, I'm home," was their condescending attitude.

I wasn't paid for subbing with Zoot and Al, and since Jerry and I were new in town not much work came our way in those early months of 1961. Then summer hit. For musicians, summertime is terrible in New York; work dries up except on the road. Luckily, Jerry and I stumbled into what turned out to be several years of annual summer gigs at different Pennsylvania resorts.

"Doesn't your wife play drums?" asked tenor saxist and band leader, Bob Newman, when he met Jerry at a jam session in the city. Jerry replied in the affirmative and Newman said, "I can get you some gigs up in the Poconos where I have a band working at Mount Airy Lodge.[2] I'll give you a list of piano players you can call; most of them have already played up there." There were several piano players on the list we didn't know but we had plenty of time to get acquainted during the hundred-mile ride up into Pennsylvania and over to Mount Airy Lodge.

Bob Newman's orchestra was in the main large ballroom where they had dinner and dancing. Our trio—piano, alto, and drums—played strictly for dancing in the smaller more intimate lounge on the other side of the club. After we finished work, we'd play sessions. Bob Newman and a few of his guys would find some club to jam for a couple of hours, or he'd take us down to the Deer Head Inn[3] to hear, and sometimes sit in with, the remarkable pianist, John Coates Jr. As John put it: "they would often come to the Deer Head because that was the jazz spot in the Poconos."

If Jerry got a summertime gig that took him on the road I would strike out on my own, playing casuals, weddings, and proms in the Jewish part of the Poconos or in the Borscht Belt of the Catskills. (I've never played so many Horas in my life.[4]) There were some pretty droll scenes in those mountains. Comedians who weren't funny would throw their hands up in the air after a punchline and I'd fire a "ba-doom" to catch it. I was good at that because of the show-biz schtick I absorbed in strip joints from my father, and, even though I didn't read, I could play dance acts, like professional ballroom dancers, because their moves were second nature to me. I remember this one team that had charts prepared. As they danced, I kept turning pages and they were so impressed: "We love what you did for us, Dottie!" I had to fake it; I had to fake it a lot!

One of the darkest episodes of my life happened during the early summer of 1962, when Jerry was gone for six weeks to Russia with Benny Goodman. I was working jobs and hanging out in the Poconos. One of those jobs was an extended gig with singer-songwriter-pianist, Bob Dorough, and his Quartet at Mount Airy Lodge. As Dorough recalled, "I had another drummer and he was kind of goofing on the job, drinking and using drugs and nodding off—Al Levitt. . . . So when I got rid of Al Levitt, suddenly there was Dottie. . . . So it was just sort of natural for her to start up the very next night."

Bob Dorough at the piano was the main vocalist but I also did some singing from behind the drums. Dorough described me as "sort of in the Peggy Lee or Lee Wiley mold, swinging and musical. Musical like a musician can be musical, more so than just a singer who doesn't know music." The other musicians in the group were guitarist, Al Schackman, and bassist, Les Grinage. I was happy to have the work, but I wasn't thrilled with either the group or the music. It wasn't a jazz band; mostly we played dance music.

We did two ninety-minute shows a night, and after a while Dorough's singing got tedious; it was like humming that seesawed back and forth. His piano playing was very wide, soft, and lazy, the same as he talked. I wanted an edge in what we played so at times I'd try to put in a kick or two, but then I risked going against the way the others were feeling. To make matters worse, the bass player, a supposedly hip cat from Harlem, wandered all over the place. Because he was a soul brother, Dorough and his guitarist thought he could swing, but that bassist couldn't play four bars in the same groove. When that happens, when somebody is inconsistent and the other musicians don't notice it, the tempo you end up with isn't where you started. It was all I could do to keep him from rushing or dragging, so believe me, I was floored when this Black bass player told Bob and Al he couldn't play with me because I didn't swing!

From that point on there was no love lost between Grinage and me. He kept putting a bug in Dorough's ear to fire me! Bob Dorough remembered the trouble we had: "Near the end of the season she had a big fight with the bass player . . . over the concept of 'swing' and they didn't get along at all. They were fighting on and off the bandstand."

Things came to a head one night when Dorough and Schackman brought a tape recorder to the gig. "We're going to find out who's wrong," they said. God, that really killed me! I thought to myself: "You nincompoops. You're gonna audition me? Do you realize the people I've played with and yet you're going to tell me that this guy can swing just because he's Black??" Not all Black musicians can swing. As the Black musicians I ran with said: "It doesn't mean a thing, baby."

Well, that did it. "You don't have to fire me," I told them, "I'm gone so go ahead, swing yourselves to death!" I gave my notice that night; I quit before they could find out if I was right or not. I packed my things in the car and was pulling out when, unbelievably, the bass player ran out to the parking lot and tapped on my window. "What do you want?" I snarled. "Could I get a ride to New York?" "You gotta be kidding me!" I shrieked and hit the gas. The nerve! He was the reason I was leaving!

That was the only time I ever got rejected and it was demeaning. Who were they to say that? Al Schackman may have been a fair guitar player, and Dorough wrote clever lyrics, but they were the ones who couldn't swing; they sounded like beginners. I was deeply hurt that they would do that to me.

When I turned onto the highway it was dark and foggy so I drove slowly. The gloom matched my mood; faced with a two-hour drive and nobody at home to talk to, I felt very lonely behind the wheel. Crying bitterly, I couldn't concentrate and several times caught my car weaving in and out of my lane. An hour out, headlights on the car in front of me lit up a stretch of road ahead, and through weepy eyes I saw a large brick wall set back off the road to the right at the beginning of a long curve. Impulsively, I stepped hard on the accelerator, passed the car in front of me and made a split-second decision to keep driving straight when I got to that curve. I was going to hit the wall!

A siren blared and jolted me out of my trance. Slowing down, I didn't see the motorcycle cop until he pulled up alongside and gestured me toward a vacant lot. The two of us parked, he made a beeline to my open window and between sniffs and sobs I meekly asked, "What did I do?" He described how my erratic driving got his attention and made him wonder if I could see where I was going. "Do you have fog lights?" he asked. I told him yes and he immediately dropped the subject of my lights to give me an earful about weather conditions in the mountains that time of year. It was all a ploy. Sizing up my emotional state he talked me down. Talked me down and saved my life!

The whole episode was bizarre. Feeling sorry for myself was not my style, and suicide had never before crossed my mind, but everybody has their day and that row in the Poconos was mine. It continued to bother me until several months later when I had my first taste of vindication. Listening to Zoot and Al one night in the Half Note I heard someone call my name. It was Al Schackman. "If it's any consolation, you were right," he said. "The bass player was the one who couldn't keep the time." "No kidding," I replied, feigning disbelief, "thanks a lot."

More recently, Bob Dorough weighed in: "I'll always regret it and I don't remember why I chose him over her, but I fired Dottie, although I admired the way she stood up to him . . . while he was demeaning her opinions with statements like, 'What do you know? You're just a girl, trying to be a drummer.' . . . I knew too late that I had fired the wrong one. Anyway, back in the Apple, in the following months, I tried to make up with Dottie and atone for my having fired her."

I wasn't impressed. Was I livid? Damn right I was. I'll never forgive them. Never!

Strollers

Jerry returned from the Russia tour with Goodman in July 1962. A short time later, an idea was hatched at Eugene's apartment to make a demo to market our trio, the one that had been jamming privately as a "family" for close to a decade: Eugene on bass, Jerry on alto, and me at the drums. But before we set foot in a studio our intimate trio swelled to a quartet. Jerry had recently played with Latin jazz percussionist, Willie Bobo, and he was impressed with the young, unknown pianist in the band named Chick Corea. Jerry made the call and Chick was available.

The four of us met one afternoon in Manhattan at Stea/Phillips[1] recording studio. Co-owner, Billy Phillips,[2] arranged the studio time and engineered the session. Using Jerry's charts, we did six tunes[3] and Eugene smiled all session long because, boy, it was cooking. I took one of my best recorded drum solos on a tune composed by Jerry, "The Forward Look"[4] and did a vocal[5] on "Better than Anything."[6] We programmed "Better than Anything" as the first cut on the recording, figuring that a vocalist in the group would be a selling point with record executives. ▶ Live and learn.

On the heels of finishing the demo, Jerry went west with Red Norvo to Tahoe and San Diego, and I went with him. We took a dub of the recording to try and stir up some interest, but it was a bust. Our stop in Los Angeles was the worst. Dick Bock, owner of Pacific Jazz Records, agreed to audition the dub overnight but, he was thumbs down the next day. Adding insult to injury, his blunt verdict on my vocal was "You're no Nancy Wilson." That was a shock. Clearly, he hated my singing, but more painful was the nagging suspicion that when he heard my vocal on the very first track he may have assumed I was featured on all the tunes and stopped listening. Obviously, the reverse was true. The rest of the dub was instrumentals with charts so great I still wince at the blunder of putting me up front.

Dave Brubeck was the second illustrious pianist I worked with in the early 1960s. His quartet had achieved a level of international celebrity reserved for only the biggest stars in jazz. My chance to play a concert with that fabled group was due entirely to the senator, Eugene Wright. Although neither Eugene nor I (nor anyone else we could find) can remember exactly when or even where that concert took place, Dave Brubeck's wife, lyricist Iola Brubeck, kindly cut to the crux of how it happened: "I can verify that Dottie Dodgion did substitute for Joe Morello in the Dave Brubeck Quartet one time when Joe was ill and unable to make the gig."[7]

It was all last minute. Dave, scrambling to find a replacement, went to Eugene and asked who he'd like to play with. Eugene remembers saying: "Well, what about Dottie Dodgion? . . . She can do what you have to have done." Now, Dave knew me from San Francisco and that I was an accomplished drummer, but since Eugene could have had his pick of virtually any musician in New York City, he was surprised when Eugene chose me. It wasn't a mystery: Eugene, bless his heart, wanted me because he had schooled me on how to listen to him.

I do remember taking at least one plane flight to get to the concert venue. Gene was the straw boss for our trip—he took care of all the travel plans, like checking our instruments. After getting me squared away for the flight he said, "Okay, 'Queen'"—Gene called me Queen because he treated me royally—"you go to the bar now." Since Paul and I were the only drinkers we repaired to the airport lounge until our flight was announced.

When we boarded, I was amused by the seating arrangements. Instead of sitting in adjoining seats, Dave, Paul, and Gene were spread out around the cabin; I guess after playing together so much of the time they stayed far apart when traveling. Eugene sat next to his bass—"Miss Bass," as he called her. He booked her seat and ate her meal—Gene was a big man.

I sat next to Dave on the way out. We both rested quietly through most of the flight, but as we started our descent Dave woke me and said that we'd be landing in about ten minutes. "It's almost martini time!" I cheered. "'Once we land," I told him, "I'm off straight to a bar for an 'In and Out' cocktail." Dave was puzzled by the name. He was not versed in the fine art of booze so I clued him to the recipe: "Put half a shot of vermouth in a shaker of ice and immediately pour it out—in and out as quick as you can. Add a shot of Grey Goose and shake well. Pour the cool clear liquid into an ice-cold glass and drop an olive!" Dave, drunk on the thought, said, "Dottie, I don't drink, but I want one!"

Later, when we gathered in the performance hall for a rehearsal and sound check, it was my turn to feel puzzled. Dave's charts were complicated and a lot of the pieces were in unusual time signatures. Jazz, for me, had always been in 4/4 time, so I was thrown. How, I wondered, would I be able to hear and feel the natural time of where to place "one" in such complex compositions?

With my confidence limping, Gene took me aside and told me to think in two: 1–2, 1–2, 1–2, 1–2, and to follow him for the endings. It was good advice. I learned that no matter what time signature it is, it will work out eventually. Unless there are accents on things, but I hear those anyway, and I never had to count, like 1–2–3–4–5. The time signature was an indentation in the music so I'd go wherever that indentation was. It was just feeling, or maybe intuition, but whatever it's called, I trusted it.

I have no memory of the concert except that once again Gene took care of everything. He even set up my drums so when I went on stage I just sat down! Beyond that, I have only the few details provided by Iola Brubeck: "I recall Dave describing to me how Dottie walked on the stage in high heels and slipped them off when she sat behind the drum set. I don't remember whether she had another pair of flats behind the set or if she played in her stocking feet."[8] Best I can recollect, I fit the band just fine, an impression backed up by Eugene: "So Dave used her and he was happy with her. . . . That was one of the big moments in Dottie Dodgion's life, is the fact that she played with Dave and everybody was so surprised that she did what she did with Dave.'"

My next hookup with a renowned jazz pianist was anything but a one-off. From early 1963 into 1964, I was the regular drummer in Marian McPartland's Trio that appeared at the Strollers Theater Club on East 54th Street in New York City. I had great respect for Marian, and since I was evidently the first woman musician she ever hired, I believe the feeling was mutual. A little over a decade later, in an essay she authored for the 1975 edition of *Esquire's World of Jazz*, Marian confided how she had taken "it for granted no women played good drums. And so when I heard Dottie Dodgion in the early 1960s, I was amazed at how solid, how swinging, how tasty this woman's playing was! . . . Every time I hear her I marvel at her excellent time sense (at any tempo), and her swinging, hard-driving beat."[9]

Our bassist at Strollers was eighteen-year-old Eddie Gomez, who not too many years later became one of the most sought-after bassists in jazz. "It was a great experience being around Marian and Dottie," Eddie said. "Both of them were, of course, great players but also very maternal towards me." Eddie had no attitudes at all about playing with women: "I'd never thought too much about the fact that I was surrounded by two women. . . . Nowadays it's very common to have women as side-persons. But back then it was a bit unusual and maybe a rarity, but I thought it was great that I was playing with them. . . . It was a great little trio."

"It was a lot of fun for me playing with Dottie," Eddie reminisced. "She has a kind of energy and a vitality in her music and in her personality; one translates into the other." From the get-go, Eddie understood my approach to the drums and to the trio. As he described it, my conception "was about swing and about making it all feel good." He continued by saying, "There are a lot of drummers but I think it thins out pretty quick when it comes to that kind of swing. . . . So I think it was just the way she swung. It was kind of a real happy-time feeling . . . just this really deep profound swing."

At Strollers we worked a theater program and a jazz gig. Each night we'd start off playing incidental music for "The Establishment," a British satirical revue written by Peter Cook of "Beyond the Fringe" fame. After the stage show, Marian, Eddie, and I would reconvene in a small pub lounge at the back of Strollers for a couple of sets. Strollers was one of several clubs in the East 50s frequented by famous people of all stripes, from the distinguished English actor, Sir John Gielgud, to singer and activist, Harry Belafonte, to White House Press Secretary, Pierre Salinger. We also had our share of drunks, but Marian didn't suffer fools. Normally a model of British propriety, when some boozed-up guy would hang on the piano Marian would summarily tell him to "Fuck off, Ducks"!

Unforgettable was the night Dizzy Gillespie unexpectedly showed up in the break between sets. I hadn't seen Diz since Jimbo's, but I was backstage and didn't know he'd come in. About midway through the intermission, I had some business with Marian, so I hurried back to the theater and began climbing the off-stage, very narrow, one-person-at-a-time ladder that went straight up to the loft she used as a dressing room. I was about half way up the twenty steps when I saw a large male figure heading down. His head in shadow and his bulk filling the passage, he squeezed to one side when he saw me and lowered himself until our faces almost met. "Oh, hi, Dizzy," I said casually, as if we met that way regularly. "Stay there a minute, Dottie, I've got something for you," and he reached in his pocket and took out a little bottle and scoop. "Oh, no, Dizzy," I said politely, but he was cheerfully insistent. "You don't turn the Diz down," he said laughing, and with the scoop he gave me a "one and one," which is a snort of cocaine in each nostril. I've never told anybody that, but what the hell.

That wasn't my first time using coke but it sure was the craziest. I had turned on previously because I wanted so bad to be one of the guys, but I never got hooked because I couldn't tolerate more than a small amount as a pickup. I was never hard core; I was in my early thirties when I worked Strollers, but I might as well have been eighteen because I was such a babe in the woods around all the drugs that were being done. I mean, at that point in my life I barely drank compared to a lot of musicians, and I never got close to heroin. I knew better about heroin, I'd seen so many junkies in my life. Besides, I'm an up person. No way would I do anything to bring me down, but sometimes you can't win for losing, I guess, because it wasn't long before I smacked head-on into problems with another nasty habit: smoking!

My mother was a smoke stack, lighting up four packs a day. I followed suit and was a heavy smoker at fourteen. At first I smoked mentholated "Spuds" and other brands made of poor-quality tobacco because the real cigarettes went to the boys in the war. I switched to unfiltered Camels when I got to New York, only to find out two years later that I was allergic to tobacco! I had no idea at all. My first clue was the night I inconveniently passed out at Strollers.

At intermission, I went behind the stage to sneak a cigarette. I don't remember tumbling down a flight of stairs. I do recall waking up in the basement draped over a butcher's block in the kitchen right next to the dumbwaiter, with a guy over me listening to my lungs through a stethoscope. Clearly, someone had called for a doctor in the house. "You should not be smoking, young lady," he warned. "If you don't listen to me, it won't be long before you'll need a hole drilled in your throat!" Smoking had for years been my Linus blanket, my thumb in my mouth; I couldn't quit! But finding out I was allergic to nicotine, I had to quit. I had to!

The Strollers gig ended shortly thereafter and the very next day I went to work across the street at the Embers with the Jerry Dodgion Quartet that included the Boston-based Neve Brothers, John on bass and Paul at the piano. We played opposite the entertaining virtuoso pianist, Dorothy Donegan.[10]

J. C. Heard was Dorothy's drummer and since he was there first I shared his drum set.

In those days, when a club had a stage that wasn't big enough for two drum sets, drummers from the different bands on the bill used the same set. I was used to it; I'd played on so many different sets since Jimbo's that the arrangement didn't bother me. Fortunately, it didn't bother J. C. Heard either, even though I had nicotine withdrawals so bad I was ruthlessly pounding his drums. J. C. Heard, bless his heart, was sympathetic: "Beat the hell out of them, Dottie, go ahead Honey, beat the hell out of them!" but it wasn't enough. No doubt, I needed something to ease the nicotine crash, but it was the cold turkey of not having that "thumb" to suck that was really driving me crazy.

Jazz percussionist, Willie Bobo,[11] came to my rescue. We had been friends since the late 1950s, when Willie was with vibist, Cal Tjader, at the Blackhawk, and he knew what I needed: a big bag filled with lemonade pot. Technically, lemonade pot is "the shake," the loose buds and leaves that drop off the stems of cannabis flowers. Smoking lemonade pot doesn't get you high. I had to smoke 10 joints before I felt anything, so as pot it was basically worthless, but it didn't matter. Whenever I got the itch, I rolled my own (thank you, Buckwheat[12]) with that phony pot. A joint in my mouth satisfied my oral craving and helped me beat the habit.

I quit tobacco and my lungs got pink.

The Village Stompers

We did a week at the Embers, which by New York standards was a generous amount of time for a gig. Most musicians in the city worked short gigs.
There just wasn't that much room and there was such an abundance of great
musicians that clubs could get the best and make out like bandits.

In my case, there were so many top-flight drummers in New York that,
after Marian, I had to make due with occasional mostly one-nighters, pretty
much through the rest of the 1960s. Despite the scarcity of regular work, my
reputation as a swinging drummer spread. I saw to that. Eugene was there
and he remembers that, "When she was in New York she was playing with
all the top guys. . . . All those guys knew Dottie, knew she could play."

Still, getting the respect of my peers meant never letting up. As the late,
esteemed bassist, Bob Cranshaw, remarked: "Dottie was a pioneer. . . . She
definitely was blazing a path for a lot of women. . . . It had to be very hard.
It had to be extremely hard. . . . She had to fight through the crowd of drummers, because it is always very hard for the women to get into. . . . The guys
hang together so they pass on things to each other. Most of the women are
usually left out of that equation. Dottie made sure she was part of the equation because of the way she played. . . . The guys knew she wasn't taking a
back seat. . . . We couldn't deny her if we wanted to. . . . She was definitely
one of the major drummers and one of the major drummers here in New
York. . . . She threw her hat in the ring with all of the guys who were playing,
she was just as good and she stood just as tall."

Insider respect is a precious commodity, but it didn't inoculate me against
sexism. Like the time Billy Butterfield's band needed a drummer and some

of the guys called me: "God, Dottie, you'd be really great for the band." "But I don't read," I replied. "No, no," they assured me, "You wouldn't have to, Man." It sounded good so I agreed, but I should have saved my breath. When those same guys proposed me to the band manager he exploded: "No fucking girl drummer's going to play in this band. Are you kidding? They'd say the band didn't have any balls!" That was a drag and just plain wrong. As I've said: "You don't have to be big and strong to play; first it's in your heart, then your head, and then your arms and wrists—that's where it is, how ambidextrous you are. Roy Haynes is no great big cat, but he cooks his ass off."[1]

Between gigs, Jerry and I would go on occasion to sessions at a rehearsal studio in Long Island. The studio was owned by trombonist, Marshall Brown, who didn't care for my playing. The way I swung, my conception at the drums, didn't suit him. And that was okay since I didn't care for the way he played, either. It was definitely Dixie, hard Dixie, very staccato. Despite our stylistic differences, we tolerated each other, and I'm glad we did. It was at Marshall's studio where the inimitable cornetist, Wild Bill Davison, heard me play, and in the Spring of 1963 he hired me for a two-week gig at the Colonial Tavern in Toronto.

Aside from yours truly, the band Wild Bill took to Toronto included clarinetist, Joe Barufaldi; Hayes Alvis at the bass; pianist, Don Coates; and my Long Island nemesis, Marshall Brown on trombone.[2] As usual, I stuck out in the band because of my gender, but as jazz writer, Hal Willard observed, that didn't bother Wild Bill: "A female jazz artist was unusual, but a female jazz drummer was very definitely an object of curiosity. But not to Bill. She could play." "Dottie's a damn good drummer and she sings a hell of a song,"[3] Davison said.

Opening night of the Colonial engagement I sat at my drums against a wall with the band arrayed in front of me. Wild Bill kicked off a medium tempo for the first number and a few bars in, Marshall turned part-way around toward me and punched out a run of staccato notes marking off the time. It was his boorish way of telling me I wasn't playing it right, and to him I wasn't. In his mind I was not playing strict enough. I was maybe too swinging, and he was trying to intimidate me into that almost marching-band cadence he preferred.

I tried shifting gears to fit with him but it didn't work, and next thing I knew his slide was pointing right at my face. With his back to the audience, he was making a more obvious display of where he was placing the time and where he thought I ought to have it. At this point in the tune, Wild Bill started to take his solo, but, distracted by the commotion behind him, he craned his neck, saw that Brown was giving me a hard time, and out the corner of his mouth he spat, "Quit it, Marshall, and turn around!" That was the end of that. Although it wasn't my fault and I had tried to adjust, it wound up as one more time in my life when I had to stick to my guns.

An amusing postscript to the Colonial Tavern job occurred when we played an American resort on our way back from Canada. Over the years and before I ever met Wild Bill, I had heard story after story from other musicians about his reputation as a kleptomaniac—how every place he went he took something. On this occasion, Wild Bill had a rocking chair in his room. Now, I don't know how it got up there, but the morning after we finished the gig I was smiling inside and wondering because, with everyone packed and ready to go, that rocking chair was on top of our car! As we were about to leave, the owner of the resort came out to see us off. Beaming, he said, "Boy, Bill, it's been wonderful having you here," and away we went!

I worked with Wild Bill again in June, this time for a gig at the Belle-Mar Supper Club[4] in Syracuse. Then it was back to New York and a dry spell that lasted until by accident, literally, I fell into something. Jerry and I went one night to an eastside club, the Gordian Knot, to hear the Al Grey/Billy Mitchell Quintet. Trombonist Grey and tenor player Mitchell were both veterans of the Count Basie band. Rounding out the group were pianist, Richard Wyands, Major "Mule" Holley at the bass, and drummer Grady Tate, who was one of our New York pals. The place was packed when we got there; the only seats left were right behind the drums at the back of the bandstand. Jerry and I sat down, said a quick "Hello" to Grady, and proceeded to dig the first set.

Dumb luck struck a few tunes later. Billy was soloing when Grady snapped his left hand down to hit a rim shot and at the crack of the stick cut one of his fingers on the edge of the snare. Bleeding profusely, he spun around and motioned with his head for me to get up there and help him. Jerry was shaking his head, too, but he was signaling "no" just like he had at the Vegas Flamingo before I sat in with Hamp. Deciding what to do wasn't hard; I mean, Grady had turned to me automatically, and if he had that much confidence in me why should I listen to Jerry? Once again, Jerry was afraid for me, but Grady had no doubts that I could do it.

The transition was seamless, like it'd been choreographed. Grady, keeping time on his ride cymbal, slid off the stool as I grabbed one of his spare drumsticks, scooted myself onto his seat, and eased into my triplets without missing a beat. Billy Mitchell kept playing; I had snuck in so smoothly that he was oblivious to the switch. Of course, the audience saw everything, agog that a woman was taking over for a male drummer, so when the crowd gasped followed by a collective "wow!" Billy thought he was killing them! And, of course, he was. Billy was a great tenor player, he just didn't know about the new ingredient stirring it up behind him. Billy went on to play several more choruses and I cooked him subtly underneath, playing the time like Grady knew how to do. When we finished, Billy turned around, flashed a big smile, and said, "damn, Grady!" followed immediately by, "wait a minute, you ain't Grady! You wanna go to Chicago?!"

That was great undercover. I took over for Grady and Billy didn't even question it. There was no reason to. I was grooving him and that was enough; he didn't need to know who it was that was grooving him! It was a cool thing to be able to do. I always say I like to be kind of unknown, to give you before you've gotten it—in other words, making you excited before you even know it! That's always been more my style than blowing my own horn—let somebody else do that. Low profile, that's old school; the secret power of the old pros.

The old-school clique I was part of in NYC was small but very select: a group of heavy, seasoned jazz musicians who knew the true way to play.[5] Nobody was spotlighted when we played; it was a unit that could swing together forever without rushing or dragging. Everybody found that spot and it was as if we were one in the overall sound. That is really old school; and that's when I really had fun.

If you wanted to sit in with an old-school jazz group you didn't bring music to play. You had to listen and know those standards or bebop changes or at least have the talent to be able to recover if you didn't. The real pro musicians that I got to play with, that's how they looked at it. Why I was blessed to be placed in the path of so many musical geniuses I do not know, but I paid attention and they pushed me hard. The reward was that I played better. The passion I felt from the big boys never left me wanting. How many situations in life can you say that about?

When the Al Grey/Billy Mitchell Quintet closed at the Gordian Knot, Grady said that he couldn't make Chicago. So I got the job! A week later we left for a one-week gig at the Gate of Horn club on the north side of Chicago. It was January and it was windy, or as the natives say when blustery Chicago weather hits: "The 'Hawk' is out!"

The mighty "Hawk wind" was so strong that whenever Wyands and I walked the long blocks from the Blackstone Hotel to the club, we'd hang onto walls, corners of buildings, and each other. When we reached the club, which was in the Rice Hotel, we'd walk into the street-level lounge and then downstairs to the room we played. A mirror was hung at the top of the stairs, and before every performance I stopped in front of that mirror, stared into my eyeballs, and repeated to myself that everything would be fine. I picked up that technique from a self-hypnosis book and it worked to calm my nerves. Gray and Mitchell were the "big time," and despite starting out with Goodman, I was still in awe of that rarified level of musicianship.

We traveled to the gig as a quartet—Gray, Billy, Wyands, and me—and picked up a bass player in Chicago. It turned out he was a junkie. During rehearsal he just sat in a corner, so it was clear from the outset that he wasn't going to be much help. On the bandstand he didn't miss notes, so in that way he seemed qualified, but he couldn't give us his full support because junk sapped his energy. It was so bad that every little bit he'd nod off. Billy or Al would nudge him and he'd come back, maybe in the right place, but it was nerve-wracking for the rest of us.

On the third night, a large Black woman came in during intermission. Her name was Bertha and she was a bass player from Chicago. Billy had played with Bertha years before so he gave her a big hug and asked if she wanted to sit in. "Sure," she said, and Billy turned to the junkie bass player and told him to lose his sorry ass: "Get off the stand, man; find a chair and sleep all you want."

Back then, women bass players weren't taken seriously[6] and since Bertha wasn't a regular on the circuit I hadn't heard of her before, but she was a powerhouse! Bertha from Chicago was the only "ging-ganger"[7] acoustic-lady-bass-player I ever heard, and there wasn't any gender there at all. She played the entire second set and cooked us into bad health. After we finished, Billy walked over to our groggy pickup bassist: "Aren't you embarrassed to have a woman come up and put you to shame?!" That cracked me up, but at the same time it hit home. As the only ofay in the band and a girl at that, I stood out even more than Bertha. People used to tell me, "Being a girl drummer is something, but being a white girl drummer, you really brought it on yourself. If you were Black, the road would be a little easier."

In early 1963, shortly after closing the Gate of Horn, I parted with Billy and Al and went on tour with the Village Stompers, a New York–based band that played high-class Dixie. The Stompers had in their ranks one of the top Dixieland banjo players, Marty Grosz, and also clarinetist Joe Muranyi, who, a few years later, joined the Louis Armstrong All-Stars. One of the Stompers's tour stops was at Harvey's Top of the Wheel in Lake Tahoe. I had done a week there two years earlier, but this second visit was memorable for two reasons: Deborah and Maury Wills.

Tahoe was only a two-hour drive from Sacramento so every weekend of the gig at Harvey's I was able to spend with Deborah. I'd pick her up on Friday after school and get her back late Sunday. Deborah and I had the pleasure of each other's company in Tahoe; the presence of baseball icon, Maury Wills, was a bonus. Maury Wills, the brilliant Los Angeles Dodger shortstop and consummate base stealer, was playing banjo as a solo during intermissions at Harvey's! After the Stompers got off, Maury would take center stage on a stool and play for thirty minutes, and he was damn good.

Working opposite each other, Maury and I became friends and when he met Deborah he took an immediate liking to her. The feeling was mutual: Deborah, oh, she just loved him. Sometimes on our days off we'd do things together, and one of our excursions in particular left an indelible impression. It started simply enough on a Saturday: "What are you doing tomorrow?" Maury asked me. I told him that I had to take Deborah back to my folks place in Sacramento in time for school on Monday. Maury thought for a moment and then volunteered, "I'm not doing anything. I'll drive you down, how about that?" "Great!" I said.

On Sunday, driving to Sacramento where my folks were living in a mobile home, I gave Maury a heads-up about what he was getting into with my stepdad. "Bob's a full-blooded German from Valparaiso, Indiana," I told him, "and he's not used to being around anyone who is Black." Although I'd never heard Bob make derogatory racial comments, I thought it necessary to warn Maury that seeing a Black man walk into his trailer might be a bit of a shock to Bob. Maury winked and quickly assured me: "Don't worry about that, I've been there before and I know what to do." I took his word for it and he was right; from the moment Bob was introduced to Maury Wills, "the famous ballplayer," he was impressed. Maury really knew how to work Bob; he was a real gentleman, a real charmer. Maury acted as if there was nothing wrong, and of course there wasn't.

When the visit with my parents ended, Maury and I were ready for the drive back to Tahoe, but Deborah had other plans. "Uncle Maury," she said—anybody she felt close to at that time she called "Uncle"—"could you come with me to school tomorrow? I have to do a 'Show and Tell' and my dog died." (Deborah had taken her dog the year before for Show and Tell because she had trained him to do a trick with a cookie and a string, but, sadly, he didn't make it for the encore.) Neither of us had to work on Monday, so Maury agreed, touched I bet by Deborah's innocence.

I stayed with my folks, Maury got a motel, and at eight a.m. sharp on Monday morning Mr. Maury Wills was on our doorstep, a baseball in his hand. He had brought it on the off chance someone at the school might know who he was and fancy an autographed souvenir. Truth be told, though, none of us had a clue if anyone in the convent knew anything or even cared about baseball. As things turned out we were surprised, to say the least!

Picture Deborah, if you will, standing in front of her class holding Maury's hand and proudly announcing: "This is my Show and Tell; this is Maury Wills!" Now imagine deafening silence followed a moment later by complete pandemonium! Those normally demure nuns went crazy. Exclaiming "Oh, Maury Wills, Maury Wills!!" they competed for his attention and lined up to get his autograph on any surface that was handy. (The signed baseball found its way to the Mother Superior!) Deborah said she was "Queen-for-a-Day," and it tickled Maury as much as her.

When the Stompers tour ended and I returned east, Jerry was getting more work, thanks in large part to Jerome Richardson. "He did so much for me," Jerry recalled, "he got me subbing for Phil Woods with Quincy Jones . . . and then later I met Phil and then I started playing with him." Eventually Jerry and I became friends with Phil and his wife, Chan Parker, Charlie "Bird" Parker's widow, and visited them, sometimes for dinner, out in New Hope, Pennsylvania, where Phil taught at the Ramblerny School of the Performing Arts. To return the favor, Phil would sleep on our couch when he came into New York from New Hope for a gig.

I got very close to Chan Parker because she was the one woman in New York I could go to a club with who didn't talk while a band was playing. Chan was a hard-core, no gossip, closed-mouthed lady. We didn't have many fun times because having been married to Bird, a junkie, there weren't too many funny things for her to tell. Chan wasn't an easy woman to please and that's fine, neither am I, but she was very honest, a straight arrow when it came to what she thought about you, and she was dead serious about music.

Chan was very skilled at transposing, which gained her respect from musicians. If a chart was written out for the piano in one key; she could transpose it for the horns. It was amazing she could do all that, but being married to Charlie Parker taught her to listen, and, boy, she had good ears. She was a real musician and I think we had mutual respect for one another.

Ditto for Phil Woods and me; he was in my corner from the beginning. One of the most memorable gigs I had in New York was the Sunday afternoon Top of the Gate session I did in 1967 with Phil on alto, pianist Hal Galper, and Richard Davis at the bass. A dynamite lineup! Phil could be hilarious and endearing, like the time, about 1973 or 1974, when he hired me, pianist Kenny Barron, and a pickup bass player to open Club Etcetera in DC. We were playing for the door but it was during a blizzard so getting much of an audience seemed iffy. But Phil was confident. "It'll pay $400," he crowed, "because if there's anything I'm positive about it's my drawing power." But it turned out there was no door to split because nobody showed up! We didn't make any money at all! An abashed Phil was forced to eat his prediction, but in the end, he was good for it. Almost two years later he paid Kenny and me $400 each!

Phil and I occasionally bumped heads when he was in his cups. Etched in my memory is the fuss one night at the Deer Head Inn when, along with bassist DeWitt Kay, I was part of a trio led by underground piano legend, John Coates Jr. This was long after I had established myself in New York and long after anyone had to tell me how to play. That is until Phil decided to try it one night in the Poconos.

The trio was deep into a John Coates's original when Phil walked in—he lived just up the hill from the Deer Head. Now, Phil Woods is a genius and he was welcome to sit in any time at the Deer Head, and normally it wouldn't matter if we were in the middle of a tune that Phil wasn't familiar with because he could hear way ahead. But things were different on this particular night because Phil was bombed. So much so that he had the chutzpah to take his horn out, barge onto the stand, and, in the middle of John Coates's solo, launch into his own solo! Then, after finishing his choruses, he reeled around, for all the world like a traffic cop, and started spouting adjustments he wanted me to make! The band was still in the middle of the tune so I could barely hear what the hell he was saying, but his buffoonery alone got me hot!! Gritting my teeth and mouthing, "Really? Is that right, Phil? Is that what you want, Phil?" I kept playing the same way.

When the set ended, I saw Phil leaning unsteadily against the bar. I took the empty stool beside him and let him have it: "Phil, you can tell me how you want me to play before a tune or after a tune but don't you ever turn around and tell me how to play in the middle of a tune, and especially when I can't even hear what the hell you're saying!" Dry-mouthed and squinting, he smacked his lips together and blurted, "How dare you tell me not to tell you how to play!" At first, I thought he was serious. Then it dawned on me: his head had cleared enough so he knew he'd done wrong and now he was putting me on. Kind of like when he gloated about his drawing power in a blizzard and had to eat humble pie!

That was the most maddening thing and the funniest thing I ever went through with Phil, and reminiscing in later years we always had a good laugh about it.

PHOTO 1. Dottie
Dodgion's mother, Ada
Martha Giaimo, c. 1933.
Courtesy of Dottie
Dodgion.

PHOTO 2. Dottie
Dodgion, Harold
Mack Jr., Photography;
Romaine Studio, San
Francisco, 1941.

PHOTO 3. Dottie Dodgion, Romaine Studio, San Francisco, 1946.

PHOTO 4. Mary Kaye Trio (left to right: Frank Ross, Mary Kaye, Norman Kaye).
Courtesy of UNLV Libraries Special Collections. Courtesy of Tracy Kaye, son of
Norman Kaye.

PHOTO 5. Jimbo's Bop City (back, left to right: Roy Porter, Specs Wright, Bernie Peters, Jimbo Edwards, unknown, Dottie Dodgion aka Betty Bennett, Kenny Dorham, Dizzy Gillespie, Miles Davis, Howard Jeffries, Percy Heath; front, left to right: Ernie Lewis, Sonny Criss, Milt Jackson, Carl Perkins, Jimmy Heath, "Cowboy" Noyd, Oyama Johnson). San Francisco, c. 1950. Collection of Jimbo Edwards, photographer unknown.

PHOTO 6. Bassist, Monty Budwig, 1983. Courtesy of Brian McMillen.

PHOTO 7. Mrs. Dorothy Budwig holding divorce papers. *Call Bulletin*. San Francisco, September 8, 1954. Courtesy of San Francisco History Center, San Francisco Public Library.

PHOTO 8. Benny Goodman Band: Jimmy Rushing (vocals); Chuck Israels (bass); Zoot Sims (tenor sax); Dottie Dodgion (drums); Carl Fontana (trombone); Buddy Childers (trumpet); Jerry Dodgion (alto sax). Basin Street East, NYC, March 1961. Courtesy of Dottie Dodgion.

PHOTO 9. Dottie Dodgion, Basin Street East, NYC, March 1961. Courtesy of Dottie Dodgion.

PHOTO 10. Left to right: Wild Bill Davison, (cornet); Dottie Dodgion, (drums). Colonial Tavern, Toronto, 1963. Courtesy of Dottie Dodgion.

PHOTO 11. Left to right: (pianist) Richard Wyands; (drummer) Dottie Dodgion; unknown; (bandleader and tenor saxophonist) Billy Mitchell. Gate of Horn club, Rice Hotel, Chicago, 1963. Courtesy of Dottie Dodgion.

PHOTO 12. Marian McPartland Trio. Left to right: Dottie Dodgion (drums); Eddie Gomez (bass); Marian McPartland (piano) Strollers, NYC, c. 1964. Courtesy of Marian McPartland.

PHOTO 13. Left to right: (pianist) John Bunch; (bassist) Eugene Wright; (alto saxophonist) Jerry Dodgion; (drummer) Dottie Dodgion. Dodgion apartment, 20th St., NYC, 1964. Courtesy of Dottie Dodgion.

PHOTO 14. Jerry Dodgion and Dottie Dodgion, c. 1965. Courtesy of Dottie Dodgion.

PHOTO 15. John Coates Trio. Left to right: John Coates Jr. (piano); DeWitt Kay (bass); Dottie Dodgion (drums). Deer Head Inn, Delaware Water Gap, PA, early 1980s. Courtesy of Dottie Dodgion.

PHOTO 16. Dottie Dodgion (left); Carol Sloane (right). Milestones, San Francisco, 1986. Courtesy of Dottie Dodgion.

"Some men just sing in the bath"

You are cordially invited
to attend a Piano Party
at the Dodgion's, on Sunday,
September Seventeenth, 1972

There is a dual purpose for this celebration.
First of all to commemerate the rebuilding of a famous piano
lovingly bestowed on us by the Phil Woods Family ----
A Steinway nine foot Concert Grand (1875) rebuilt with love by
John Marabuto of El Cerrito, California.
The second purpose is to afford an opportunity for pianists
to get together socially, since they rarely have the occasion to
do so, and everyone knows that piano players are crazy! Smile!
It is open house all day for piano players----Smile!
Please come by and enjoy -----

PHOTO 17. Piano Party invite, September 1972. Courtesy of Dee Marabuto.

PHOTO 18. Dottie Dodgion and organist, Ron Rose, Lake Tahoe, 1975. Courtesy of Dottie Dodgion.

PHOTO 19. Left to right: (bassist) Steve Novosel; (tenor saxophonist) Al Cohn; (tenor saxophonist) Zoot Sims; (drummer) Dottie Dodgion; (pianist) Jimmy Rowles. Kennedy Center, Washington, DC, 1976. Courtesy of Dottie Dodgion.

PHOTO 20. Marian McPartland Quintet. Clockwise from the left: Mary Osborne (guitar); Vi Redd (alto saxophone); Marian McPartland (piano); Lynn Milano (bass); Dottie Dodgion (drums). Monticello Room in the Rowntowner Motel, Rochester, NY, June 1977. Courtesy of Marian McPartland.

PHOTO 21. Left to right: Deborah Dodgion, Chuck Giaimo, Dottie Dodgion. Washington, DC, November 1977. Courtesy of Dottie Dodgion.

PHOTO 22. *Melba Liston and Co.*, Far East tour in Malaysia. Left to right: (trombonist) Ted Kelly; (pianist) Ahnee Sharon Freeman; (road manager) Cobi Narita; (tenor saxophonist) Erica Lindsay; (bandleader and trombonist) Melba Liston; (American Ambassador to Malaysia) Barbara Watson; (drummer) Dottie Dodgion; (electric bassist) Carline Ray; (alto saxophonist) Luther Francois. Malaysia, October 1980. Courtesy of Ahnee Sharon Freeman.

PHOTO 23. *Papa Jake and His Abalone Stompers.* Left to right: Alan O'Day (tuba); Eddie Erickson (banjo and guitar); Jake Stock (bandleader and alto saxophone); Doug Curtis (trombone); Dottie Dodgion (drums); Jackie Coon (flugelhorn). c. 1992. Courtesy of Dottie Dodgion.

PHOTO 24. Dottie Dodgion, February 2, 2019. Photo by Julie S. Ahearn.

Eddie Condon's

In 1964, Jerry finally made it into the studios and although we weren't flush we were doing a better job surviving. We moved from Maria Marshall's $150-a-month one-room apartment to a two-story townhouse with twelve-foot ceilings and a dumbwaiter at more than double the rent on 20th Street, between 8th and 9th, in Chelsea District. Jerry and I were impressed—there was a tree on our block.

We had upscaled, but the downside was that our new roomy digs made the emptiness I felt without Deborah all the more stark. Over ten years had passed since I dropped my baby off at my mother's, and the ache never left, the gnawing guilt that I hadn't done right by her, that I had cheated my own flesh and blood. I missed my daughter so much and wanted her back!

After we migrated to New York, I tried several times to get Deborah out for a visit, but except for the one time when she was nine, my mother refused to let her go. It was no secret that part of the reason for her opposition was the impoverished lifestyle Jerry and I had led, including our severely cramped living quarters. But now that our stock had risen I made the leap from asking for short visits to thinking that the time was right for Deborah to move in permanently with us. Surely my mother would see the wisdom of it.

I should have known better. My mother had as good as adopted Deborah so any mention of taking my daughter back riled her big time: "I'll sue and take you to court," she fumed. "I've gone through everything with Deborah, all the worry, work, and childhood diseases, so you've got no cause to claim her!"

She was right; I'd been out of the loop. I seldom knew when Deborah was ill, and when I found out afterward I'd complain that I never got a call. "What could you have done?" my mother would say, and sadly it was true. I was a broke gypsy-jazz musician who could do nothing except worry and bitch at her, although secretly I was grateful.

My mother's resistance softened slowly over the next few years as Deborah, attempting to break out of her shell, became a handful for her and Bob. A turning point arrived when Deborah started dropping acid under the influence of Timothy Leary! Leary, the so-called "inner-space pioneer," was in Sacramento advocating for LSD and gathering his flock. When Deborah learned he was to speak at a local convention hall, Momma and Bob gave her permission to go. Neither of them realized what it was about. According to Deborah, Leary was "mind blowing." He explained how to use the drug, to not let the drug use you, and told her to: "Take as much as your body can handle and use it to open up your mind and dig deep into yourself." She started tripping when she was about eleven and after hundreds of trips she quit at twenty-eight.

Deborah had never smoked pot or experimented with other drugs, so the news of her psychedelic experiments hit my mother like a bombshell. For the first time, she seriously, if grudgingly, considered that Deborah might need Jerry and me to be more actively involved in her life. I knew the transition had to be gradual. As an inaugural step, I proposed that Deborah fly east in June 1964 to coincide with the New York World's Fair in Queens. My mother, who had never been to New York, agreed on the condition she accompany her!

The night before Deborah and my mother arrived, Jerry and I threw a party at our house; the fun was sweetened by a plate of pot cookies brought by one of the guests. The day after, before collecting Deborah and my mom at the airport, Jerry and I quickly tidied up. In our haste we overlooked a blue plate of leftover cookies on the dining room table.

That evening, with Mom and Deborah settled, the four of us made plans to head to the Fair first thing the following day. In the morning, as we gathered in the foyer to leave, my mother's stomach was queasy so she made a detour to the dining room and snagged a cookie off the blue plate! That took me completely by surprise because she never ate sweets; it would never cross her mind to have a bun or a muffin in the morning, much less a cookie. Coffee and cigarettes always started her day. So how could I have known?! As she scarfed the cookie down, Jerry and I looked wide-eyed at each other and had the same thought: "Thank God she didn't take two!" Fortunately, the gods were with us. Those cookies, made from good Colombian hash, weren't killer.

The World's Fair was packed, a crush of visitors milling around one magnificent pavilion after another. Shortly after we arrived, the cookie kicked in and Momma got very relaxed. Smiling and with tears in her eyes, she gushed, "Dorothy, this is the most beautiful day I've ever had in my life." She had suffered so much, God love her, that I was grateful to see that look of contentment on her face. I'm really glad that accident happened; if I never gave her anything else, at least I gave her that cookie.

They stayed for a week. Long enough for Deborah's eyes to be opened to big-city excitement, making her cloistered world in Sacramento much less appealing. Long enough for my mother to realize the importance of exposing Deborah to a kind of stimulating intellectual environment that was out of her and my stepdad's league. And long enough for my mother to fully realize that she and Bob were in over their heads with their acid-tripping granddaughter, that at their age they weren't "with it" enough about the drug scene, and that, since I was hip about such things, I could control her more. "It's time for you to take her," my mother admitted. I knew she wasn't ready for a complete break, but the door had opened for Deborah to become a more regular and integrated part of our lives.

The three summers we spent with our daughter in the Poconos in the mid-to-late 1960s helped us bond as a family unit. Jerry and I played at Mount Airy Lodge where we found this lovely lady, Mrs. Brown—God love her, little old church lady—who rented us a cabin close to the lodge, with two bedrooms, bath, living room, small dining room, kitchen, and a back porch, for only $25 a month!

I recall in some detail the summer of 1967 when Jerry and I worked weekends in the small room at Mount Airy Lodge with a quartet that included pianist Dave Frishberg.[1] It was like a club date; the music was straight-ahead, and I did the occasional vocal from behind the drums. "She'd maybe sing two or three songs a night," Dave recalled. "But she was really good; I loved her singing. It was totally a jazz approach. It was very hip singing."

Now and then I'd work as a single in the Poconos. I subbed a couple or three times in Bob Newman's big band when he didn't have his regular drummer, Jerry Segal. I also got calls to play with John Coates Jr. at the Deer Head Inn. John played solo piano much of the year, but in the summer he would have DeWitt Kay on bass, sometimes adding a drummer. Those informal trio sessions over several summers helped me establish a working relationship with John that paid off more than a decade later.

Although I did some singing in the Poconos and other places like Toronto, my work in New York City focused exclusively on the drums. In the Big Apple jazz leagues of the 1960s, you had to commit to an axe, to specialize on one instrument. These days, a jazz musician is expected to double on other instruments, but back then doubling was frowned upon and that was okay with me. Heeding Jerry's advice from some fifteen years earlier, I didn't want to be known as a dabbler: a singer who played a little drums or a drummer who also sang. I was a drummer, plain and simple, so I didn't sing a note during my first two decades in the city, except for the time that was an unmitigated disaster: a trio gig in the mid-1960s led by tenor saxophonist, Zoot Sims, at the Tavern on the Green in Central Park.

We kicked off the night playing a wedding party in the lounge, cooking smoothly with a clear horizon until the Tavern owner stormed onto the bandstand and demanded: "Doesn't anybody sing in this band?" That threw us a curve because our trio didn't have a singer, at least as far as Zoot knew. Zoot wasn't a singer at all, the pianist ignored the request, and I begged off. Striking out got the owner so incensed that a desperate Zoot said, "Okay, I'll do 'September Song.'"[2] Zoot hit me in the arm: "You do 'Straighten Up and Fly Right,'"[3] and when our pianist caved we got over that bump in the road[4]

Bullied into singing was humbling enough, but the Fates weren't done. Later that night, we backed a show with comedian, Alan King, as the emcee. King, like other comics of that era, had a reputation for picking on musicians in his backup band when he ran out of material. I never liked that; my thinking was: "Get your own jokes, man, it's enough they have to play for you!" Well, who do you think was singled out that night in the Tavern on the Green?

King was deep into his shtick when he spied me on the stand. A woman in the band? He couldn't resist: "Ohhh! What do we have here? Must be the tenor player's girlfriend on drums!" I shot him the dirtiest look in my arsenal but his impish grin told me my message only fueled the flames. "Well, we don't want to mess with romance," he scoffed. The audience snickered and it embarrassed Zoot something terrible. I looked at Zoot as if to say, "Don't let it get to you," but it was too late. "Leave her alone!" Zoot gallantly warned, but that gave King more ammunition. "Oh! Leave her alone! Oh, oh, do I hear wedding bells!"

Zoot didn't have to defend me; we could have ridden it out, but the damage was done. Zoot never hired me for a lounge gig again. He gave me jazz jobs; they were still okay, but not Vegas-style, commercial shows, and it was all because of Alan King's crass remarks. They put Zoot in an awkward position and he was just too laid back to ever go through that again.

That Zoot's respect for me as a player didn't suffer from this incident is confirmed by a touching anecdote told by his widow, Louise Sims: "Somewhere along the way Zoot got the idea that in our den downstairs . . . he was going to build his 'Wall of Fame.' He was going to get 8x10 glossies of all these musician friends and he was going to build a wall-sized frame and he was going to put their pictures in it. . . . He went to a lumber store and he ordered the wood, measured it and everything. And on the top row he started with the bass players and drummers and in that row . . . are, among others, Shelly Manne, Jake Hanna, Cliff Leeman, Buddy Rich, Dottie Dodgion. And right below her are Gerry Mulligan and Ruby [Braff] and Sinatra and Norman Granz to name a few. So, she's surrounded by heavyweights. I think Dottie's one of maybe three women on that wall."

Almost twenty years passed before I sang a second time in New York and it was another fiasco, only to be redeemed at the last moment. Singing was back on my radar because in the early 1980s jobs for women drummers were scarce as hen's teeth. Desperate to get more gigs I started to experiment with vocals. Since singing from behind the drums was looked down upon as a "lounge act" in those days, I decided to try standing out front, a plucky move that would give me the chance to regain the melodic end of music that I had missed by focusing entirely on drums. I started sitting in and singing with different bands; I even had Phil Woods do eight charts for me, but the more I tested the waters the more hesitant I became.

I had my excuses: I hadn't sung for all those years in New York; I didn't have a large enough vibrato in my voice; and my chops weren't what they could have been because for years I had smoked three packs of Camels a day. My confidence slumped, but a surprise visit from Jerry Harris, a vocalist and good friend from Delaware Water Gap, picked me up. Jerry had heard me sing one time at the Deer Head Inn and knew I could carry a tune. Telling me that I sang great and shouldn't worry, he gave me this advice: "Free your flux, baby cakes!" "Do what?" I wondered. "You can talk, can't you?" he asked. I replied, "of course," and he told me to put my hand over my stomach and talk. I could talk about anything, but it had to be loud enough for me to feel the vibrations in my stomach. "Talk loud and put the air behind it," he said, "and it's the same as singing. Just add the melody!"

I realized that Jerry Harris wasn't telling me anything new. I'd gotten similar advice from my vocal coach almost forty years earlier,[5] but hearing that message again, dressed this time in inner-city cool and delivered in Jerry's Black soulful voice, was the pep talk I needed. "Freeing my flux" gave my voice more authority, and a few nights later I sat in singing at the newly reopened Eddie Condon's on west 54th street.

Eddie Condon, a famous figure in traditional jazz circles, had died in 1971, but the club carrying his name remained a prestigious place to play. So, when cornetist and co-owner, Ed Polcer, rang me in 1985 and asked, "Dottie, want to play a week at Eddie Condon's?" I was thrilled! I had worked with a lot of big names but I'd never headlined my own group at a club in New York! The only condition, I said, was that as long as it was my band I wanted to alternate between singing out front and playing the drums. "Agreed!" Ed replied, "however you want to handle it."

A few days before we opened, I went to the club and stopped dead at the entrance. "THE DOTTIE DODGION QUARTET" shouted the marquee! I was excited and proud. Then I panicked! Worried that no one would show up and I'd be humiliated, I needed any kind of reassurance I could get. I sought out my friend, Stella Giammasi, who was married to pianist Dave Frishberg. Stella was Communications Director for the PBS channel in New York, and she knew her way around.

She took me to a seer in midtown Manhattan. In the lobby of an office building, we joined a small group seeking prophetic wisdom. Each of us submitted a question on a piece of paper that was put into a bowl. A short time later, we were seated in a small theater as the seer pulled questions from the bowl and made his predictions. My question was succinct: "Will anybody show up?" (I made no mention of Eddie Condon's.) The seer was equally terse. "It only takes one," he answered, which as things turned out was right on the money.

In the process of forming my quartet, I decided to add a drummer to fill in and play simple time behind me when I got up to sing. I selected Ron Marabuto, the son of my dearest friend, Dolores, "Dee," Marabuto. I had known Ron since he was seven, and although he wasn't really a tasty drummer, he'd recently worked with baritone sax great, Pepper Adams. Plus he was in New York and available. He seemed the perfect choice, but in retrospect I should have given it more thought.

The other members of my group were pianist, Richard Wyands, whom I knew from my stint with Billy Mitchell; Danny Moore, who played fourth trumpet on the Thad Jones/Mel Lewis band; and bassist Boots Maleson from Brooklyn. Boots wore white socks hanging over formal tuxedo shoes but I wouldn't have cared if he was shoeless, he was that good a bassist.

On opening night, I was relieved that the place was packed. After a few instrumentals I stepped in front to sing and introduced Ron Marabuto as my back-up at the drums. On my first vocal of the night I felt absolutely naked, but I was bound and determined. Then, just after the bridge, my concentration took a big hit. Ron was too loud, he got in my way, and he wasn't swinging. I ended the number abruptly, figuring that he had first-night jitters, was showing off to cover it up, and needed a moment to calm down. We went downhill from there.

During my second vocal, Ron rushed and dragged so much I was forced to turn around and snap my fingers so he would cool it with the beat. After three tunes, we were losing the crowd, and the other band members were whispering: "C'mon, Dottie, get back on the drums." I felt like I was making a fool of myself!

I cut my losses and called an early intermission. Backstage I told Ron it wasn't working and fired him. When we got back on the stand and I sat at the drums the crowd roared with applause. "Wow," I thought, "the audience, and even my own band, didn't like my singing and wanted me back on drums." That really discouraged me. I took the whole thing upon myself and, in his absence, I absolved Ron of any responsibility for what had happened.

When we got off for the night, the guys in the band told me how upset they'd been with Ron's playing and that the audience felt the same way. "Dot," they told me, "don't bring him up anymore." When I learned my singing wasn't the problem my mood brightened, but the die was cast. Without a backup drummer I was forced to cancel my vocals for the rest of the gig. To make matters worse, Dee was really hurt when she learned I had told her son "to get off the stand," but I couldn't sacrifice my reputation to protect him.

The seer's prediction was validated a few weeks after I closed Condon's. My clarinet-playing dentist was in the audience that first night, and he loved the way I sang. Loved it enough to set up and pay for a private recording date, my first one as a solo vocalist, although I did play drums on one tune. I recorded with the same band I used at Condon's, including, believe it or not, Ron Marabuto. I put Ron in an isolation booth, gave him strict instructions on how to play for me or else, and thankfully he really took care of business. Ron was a completely different drummer at that session and it worked out great, which helped me mend fences with Dee.

The session was never intended for release. I had no thoughts of promoting myself as a singer because I had already passed the acid test as a drummer in the fraternal order of the New York City jazz world. My dentist arranged it for posterity's sake, and that's how I looked at it, too. Years later I did a lot of the same tunes on "Dottie Dodgion Sings,"[6] using even better musicians playing those glorious charts by Phil Woods.

Pearls to Swine

Making it as a jazz musician in New York City wasn't only about gigs. Just as key was learning the code of the streets and coping with the politics of the music scene. To succeed it came down to finessing attitude. Everything was attitude, as my street-wise tutor and lemonade-pot pal, Willie Bobo[1] taught me.

I remember a walk with Willie in Harlem. We were headed to Count Basie's club, and about a block away there were drunks laying up against the curb. As we hurried to pass them, the comments started to fly: "Heyyy, look at that sweet little thing!" "Hello, baby, got cab fare for two?"

They were pitiful, and taking pity I naively stopped to say hello to one of the saddest of the bunch. In an instant, Willie spun around to face me, jerked my arm forward, and with a stern expression he whispered: "You don't give pearls to swine!" In that teaching moment, I learned that if I showed the slightest sign of being friendly, even uttering a simple, "hi," it was a blatant invitation; the door would be opened and it would be very hard to close. That was early in the game for me, when I guess I was in a kind of an "Alice in Wonderland" daze, so I have Willie to thank for waking me up to the social sciences of the street.

I had to get my "street chops"[2] because practically every time I went out by myself there were way too many people messing with me. When you walk out your door in New York, you don't lollygag or laugh; you think straight ahead but watch on both sides. You don't give people an inch. If somebody asks for a match, you don't have one. If somebody asks for the time or directions, say "I don't know" and keep walking. I can read people when they're dishonest. You learn what to look for; it's self-preservation. Jazz went with that kind of life.

When I wasn't hoofing it in New York, I was in a car; every drummer needs a car. Plus, Jerry and I regularly hauled musicians, often in numbers that wouldn't have fit in our Volkswagen, so we replaced it with a succession of used Mercedes—I remember how vandals kept breaking off the hood ornaments. Stories abound from those cramped commutes. Like the summer night we were going down 7th Avenue with our windows open and five in the car. I was sitting on the front seat in the middle between Jerry, who was driving, and a guy named Don, who was squeezed against the passenger door. Don owned a bar and loved musicians. In the back was my daughter, Deborah, and a young Jon Faddis, future jazz-trumpet virtuoso.

We stopped for a red light at Broadway where "the whores on Seventh Avenue" were hanging on the corners.[3] One of the ladies crossing in front of us stopped, then sauntered over to the driver's side of our car and peered inside. "Hey, Don," she said, and Jerry and I sank back into the upholstery to give her a clear sightline across the front seat. After she and Don shot the breeze for a few moments, she noticed Jerry: "Hey, you're pretty cute, too." I sat exasperated as the three of them yakked and the traffic light changed for a second time. I began to sweat the honking horns, afraid a cop would wander over to see what was holding up traffic and discover a plot that was thicker than casual conversation.

That was because I was holding the bag. Literally. I had a bag of pot hidden in my purse! Our stash always went with me; nobody would suspect innocent Dot, and I was usually the coolest, except of course when we were attracting attention to ourselves in the middle of Times Square! I think Jerry forgot he was driving, so out of desperation I reached over and poked him, "C'mon! We have children in the car, for God's sake!" I sighed a very audible "whew!" as Jerry pulled away. The coda is that Faddis told the story to everybody he knew, including his mentor Dizzy Gillespie, who thought it hilarious. Little things that happened in the hothouse of a car could quickly enter New York City jazz lore.

Jazz musicians in New York were forever crossing each other's paths, and rules of the road for informal "how-do-you-do's," were common currency among them. Jazz protocol frowned on one musician asking another, "You workin'?" Nobody wanted to be reminded if they weren't, and worse yet, they'd be jealous if you were. When musicians ran into each other they didn't say, "How's it going'?" Or "Hey, man, what's happening'?" I can't remember one New York professional asking that because someone might tell them and they didn't have time for that. Everybody had someplace to go, afraid they'd be late for a date. New Yorkers kept it simple: "Hey, man," "Hey, baby," or "Give me five," and leave it alone. Otherwise, it's wasted energy; they'd take up your time and not really mean it. That's one thing I loved about New York: "Mean what you say!"

Look deeper and the insider jazz community could be a haven of sociability. Like at Jim and Andy's, the musicians' bar on west 48th Street where Jerry and I were regulars. The owner was a marvelous Greek man, Jim Koulouvaris. Jim kept order in that bar, standing with arms folded and a steely eye, but he was my savior, a real-life angel who looked out for Deborah.

Deborah was one of the few children allowed in Jim and Andy's; whenever we'd drop her off in a rush to a gig, Jim would personally escort her to a booth at the back of the club to eat. Deborah always ordered a hamburger, and, despite the fact that the cook, Pete, "Petie" Salvato, was an Italian chef who never made hamburgers, he'd fix just for her a hamburger on an Italian roll with his "Petie Potatoes," cubed, fried, and sprinkled with olive oil and lemon juice. God, they were delicious! After Deborah ate, the staff at Jim and Andy's took turns watching over her like nannies until we'd get back. One night, Jerry got off a gig at midnight and drove home. When he walked in, I asked, "Where's Deborah?" "Oh, my God!" he cried and dashed to the phone. "Yeah, she's here," Jim said, "I'll wait with her. Take your time, Jerry."

Throughout my professional life male musicians were at the center of the jazz nation in New York. Women, particularly the wives but also women who represented a threat to the wives—girlfriends and groupies—were on the margins. I was unique. As both a player and a woman I could occupy either position depending upon who was looking, but despite the ambiguity of my role, I had a good relationship with many jazz wives.

In my circle of spouses was Louise Sims, wife of the dear departed Zoot. For several years, Louise and Zoot hosted hilarious "Ping-Pong-Parties" in their apartment. I first met Louise when she and Zoot were dating. They married in 1970 and the Ping-Pong-Parties began not long after that, lasting until about 1975. Louise remembered how Zoot called her at work on her birthday and told her that instead of using her key she should ring the doorbell when she got home "because he had a big surprise." Sure enough, as Louise tells it, when she rang the doorbell Zoot "opened the door and he hugged me and said, 'Happy Birthday and here's your present.' And he turned around and he pointed to a ping-pong table in the middle of our living room. It wasn't exactly what I was expecting for my birthday but it certainly was unique."

The parties started around four in the morning after Zoot's gigs and went on for hours; I usually got home way after daylight. I really enjoyed it when Zoot and Al had matches. Even though they'd finished playing for the evening at the Half Note, it was like they were still on. With their horns replaced by paddles they'd tell snappy stories with colorful turns of phrase while swatting the ball. As Louise described it: "They played vicious ping pong as you've seen in the Olympics." That competitive, "cutting-contest" mentality was at its height when, as Louise explained, Basie trumpet man, Joe Newman "bragged that he was at one time the champion of a southeastern group of top ping-pong players and he challenged Zoot to a tournament. . . . One night, Joe Newman, in his attacking the ball, leaned over and ripped his pants all the way up the back. Zoot said, 'Emergency, Emergency, we have to solve this.' He turned to me and said, 'Quick, get your needle and thread and sew these up.' He made Joe take off his pants [and] threw the pants over to me. I didn't know how to sew for the life of me. Joe played in his underpants and they continued the tournament until I had the pants sewn as best I could. . . . It was a funny, hysterically funny championship."

Although I have had close and enduring friendships with many spouses of musicians I worked with, truth be told, some jazz wives took exception to me, leveling accusations that were patently untrue. Like when Jerry and I attended an A&R (Artists and Repertoire) party, held annually in honor of the writers, arrangers, and jazz musicians who had worked the studios the previous year. In the shank of the evening's festivities, I was chatting with a musician when his wife swept up alongside and made a not so subtle dig: "I see my husband's paying a lot of attention to you. Don't you be giving my husband eyes and don't you be getting any ideas!" This was followed by the coup de grace: "Are you fucking him off the bandstand, too, like the others?"

She was jealous for no good reason because nothing was happening between us, and if there were, he wouldn't have been dumb enough to make it obvious in front of his wife in a public setting. My first response was to give her a look that said, "What the hell are you talking about?!" Then I ignored her. It was such an honor to be invited to the celebration I decided to be "cool Dot" by keeping my mouth shut and not making any more of a scene than she had already made. Jerry and I tried to stick it out a bit longer—I didn't want to leave that minute and give her the satisfaction of immediately running me out, but she kept at it and Jerry finally asked me, "Had it?" "Yeah, kinda had it," I replied.

As soon as we got outside, I took a paper bag out of my purse—we had double-bagged something earlier in the day—and pulled it over my head. What a picture I must have made, ambling down a busy New York City street with a bag on my head! But it was a gag for Jerry—after all the insults that woman had lobbed in my direction I figured maybe he didn't want to be seen with me!

Another time I wasn't so laid back. There were seven of us packed into our dark green Mercedes on a Monday night, heading from Jim and Andy's to the Vanguard for the gig with Thad and Mel's orchestra. I was scrunched in the middle on the front seat; three musicians were in the back, one of them had his wife sitting on his lap. As we were going down 7th Avenue, there was dead silence in the car; all the guys were lost in thought about the evening's work ahead of them.

The quiet was undisturbed until, suddenly, the wife snapped, "You know, Dottie, I've never really liked you." The calm in the car turned uneasy and I knew everybody was waiting for me to say something. Now, most people would have said, "Well, I never liked you either," and started an argument, but that was the last thing I wanted to do. I waited about a minute and then, with just a hint of defiance, I answered, "Well, I can't answer everybody's ad." That shut her up. It was all I needed to say; I was known as "One-Line Dot."

I understood why some wives were jealous. Women fell in love with musicians because it was glamorous. They'd go to a club or a dance and when the trumpet player smiled at them it was exciting for the woman because she was a nobody, but the musician he was somebody. So, if she dated a guy from the band, suddenly she's somebody all the time and all the while they're wooing she gets to come to the gigs. After they get married, she never gets to go to a gig again. The wives stay home. Nobody wants the wives at the gigs, especially the bandleaders, because they usually cause trouble.

The last straw for the wives was the double standard in the jazz world. Guys on the road had girls on call but the wives back home were sacred. The wives in turn knew their guys couldn't make money by staying in New York, so they did their best to turn a blind eye to their husbands' trysts as long as the men came back to them. Even so, the wives resented the fact that they no longer came first, so it didn't take long before the glamour of marrying a musician faded.

In the middle of all this marital discord was yours truly, the enemy on the bandstand, a woman who was not only a drummer but a female musician who was fully accepted into that exclusive mens' club with the respect of all those heavy guys! Of course, what the wives really thought was that I was going to bed with every one of their husbands! They couldn't imagine a man and woman having a friendship and sharing the music, and, true enough, it was rare. I was very lucky. I did break that barrier.

Park Ridge

When Jerry and I left Jones Street for the townhouse on 20th we felt like we'd moved to the outskirts of town, or what we kiddingly referred to as the "suburbs," because back then the Chelsea District wasn't built up like it is today. Little did we know that in a few years we would leave New York City for real suburbia, across the river, New Jersey style. What finally got us off the dime to move into the middle class is yet another screwball New York story.

It was early am on a Tuesday. Jerry, back from a gig, was looking for a parking spot, a task more complicated than it sounds because on Tuesdays we had to find alternate parking before eight in the morning so a sweeper truck could clean our street. Good fortune didn't smile on Jerry that night. He had to park four long blocks away, and shortly after he started the hike back, a big drunk confronted him.

"Gimme a cigarette!" he barked. "Don't smoke," Jerry replied. The drunk, holding a shabby sack of empty beer bottles, wasn't buying any of that. Shaking his fists, he bellowed, "I said give me a cigarette!" At that moment, the paper bag split open, its contents clattering on the sidewalk. Betting that the wino wouldn't risk losing his haul by chasing him, Jerry took off running. He'd never been that scared or had to run for his life before in New York, so when he burst in our door he didn't mince words: "It's time to get out of New York! We're moving to Park Ridge, into the house Billy found for us."

That was the same Billy Phillips who co-owned Stea/Phillips Studio where in 1962 the informal session with Eugene, Jerry, Chick Corea, and me was recorded. Billy lived with his wife, singer, composer/arranger, Anne Phillips,[1] in Park Ridge, in the northeast corner of New Jersey. We first met Billy and

Anne in the Poconos, the year previous to that recording date, through bandleader, Bob Newman, and his wife, jazz trumpet player, Norma Carson.

Not long after, Jerry and I did a job with Anne, when, as she tells it, "My aunt was in charge of getting the music for the big June fete celebration at this country club outside of . . . Main Line, Philadelphia. She decided instead of hiring the Lester Lanin band she would ask me to get music for her dance. Well, boy, did I get a great band! I'm quite sure it was Dottie and Jerry and Norma and Bob Newman. Norma Carson was a great trumpet player. . . . She was originally from Oregon and lived near the Severinsen family that included future trumpet star, Doc Severinsen. An interesting story is that Doc Severinsen's father would say to him, 'Why don't you play like that girl down the street?'"

The four of us became friends, and when we'd visit Anne and Billy in Park Ridge, Billy would try to talk us into moving nearby. One time he told us about this great little house across a brook from their place that would be on the market soon, but at that point Jerry and I weren't ready to think seriously about a move. The menacing wino changed our minds.

That great little house sat in the woods on Bear Brook Road; the road was unpaved and the next nearest place was at least a half-mile away. Made from Italian stone, it had an attached garage, hardwood floors, a huge fireplace in the living room; what we envisioned as Deborah's room had a smaller fireplace and windows all around looking right into the forest. We loved the house, but it was so far out in exurbia that only one bus came in. That worried us until we saw the asking price. The "inconvenience" of the dirt road made it dirt cheap. At $50,000 we had enough money saved to put down, and suddenly our doubts about moving to the boondocks melted away.

In 1967, not long after we moved into Park Ridge I was back in Las Vegas. I didn't have any work in New York and money was tight, so when I got a call from Gus I went. We worked one-nighters and sporadic gigs in the lounge at the Four Queens Hotel, but our regular job was at the Silver Slipper from midnight to six in the morning, six nights a week.

That was a swinging time in Vegas. Night after night, one big name after another was headlining the hotels: Count Basie, Harry James, Tommy Dorsey—it was a battle of the big bands on a grand scale. During one great run of twelve to sixteen weeks, wonderful musicians from those bands poured into the Silver Slipper after their gigs to unwind, listen, and sit in, and I got to play with all of them. The pressure of cooking that revolving door of heavyweights egged me into "my binge days." Every night a guy would show up in the Slipper with Bennies[2] and before we hit, each of us in the band would grab one of those little pills (I'd break mine in two). I was also drinking ten to twelve shots of Courvoisier a night. It's a wonder my heart didn't stop. Looking back, I probably didn't need stimulants to keep up, but once again, I wanted to fit in.

Things really got hot when four big-band veterans, who happened to be in town at the same time, sat in for two months as a driving front line for our band. They played so hard and so fast for an hour each set that I dared not make a mistake, an "oops," with those pros. It was really heavy for me, but my wherewithal was stoked after a few nights as hints of bandstand sexism crept in.

I sensed a patronizing vibe almost from the first from this first-string front line. It probably didn't help that at five-foot-three, 123 pounds, and dwarfed by my great big ride cymbal, I didn't look the part of a full-throttle powerhouse drummer. As the condescension dripped, I could tell that at least some of guys were waiting for me to commit an oops so they'd have reason to dump me. To try and hasten the inevitable, each of the four by turns started taking several choruses at a furious clip, convinced that I'd be unable to keep the tempo. But they couldn't beat me because I was used to being tested. When I didn't fold the expressions on some of their faces were priceless. A mixture of disbelief with an obvious distaste for what to them was an unladylike display. I couldn't win for losing!

My personal life, too, had its ups and downs this third time in Las Vegas. The highlight was a weekend visit with Deborah. At sixteen, this was her first trip to Sin City and she was dazzled by the glamor, the slots, and Gus copping a bow tie worn by British singing sensation, Tom Jones, as a memento for her. On the flip side was an early hint of trouble in my marriage.

I was making good money in Vegas, $400 a week, and according to Gussie, I had "a great reputation for being a good, good drummer," but after four months I was lonely. Feeling especially down one day, I called Jerry. "I'm getting awfully lonesome for you, honey," I said. His indifference surprised me: "I think you better stay there, there's nothing here. Make the money while you can." That was the very first time I said I missed him and he didn't say, "I miss you, too, honey. Come on home," and it hit me hard. I remember feeling rejected, really rejected that money was coming between us, but I squelched the sting, uttered a simple "Okay," and stayed in Vegas out of spite.

When I did get home, I was back to scuffling, until an unexpected small-jazz world intersection paid off. Every Monday night for years I had accompanied Jerry to the Village Vanguard where he worked on the Thad Jones/ Mel Lewis Band. At intermissions I'd stroll into the kitchen and usually bump into Lorraine Gordon, wife of Vanguard owner, Max Gordon. At the time, Lorraine was booking some of the older, classic Dixieland players into Brooklyn joints. She'd heard me play somewhere, so when my presence backstage coincided with some jobs she was arranging, she told those old timers, "I've got a drummer for you."

After I worked a few dates in Brooklyn, the Dixieland cats wanted me back so I got to play with quite a few of the old-time greats. I enjoyed playing with them and never thought it beneath me. Besides, they were too hip to be called corny Dixieland—Buck Clayton, for one, was a great, "old school" trumpet player who just swung. Another classic who carried that swinging stamp was trombonist, Vic Dickenson. Truth be told, when I got the call I hadn't even heard of Vic Dickenson! I didn't catch on until an awestruck Jerry said: "You're working with Vic Dickenson?! Oh, God, he was one of the originals!" Jerry was very proud of me; it was a long way, Baby, from those girls over the bar in San Rafael!

Vic Dickenson, a real skinny, little grey-haired sweet old man probably in his early sixties, gave me my first real introduction to smoking pot. I'd gotten high from secondhand pot smoke, like at Buckwheat's, and I'd had phony lemonade pot, courtesy of Willie Bobo, but Vic was the one who turned me on to the real stuff.

It happened the very first time I met him, on a gig with two horns and a rhythm section at a place in Brooklyn that looked like a beach house. The bar and bandstand were downstairs; upstairs was a screened-in porch complete with lawn chairs and a green-and-white-striped canopy—like something you'd find in Miami. Between sets, once Vic and I made friends with those lawn chairs, he took out a joint, lit it, handed it to me, and said, "Take a poke." It dawned on me that it might insult the hell out of this great musician if I didn't, so I took a hit and got so high I worried I wouldn't be able to play. Catching my uneasy vibe, Vic relaxed me by saying, "I wouldn't give this to you if I didn't think you could handle it." And he was right. My playing wasn't affected in the second set, but my ears were opened just that extra amount so I could ignore talking at the tables and get right into the music.

I kind of liked that, and after a while taking a poke just before a job became so much a part of my ritual that I never gave it a second thought.

Piano Party

I felt vaguely discontented not long after moving into Park Ridge. Uneasiness with my marriage and my career would eventually mushroom into full-blown despair.

Seeds of doubt about my relationship with Jerry were planted by the episode in Vegas when he rebuffed me over money. I had an inkling that he really hadn't missed me that much but I suppressed it. The implication that my marriage was starting to unravel was inconceivable because the first ten years had been so glorious. The first ten years, Jerry and I completed each other as soulmates. I had no need for a girlfriend to confide in because I could tell Jerry anything. Plus he was a great lover. Before we were married I wondered where Jerry got his expertise because he wasn't a womanizer. He told me about a prostitute in Sacramento who had taught him and all the musicians in his gang. When I finally got to meet her, I raved: "Thank you, thank you, thank you, my darling!"

During our decade of marital bliss, we did everything together, which gave him lots of opportunities to correct my missteps in our daily routine. Like taking a shower. After our first shower together, we started toweling off and, not knowing any better, I threw my towel over my shoulders to dry my back when suddenly Jerry stopped me for a lesson. The better method, he said, was to use my hands to squeegee off my body as much water as I could before using a towel, and then to fold the towel in half and rub briskly to blot the water down the middle of my back. I was twenty-five and he was teaching me how to bathe!

Jerry was my teacher off the bandstand, pretty much like my father. I thought he was the perfect man and I wanted to be the perfect wife. I felt I had a lot to learn from him because he was so much more schooled and I wasn't an intellectual. In a way I was Eliza Doolittle to his Henry Higgins. Pretty much anything he asked me to do seemed like common sense.

Jerry told me not to laugh too loud when we were around other people. He didn't want me to be the type of female who would laugh from her belly and attract attention. Jerry never liked to draw attention to himself—ever, about anything—but I couldn't help it if I had a big voice and a hard laugh. Later in my life, I resented his attempts to shape me according to his own dislikes. It was a form of mind control, but back then I loved him and didn't care.

In the late 1960s, uncertainties in my personal life were echoed by the volatility of my career. I was working sporadic, small-time and short-lived gigs, but I also landed my first major print coverage. Early in 1969, *Down Beat* magazine published a very complimentary profile of me written by Carol Sloane.[1] Carol, a celebrated jazz singer (she has a four-octave range and perfect pitch) and occasional journalist, heard me at the drums and described my time as "razor-keen."[2]

A month after *Down Beat* hit the stands, Carol invited me to Raleigh, North Carolina, where she had just moved, to work in her backup band at a local club, the Frog and Nightgown. At our first rehearsal the pickup pianist and bass player were so bad Carol fired them and we headlined for six days as a duo on drums and vocals. To introduce each tune, I'd play a few bars of rhythm, and then as Carol sang I listened to the notes between the lyrics and filled in the background with my sticks and brushes. That's what a singer needs, a supportive swinging background of rhythm, and it's the hardest thing to find. Carol was very happy with what we did at the Frog and Nightgown: "We should have been recording!" she exclaimed.

Working with Carol started me dreaming about my own singing, using limited accompaniment in what I call a "Nat King Cole" supper club. I envisioned me at the drums with a bassist in an intimate setting with plush drapes and thick carpet making the sound acoustically smooth, just like Nat sounded. Give me a "Nat Cole room" and I'll be happy the rest of my life, but that would depend on finding that ideal room—there used to be a few around, but probably not anymore—and the right bass player, one who'd be in tune and know the chords. Today, at this later stage of my life, scaling back to a bassist would be easier because it's become increasingly difficult to find pianists who really know how to "comp."

Comping means playing the chords for whoever is singing or playing the lead. Elmo Hope, Hank Jones, and Tommy Flanagan were three pianists in my generation who set the standard for how to comp behind a singer, leaving room in her lane. Good comping pianists respect simplicity. Piano players these days don't always get it; they go into their own little world and it's difficult to stop them from hitting too many notes. When I'm singing behind the drums it's not unusual for me to remind my pianist to "Stay out of my lane!"

Later in 1969, I was a guest on Dick Cavett's prime-time television talk show. Bobby Rosengarden, leader of the Cavett show band, was a friend of mine and he recommended me to Cavett. When Bobby pulled up a ballad at the rehearsal, I told him I didn't want something that slow. Ballads are the hardest tempo to play because you have to leave a lot more space between notes, and I didn't want the added pressure of having to prove on national TV that I could do that successfully. "Okay, what tempo do you want?" he asked. "Something with a groove," I said. He counted off a really fast tune and I felt much more comfortable. Even though I couldn't read the chart and I didn't know the tune very well, after we ran through the number a few times I had a good feel for the arrangement.

I got back to the studio early for the taping and stood patiently behind the curtain prepping to go on. Nature didn't call until it was too late. At the very moment I got my cue I had to go to the bathroom soooo bad. There was no time to bolt and pee so I uncrossed my legs, took a deep breath and concentrated on walking across the stage without leaving a wake. But when I got behind the drums, and it came down to the nitty gritty, the pressure relaxed. I played the music easily, at one point trading eights with the band, but once the number ended and the show broke for commercial, I ran like a bat out of hell to the ladies room.

When the show resumed I was sitting between Dick Cavett and Bobby Rosengarden. Bobby was beaming with pride about my performance, but I could see he was nervous about my getting tripped up in the talk segment. Dick started his interview by asking, "How does a nice girl like you get into a business like this?" The studio audience laughed and, just as I was about to answer, Bobby chimed in, "Oh, her father's a drummer." The die was cast: Every time Cavett asked me a question, Bobby answered. Finally, Dick Cavett said to me, "Do you have the feeling that you're not being interviewed?" Bobby was overly protective and that was really funny and even cute, but definitely annoying!

That year, 1969, was also when we joined Eugene Wright's band, which included pianist Roland Hanna,[3] for his tour of southern colleges. This gave Jerry and me the chance for extended work together and gave Jerry the chance to at least partly follow through on a promise he made early in our marriage that someday we would get our own group to tour and record. It wasn't a perfect realization of my dream, but at least we were bandmates on a regular working band. Eugene's breadth of contacts jump-started our bookings for concerts in the Carolinas, Mississippi, Alabama, and Tennessee.

As our integrated band went about its business in that belt of southern states, racist reminders were unavoidable. For starters, we were limited to Black colleges since white campuses wouldn't hire us with Eugene and Roland in the band. Driving to gigs could be unpleasant; I remember awkwardly crouching down as we passed through towns to avoid being stopped for having a white woman riding in a car with two Black men. Eugene recalled this poignant episode at one of the schools: "We were playing our first gig in Mississippi . . . and Dottie and I . . . were setting up, and here comes one of the Brothers. . . . He says, 'Mr. Wright, you got a white drummer.' . . . This guy comes in and he's already judged her and the fact that she's white. . . . I said, 'Oh, yes, her name is Dottie Dodgion. . . . Wait until you hear her play and then you come back and tell me what you want to tell me.' . . . When we took the first break this guy comes back and says, 'Hey, Mr. Wright, listen, I apologize.' I said, 'You don't have to apologize, just remember, never judge anything until you see or hear it, and the fact that she was white has nothing to do with it.' He said, 'Yeah, I could see that 'cause, Man, she was cookin'; I couldn't imagine anybody playing like that.' . . . He went back and sat down and he came back again, he went over [and told Dottie] . . . 'Listen, you sure can play.' . . . When he heard her play he couldn't stop talking about her."

We toured on weekends, Thursdays through Sundays, but after the great reception we got at the first few colleges, I was hot to expand our bookings. I even designed a glossy PR package. When the band was offered contracts for a month or two-month tours, and before we got in too deep, Jerry sat me down to explain that he couldn't give up his Monday nights with Thad and Mel at the Vanguard. Jerry also worried that leaving the city for extended periods could mean losing out on recordings and studio work, threatening the success he'd taken so many years to achieve. There's always somebody waiting to take your place in New York.

Those were legitimate reasons to pull back, but not to stop altogether. I suggested that maybe we could scale down the dates, but even so Jerry decided to bail. He didn't even try to keep us together on the band, and with Jerry gone, the bottom fell out of the dream. Jerry reneging on his promise unraveled our marriage a few strands more, but the inevitable outcome of growing apart waited yet a few more years while my angels delivered three very welcome diversions.

I was over the moon when Deborah moved in permanently with Jerry and me and entered her senior year at Park Ridge High. I welcomed her with open arms, but the timing turned out to be a bit awkward for me because she was almost grown up and acted pretty standoffish. I did everything I could to make her feel loved, but Deborah, during those early, ticklish weeks after we were reunited, didn't run to me, and she didn't need me to put my arms around her every minute because Mom and Bob had done plenty of that. Today, she'll come up and kiss me on the cheek or she'll give me a squeeze and say, "I thought maybe you needed that." But she was a very different girl when she was first living at Park Ridge. In hindsight, I think our rocky start was an early sign that Deborah and I have very different karmas. I know I came through my mother in this life but I also know that I never knew her before that. But I'm convinced that Deborah was my mother before in a previous life because she has reversed the roles so many times on us. Whenever she'd talk to me like she was the Mommy, I listened.

Although Deborah was on the verge of adulthood when she moved in, she had been so sheltered all her life that in some ways she was very naive and determined to remain so. That left her vulnerable, an easy target like a lost deer in the headlights. Because of the guilt I carried over my absenteeism when she was younger, I felt an acute duty to shield her from being hurt during that last stage of her teenage years. One of the most pressing subjects was sex. Deborah was almost eighteen and still a virgin, so when she found a street-smart boyfriend in school I took her to my doctor to get the pill. I tried to be hip that way and help her; I wanted to give her freedom—I always demanded it for myself—and teach her that self-preservation was okay.

My impulse to help Deborah intensified after I took her to a psychic. He introduced himself between sets one night when I was working at a prominent Greenwich Village jazz club, Sweet Basil. His name was Frank Andrews and he told me how interesting it was that I played the drums. Then, out of nowhere, he offered me a free reading! That was a stunner because Andrews, who had once advised Grace Kelly, was very expensive!

I accepted his offer and asked if I could bring my daughter. "By all means," he replied. A few days later I had my individual session with him and it was fun; he told me that I was a queen in Egypt in another life, and that when it came to money in this life, it didn't look good. "Well, I'm a jazz musician, I'm used to it," was my cheeky response. Deborah's session was darker. Andrews said that she had been a nun who was unhappy as hell in her last four lives and each time it led her to commit suicide by drowning. I understood right then and there that my karmic destiny was to give Deborah a better chance to live a full life this time around; that the gods had sent her through me because I was worldly and could prevent Deborah from repeating that pattern of suicides and avoid the torment of yet another reincarnated existence.

Another happy distraction was the "Piano Party," an open house for piano players at Park Ridge that began late Sunday morning, September 17, 1972, and lasted until the wee hours of the next day. In a round-about way, inspiration for the event started in 1968 when Phil Woods left New Hope, Pennsylvania, for Paris. Before he sailed, Phil offered to give Jerry and me his eleven-foot Steinway Grand Piano, with one condition. "We can't take it to France," he told Jerry, "so it's yours if you'll pay a truck driver to have it moved."

Hauling that piano cost us $250, and we had the hassle of removing our front door to get it into the house. When the piano was finally parked in our dining room and we could get a good look at it, we were deflated. It was in terrible shape. A white elephant, really, and since Jerry and I didn't have the money to repair it, that 88-key behemoth gathered dust in our house for the next four years.

Until the summer of 1972, when we had the means to have pianist and piano tuner, John Marabuto (who had rebuilt Jerry's mother's spinet at Larkspur), and his wife, dear friend, Dee, flown-in from El Cerrito. For three weeks, with a stage light over his head and while Delores and I cooked Mexican, John restrung the entire piano, replaced all the hammers, and turned that wreck into a work of art.

To celebrate the resurrection, Jerry and I came up with the idea of a party to pay tribute to all the great piano players we knew, players who would jump at the chance to play on such a beautiful and completely restored Steinway. I put together an invitation that featured a cartoon of a guy playing a piano in a bathtub full of water while his exasperated wife complained, "Some men just sing in the bath." Invitation copy stated that one of the purposes of the party was "to afford an opportunity for pianists to get together socially, since they rarely have the occasion to do so, and everyone knows that piano players are crazy!"

What resulted, as reported by John S. Wilson in the *New York Times*,[4] was "an unusual mass assemblage of jazz pianists, each of whom took turns trying out the instrument." That assembly included many of New York's leading lights of the keyboard, including Hank Jones, Roland Hanna, Jimmy Rowles, Teddy Wilson, Dill Jones, Walter Norris, Marian McPartland, Tommy Flanagan,[5] Patti Bown, Dick Katz, John Bunch, and Pat Rebillot.

Pianists began turning up at eleven on Sunday morning. One by one, they played from two to five choruses and turned it over. Delores and I had a buffet prepared so the musicians ate, listened, and clapped, but nobody talked because hearing the tone of that reborn instrument for even one chorus was like cream for the ears. Dee Marabuto remembers that Walter Norris "wanted to take it home with him," and Roland Hanna was so impressed with the piano he returned to Park Ridge eight months later to record some tunes for his first solo album.[6]

We didn't tape the music out of respect for the musicians. The party wasn't a commercial venture, so we felt it would have been poor etiquette. We wanted to be first class. Today it breaks my heart that I don't have a recording, but the musicians appreciated what we did, and in short order it was the talk of New York.

The third event that deflected my attention from personal problems turned out to be a pièce de résistance in my professional career. I joined famed jazz cornetist Ruby Braff's quartet and took my place in one of the greatest rhythm sections in the world!

Ruby

On the stand, cornetist, Ruby Braff, was a magnificent musician, and he always had some of the greatest bass players and piano players in the world. It's no wonder I got spoiled! Off the bandstand Ruby was ornery, insulting, and brutally honest. I worked with Ruby Braff for about eighteen months and I know he loved my playing. He went so far as to boast that, "I've found my drummer; God willing, I'll never have to find another!"

Jerry and I first ran into Ruby at the same place I'd met Wild Bill Davison almost eight years before: the Long Island practice studio of jazz trombonist, Marshall Brown.[1] Once the three of us got familiar we started jamming in one of the practice rooms, and I knew pretty quick that Ruby liked my time because we fit like a glove. Our apple pie was in the same groove; without thinking about it we each felt where the other was going to place the note, and that's a rarity. And, as Jerry has suggested, it probably didn't escape Ruby that I was better tempo-wise than a lot of male drummers around. So, it wasn't a surprise when I got a call in late 1971 to join Ruby as the regular drummer in his quartet.

Our first gig was at the Half Note on the night of October 24th.[2] That engagement was repeated a few days later and then extended until November 7th with personnel that included Ken Ascher at the piano, and either Michael Moore or Victor Sproles at the bass.[3] Jazz journalist, Dan Morgenstern, reviewed one version of that band, concluding with, "Moore is a bitch, and a great soloist; Ascher is a sensitive young player, and Dotty [sic] keeps great time."[4] We returned to the Half Note in April 1972 and played a series of dates into July[5] before the owners closed the club's doors for good later that year.

In addition to regular appearances at the Half Note, the Ruby Braff quartet, this time with nonpareil pianist, Hank Jones, and bassist, George Duvivier, as my section mates, opened at Peacock Alley in the Waldorf Astoria Hotel on May 23, 1972.[6] Peacock Alley was a restaurant next to the hotel lobby. It was very "high-tea" proper; I worked it, but I couldn't afford to go there as a patron. Ruby's quartet was the first jazz group to play that room, maybe the first group, period; as far as I knew, harpists had been the norm prior to our arrival. Ruby got this gig thanks to Tony Bennett. He and Ruby had toured together and were good friends, so I guess Tony influenced the management to book us. In the May, 25, 1972, edition of the *New York Times*, our band was advertised as "Tony Bennett's favorite jazz artists under the direction of Ruby Braff."[7]

The only downside to the job was that Peacock Alley didn't have dressing rooms and that didn't sit well with Ruby. He demanded respect for himself and his musicians, and so quite chivalrously on my behalf he found some executive in the Waldorf and took him to task: "She's a woman! What's she supposed to do, sit around in the lobby like a hooker?"

In mid-August 1972, Ruby took his quartet to California for an appearance at the Concord Jazz Festival.[8] My bandmates on this occasion were Hank Jones and bassist, Milt Hinton. Milt was affectionately known as "The Judge" because of his prowess in keeping time. He never dropped a beat, his attack was great, and he had a sound so deep and so resonant he would make you feel good all over. Believe me, I knew at the time how lucky I was to be playing with Hank Jones and Milt Hinton, two of the ultimate jazz pros, but competing in my memory with the music we played at the Festival—and we did swing our asses off—were several incidents off the stand and personal.

First was a blast from twenty years past. Deborah and Jerry accompanied me to the festival and we shared a hotel room. About five in the afternoon our first day we were hanging in the room when all of sudden the three of us thought we could hear cocktails being poured in the bar a floor below. Jerry went to give the lounge a once-over and returned looking ready to burst. "Guess who's sitting at the bar?" he asked mysteriously. With both of us at sea, he eyeballed Deborah and broke the tension. "It's Monty," he said. "Monty Budwig, your Dad, and he'd like to see you!" Deborah and I were speechless.

I knew that Benny Goodman's sextet was scheduled opposite us that night, but I hadn't given a thought to who might be in his band. The coincidence was stunning! Monty, my first husband and father of my daughter, was playing bass with Benny Goodman on the same damn concert! Within moments, Deborah regained her cool and, as grown up as could be she announced, "I think it's martini time."

We took the elevator down and, in a hotel bar less than forty miles from where Monty had been stationed and Deborah had been born, I introduced my daughter to her biological father. It was my mother's fault they hadn't met before. When Deborah was ten, Monty was passing through Sacramento and he called my mother to ask if he could stop by to see his daughter. Mother thought it might be too confusing for Monty to jump out of the blue into Deborah's life for an hour so she said no!

Deborah and Monty sat next to each other at the bar and seemed to hit it off right away, so even though it had been a long time coming, Deborah's real father was finally with her and I was rosy at the prospect that it might be the start of a beautiful friendship. That hope was buoyed when it was time for Monty to leave; saying his goodbyes, he promised to be in touch, that he'd call or write to Deborah. He never did. Deborah and Monty met for the first and only time over drinks in a Bay Area bar before the start of a Concord Jazz Festival.

Shortly after Monty's adieu, the three of us were back in our room waiting for me to go on when I sensed alarm bells going off in Jerry. He was dying inside and I knew the reason. Jerry was down because he wasn't scheduled to play at the festival, and sure enough, a few moments later he said to me, "Gee, this will be the first time that I'm the one who waits in the back." In our relationship, I had always been on the road with him. He was the star, the "big kahuna," and I was the one waiting off-stage. Now our roles were reversed and it hurt Jerry a lot. "Wow," he admitted, "the shoe's really on the other foot."

This touchy situation got more awkward when Ruby came to collect me. Jerry had brought his horn all the way from New York, hoping I think that maybe at the last minute Ruby might invite him to play the set with us. But that was a no no for Ruby. No words were spoken but I could sense tension in the room, and as I watched Ruby quietly drawing his own conclusions I knew that wasn't going to happen. Once you allow another musician to sit in, the performance you'd planned turns into a jam session and any chance it will represent what you're actually doing flies out the window. That was especially true of Ruby's bands because we didn't have any charts to read. At the start of a number, Ruby would announce a key to the bass player and pianist and leave it up to them to adapt, and during a performance he'd point when he wanted a musician to solo or take the lead. Ruby cherished that freedom, the liberty of not being saddled with sheet music on the bandstand.

Before the concert that night, the emotional rush of Monty's surprise appearance and Jerry's faux pas when Ruby came into our room, left my head aching. Mercifully, those troubles vanished when I stepped onto the stage. The quartet cooked and everything was fine.

Until two days later, when a review of our concert appeared in the *San Francisco Examiner*.[9] Jazz writer Phillip Elwood submitted that I was in the quartet "(for reasons more visual than aural)." In other words, my presence on stage was merely to decorate rather than to musically enhance the group! Well, Ruby flipped when he read that. Ruby had very high standards in his music and even the merest suggestion that I was just "eye candy" on the stand made him furious! Ruby got Elwood on the phone and gave it to him good: "How dare you insult me by suggesting that I would hire somebody for any other reason than music! You're an asshole, blah, blah, blah."

Several years later I ran into a contrite Elwood: "Have you forgiven me yet?" My answer was an emphatic "no!" I was still furious. Instead of really listening to me that night in Concord he had apparently jumped to the conclusion that I could not be as good as a male drummer. He probably thought I would disappear quickly from the scene, but there I was, still working with the big boys. It was an insult to think that it took their approval to finally make him realize that the mistake he'd made was very prejudiced and very dumb.

Ten days after our return to New York the quartet began an extended engagement at an upper-east-side club.[10] As reported by John S. Wilson in the *New York Times*: "Mr. Braff's new home is Tony's Place, 241 East 86th Street, an attractively decorated two-level bar and restaurant that opened several weeks ago."[11] Hank Jones was still at the piano, but George Mraz had replaced Milt Hinton on bass. George Mraz has been for decades one of the most respected bassists in jazz, but in 1972 he was new on the New York scene, having emigrated from Czechoslovakia only a few years before.

Since he grew up overseas and in a different era from musicians of Ruby's generation, Mraz sometimes would be stumped by obscure tunes that Ruby chose to play. They weren't simple throwaway tunes—they had choice chords—but even in the States many of them weren't popular entries in the Great American Songbook. So, when Ruby started playing "In the Middle of a Kiss,"[12] I could understand why Mraz would plead, "I don't know this tune!" Without turning his head, Ruby would quip out the side of his mouth, "You will by the time we finish it."

We played Tony's for a month. Ruby paid each of us $800 a week, primo money for the time (as leader, his take was even more). Ruby would not work for a pittance; everything was first class with him. Including the music. Our quartet's brand of mainstream jazz at Tony's was well received in the *New York Times* column cited earlier: "I can scarcely think of a happier lure for jazz listeners than the quartet he is leading."[13] That same review included admiring comments about my work: "His drummer is Dottie Dodgion, who, in addition to providing smooth, solid support to both the ensembles and solos (her brush work behind Mr. Jones's piano solo is a model of drum accompaniment), adds an attractive visual element to the group by her facial interpretations of the solos she accompanies."[14]

I adored playing with Ruby and I knew he had deep respect for me as a drummer, but my relationship with him off the bandstand grew complicated. First of all, I suspect that from the beginning my presence in the band affected Ruby, but I wasn't aware of the full impact until Jim Koulouvaris, of Jim and Andy's fame, said to me, "Dottie, you've been the best thing to ever happen to Ruby. I've never seen him so happy. He's a changed man." Jim continued by telling me, "It's amazing what you've done because he's always hated women." And it was true. Ruby didn't have any women friends and he had never run into another woman musician that he admired. So, through the love of the music I changed his opinion of women, at least in so far as being able to play.

Gradually, though, the plot thickened. I began to realize that Ruby was sending me signals, signals that he was also interested in me as a woman. At least that was my assumption based on his actions, including his attempts to get me away from Jerry. I hasten to add that all the time we were together, Ruby never made a pass at me or said he loved me, but that didn't necessarily rule out interest on his part. Ruby wasn't a romantic man so if he had a crush on me it made sense that he was tight-lipped about it. I also think he didn't want to declare himself because I was a married woman and he was an honorable man. As I said, it was complicated, but deep down I think he took it for granted that I knew how he felt.

Little by little, Ruby's feelings got to be more obvious. He tried little ploys, like the several times he practically invited himself over to our house for dinner. Jerry was all for it, but if he thought that by being courteous to Ruby he would get in his band, it was wishful thinking. What Ruby wanted was to be around me.

Ruby's designs were more blatant the day he said to me, "You know we should move to England." Puzzled, I replied, "What? I'm going to leave Jerry and move overseas?" "I mean we'll make England home base," he explained, "because we wouldn't have to pay any taxes, and, besides, we're on the road all the time anyway, so what's the difference where we live?" I told him no, but he didn't want to accept my answer. Ruby was trying to find a way to get me away from Jerry. Permanently.

Things boiled over one night at Tony's. Jerry brought Deborah in to hear the band but instead of leaving his horn in the trunk of the car, he carried it into the club. That ticked Ruby off and for me it was déjà vu at the Concord Hotel all over again! At intermission after the first set, an imperious Ruby walked over to Jerry and said, "I don't know what you brought your horn in for," which was his not so subtle way of saying he wouldn't let Jerry sit in. Ruby followed up that crack with a reference to a salsa place across from Tony's: "Jerry, why don't you take Deborah across the street to hear the Latin band?" "Wouldn't you like to go over there, honey?" he asked Deborah. "A Latin band, they're a lot of fun. Something for you to do instead of sitting here." Boom, boom, boom, it was one rebuff after another!

I sat mortified on the sidelines. When I dared ask myself, "What just happened here?" I was conflicted. I could see that it was Ruby's room and that Jerry had been impertinent; I mean, he never should have brought his axe. Then again, everybody loved Jerry's playing; he was Jerry Dodgion, one hell of an alto player. On balance, I felt that Ruby should have been more hospitable, and, besides, the real reason Ruby had acted like a curmudgeon was obvious—I'm a woman of the world for Christ's sake and I know when somebody's trying to drive a wedge!

The spat was still simmering when the quartet and some additional personnel did two recording dates for the independent label, Chiaroscuro, on September 27th and October 9th, 1972.[15] In addition to Milt Hinton, me, and Dick Hyman on piano, Ruby had Sam Margolies on tenor and Howard Collins on guitar for a few tunes. As we gathered for the second session in October, Zoot Sims and Jerry walked into the studio carrying their horns—

they had just come from a date in a nearby studio. Now, it was already evident that Ruby was in no mood that day to suffer fools because when one of the engineers in the booth asked, "Do you want to run this down?" Ruby shouted, "Run it down?! Do you think when we're on the bandstand we run it down before we play?" So, when Jerry showed up wielding his horn, even though this time he had a legitimate reason, I grimaced and thought: "Here we go again!" But to my utter amazement, Ruby asked Jerry to play on the date, expanding the group to a septet for the larger ensemble selections. (I assume Ruby didn't use Zoot because he already had Sam Margolies on board.)

Both Chiaroscuro sessions were splendid. I remember Milt Hinton standing right next to me, and Ruby's playing a great chorus. It's really cooking, and Milt leaned over to me and said, "This is going to be a legendary keeper." That was lovely.[16] Less so was my conversation with Ruby in the studio right after the date: "You know why I invited your man to sit in?" he challenged me. "Because of you! I did it for you!" Putting a calm face on it I said "okay, Ruby," but inside I was steaming. Gritting his teeth and asking Jerry to play on the date was another of Ruby's tricks to try and shake me loose. What I couldn't shake was the feeling that things had gotten terribly out of hand.

In March 1973, we did a television special, "Aloha! Tony Bennett in Hawaii."[17] It was a catastrophe! Our band, which included George Mraz on bass and Bernie Leighton on piano, stayed at the Waikiki Hilton. Each of us had a suite of large rooms on a high floor, and the hotel was surrounded by gorgeous trees and sweet-smelling gardenias. We had a week to enjoy ourselves before shooting the special, and the entire tab—rooms, food, phone calls to the States—was to be picked up by the sponsor, agribusiness giant, Monsanto.

My first whiff of trouble came early that first week when Ruby and I checked the location for the shoot. We noticed right away that the stand for my drums was being constructed out of wooden planks set on the sand under a cover of trees. Well, that was going to be impossible because hitting the drums would move the planks up and down like a teeter-totter. When Ruby saw this, he went bananas. "The incompetence!" he shouted. "The incompetence abounds!" Ruby buttonholed the director, and a concrete stand was built on the sand for my drums.

The next dustup was over wardrobe! At the end of the week, after a rehearsal in the morning, and with the crew ready to shoot that afternoon, we were all asked to dress in a Hawaiian motif. (Hawaiian shirts were provided for the men and I had brought my own Hawaiian blouse.) Only Ruby ignored the request; he showed up in a close-knit Lacoste polo shirt, the kind with a crocodile logo on the front. Puzzled, the director said, "Ruby, there's a whole trailer full of Hawaiian shirts, go and pick out one you like." With casual indifference, Ruby replied, "I have on what I like." The director pressed him, "There must be one Hawaiian shirt you could pick." "Yeah, yours," Ruby retorted. Our jaws dropped when the director took his shirt off and Ruby put it on! As I was told later, apparently Tony Bennett didn't like the director but he shied away from saying anything. So, Ruby got even for Tony. I don't think Tony told him to be mean to the guy; Ruby probably decided that on his own.

The shoot was anticlimactic. It took maybe twenty minutes and when we saw a monitor replay there was precious little footage of the group. A quick pan of us playing in the sand and then, whoosh, back to Tony. Boy, I thought sarcastically, Ruby really got even! He was too clever by half with that director and it had backfired, but Ruby's hot temper wasn't spent yet.

Two days later, I went to the front desk to check out. Ruby was ahead of me waiting for a clerk, so I browsed a floor sign advertising coffee out in the lanai. It wasn't long before a young girl showed up behind the desk and meekly told Ruby that the total bill for our group's stay at the hotel was $1,582.00. "What?!!!" shouted Ruby, "You incompetent imbecile, you don't know what you're talking about! Get somebody over here who knows something!" Throwing up his hands he yelled his pet phrase: "Incompetence abounds!" and shattered the clerk.

As she sobbed, I poked Ruby in the ribs. "Get a coffee," I said. "I'll take care of this!" After he left, I gently told the clerk, "Honey, I think Monsanto is supposed to pick this whole thing up. Why don't you go check on it?" She returned a short time later and confirmed what I'd told her: "Oh, yes, that's correct, you don't owe anything." I went out to the veranda to tell Ruby, but he was still hot and contemptuous: "They shouldn't have incompetent assholes working here!" Once again, he had proved himself intolerant of human frailty, but this time his condescension tipped the balance for me. I started thinking seriously about leaving the band.

After our return from Hawaii, Ruby and I played the Village Gate as part of some citywide festival. The organizers put a bunch of musicians together in different groups in different places. The Village Gate, where we played, was the largest venue. Our band had Billy Taylor on piano and Earl May at the bass.

During intermission, Ruby started griping to me about Billy and Earl. Billy was a talented musician but he played too "light" for Ruby, and he called Earl, the bassist, "early May" because he'd rush a little bit and come in too soon. Earl just wasn't Ruby's idea of a bass player, and, admittedly, he couldn't compare to Ruby's mainstays: Milt Hinton, George Mraz, and George Duvivier.

I tried to stop Ruby before he started leveling scorn directly at Billy and Earl. Ruby was honest almost to a fault; he could hurt somebody's feelings very easily, but he didn't care about that. Some musician might gush, "Gee, I'd love to play with you sometime," and Ruby would cut him down with, "Fat chance, Buster, get lost!" If I tried to comfort the humiliated musician and looked to Ruby to soften it up, I'd hear another pet phrase of his, "You hate it when I'm right, don't you?" I'd have no snappy rejoinder because, damn it, when Ruby criticized another musician he was always right.

Nevertheless, I had grown weary of Ruby's bile. "You know, Ruby," I told him, "I love you to death on that stand, but, boy, when you're off the stand" —but he cut me off mid-sentence. Planting his feet and folding his arms in front of him, Ruby bellowed: "If you can't respect me unequivocally off the bandstand as well as on, then we can't work together!" I looked calmly at him and said, "bye."

Ruby never dreamed I would say adios; I guess he hadn't noticed how badly our relationship had frayed because of the way he was treating Jerry. Any chance of a détente between Ruby and Jerry had collapsed, and Ruby's pressure on me to leave Jerry was close to incessant. I couldn't stand it any longer because the more I let Ruby put Jerry down, the lousier I felt, as if just listening to Ruby's insults made me disloyal to Jerry. Jerry may have been asking for it in a way, but he didn't deserve the venom Ruby doled out. So that was the end of Ruby for me.

I let it go, just turned it loose.

Suburban Housewife

Meanwhile, life at Park Ridge in the early 1970s was checkered. A season of short-lived highs, shadowed and finally overtaken by clustered lows.

Money wasn't a problem. I had been pulling $800 a week with Ruby and Jerry was doing at least that on the road working hotels and recording with big stars like Peggy Lee, Julie London, and Lainie Kazan. God, we were sitting on top of the world; a two-car family with enough money for everything. Another hard-earned dividend was that Deborah was happy. Our relationship had warmed and steadied after that difficult transition when she first moved into Park Ridge. Deborah at almost eighteen was coming of age and as the months passed we were like two women on their way to becoming buddies, sisters almost. I was thrilled.

I was less than thrilled about not working much after Ruby. It's not that I didn't work at all, but it was on and off and too often no more than filling in for other drummers for a minute. Like when I subbed on two numbers for Wild Bill Davison's regular drummer during a live recording in 1973. I got a pat on the back for that performance in Hal Willard's book[1]: "Absolute proof of Dottie Dodgion's competence as a drummer came . . . when Bill made a record in the Rainbow Room . . . in New York[2] and Cliff Leeman got sick. He called in Dottie Dodgion."

Later that year, I was part of an "All Woman Jazz Sextet," that included the fine electric bassist, Carline Ray, for a performance at the New York Jazz Museum. Here's an excerpt from a review of that concert by John S. Wilson: "For one number, Patti Bown sat in on piano with the Misses Ray and Dodgion, forming a driving, powerhouse trio that must have scored [sic][3] any male musician within hearing."[4] Commenting on the same performance, Melinda Abern in the *Village Voice* said that Bown "was all over the piano with runs, stomping accents, and harmonic variations that sent Carline Ray flying up and down the neck of her bass and brought out fireworks from Dottie."[5]

Despite a smattering of good press, jobs were few and far between. So, over the next year-and-a-half I settled into what was for me the very definition of a mixed blessing: sporadic gigs as a poor second to the domestic routine of a suburban housewife.

Deborah became the centerpiece of my days and it was a golden time in her life. A high school senior, she was getting great grades for the first time and she had a nice set of friends—wonderful kids, all from prominent families. I told Deborah the house was open to her friends at any time and, boy, she had a gang. There must have been close to a dozen guys using our place every day to hang out after school, lying all over the floor and talking. Deborah remembers how much fun, how hip and cool I was with her teenage friends; they called me "Mom" and the feelings were mutual.

Keeping company with Deborah's friends was a comfort. Not only because with Jerry gone so much of the time I felt very, very alone, but also because their clubby atmosphere helped distract me from the reality that my music ad was going unanswered. With my career in a depressed state I found myself at a loss about where to turn. Worse yet, I was living vicariously through Jerry in a lot of ways, a dependency that was dripping with irony: first because our marriage remained caught in a slow downward spiral (although I still didn't want to face it), and second because Jerry was having career troubles of his own.

A big problem for both of us was that jazz, in the post-Beatles era, was itself in decline. Jazz gigs had slowed down, affecting both of us, but Jerry suffered a double whammy because the rise of a new generation of pop musicians meant that calls for jazz cats were drying up in the studios. He still played his Monday nights at the Vanguard with Thad and Mel, but Jerry had no choice but to work with many of the new rock and folk groups that the younger set was gaga over, and he wasn't happy about it. Adding salt to his wound, Deborah and her friends were in awe that her father was playing with the likes of Grand Funk Railroad, James Taylor, and Bette Midler! If it hadn't been so sad it would have been almost funny that while the kids thought Jerry was a hero, he felt his career had been reduced to ashes. Come to think of it, that's how I felt, too, that my days as a serious musician playing jazz might be numbered.

The fickle music world wasn't the only thing upsetting our Park Ridge address. Jerry and I were always capable of grating on each other, but a more troubling chink in our relationship caused by Jerry's jealousy coincided with our move to Park Ridge. I hate to use that word, but I think Jerry was envious of me professionally because, even though I couldn't read, I still was welcomed into the jazz big time with the big-time cats. In his mind, it was as if I'd gotten away with murder because I wasn't schooled in music like he was. So, while everybody else had accepted me, Jerry was still putting me down. That really irked me, and it meant I wasn't getting the kind of support I needed from him. Jerry always encouraged me to play but not to outshine him in any way.

I remember an incident that brought this home to me. One of my former bandmates told me in secret that he overheard some musicians raving about me to Jerry, but Jerry put a damper on it. He explained how I had an advantage he never had—the advantage of coming through a musical family. In other words, my lucky draw as a kid was the only reason I had talent. Jerry's parents weren't musically inclined, so he felt handicapped from the get-go; he couldn't believe that a great player could come through a family like his.

Jerry talked a lot about how hard he had to work on tempo by using a metronome because he wasn't a natural. But he was! Jerry's time was as good as any of the cats, otherwise he couldn't have played the way he did. And look at the big-band credentials he had: Thad Jones, Oliver Nelson, Duke Pearson, Quincy Jones, Count Basie. But I think he was afraid to accept it. He borrowed that trouble for himself and I could never talk him out of it.

Despite Jerry's success with those great jazz orchestras, I felt he begrudged my playing in small groups led by major figures in the music while he was working the reed sections of those large bands. I wasn't immediately aware of how important that divide was to him. I thought he loved playing lead, or even second alto with the top Black leaders. But he had to play a lot of arranged charts in those bands and maybe he'd get a one-or-two-chorus solo during a performance; I was jamming multiple choruses with some of the absolute top rhythm sections. There were other small cuts, too, like Ruby Braff dubbing me the drummer he'd use for the rest of his life, and some of the musicians from Jerry's circle having me sit in and accepting me right alongside Jerry.

I think those indignities, real or imagined, started to weigh Jerry down but, being a double Virgo and a stickler for the right thing to say, he didn't talk to me about it. What he did was turn to drink! I distinctly remember the night it started. Deborah, Jerry, and I went to a classic old-school diner in Park Ridge for dinner. We slid across the vinyl seats in our booth and no sooner started looking at the menu when Jerry announced: "I'll be right back, I'm going to get a martini."

That took me by surprise because Jerry and I had had a martini before we left the house since the diner didn't serve alcohol. Besides, Jerry was not a drinker, but suddenly, one martini wasn't enough. Bewildered, Deborah and I stared at each other and then watched Jerry walk across the street to a bar. He was gone long enough to have had two, maybe even three, more drinks before he rejoined us for dinner. Looking back, that was truly the beginning of the end of our ideal marriage.

Jerry's drinking lasted for several years. Outside the house, he'd hang with some drunks in New York and come home pretty wasted. Inside the house, he'd have his drinking cronies over, like Phil Woods, who returned from Europe in 1972. Phil and Chan had split, so when Phil first came back, Jerry invited him and his new girlfriend to stay with us. She was contagious with hepatitis and had yellow eyes. After that, Phil would make occasional visits and stay for a while and as Deborah recalls, "when I would be getting ready to go to school he'd be drinking vodka."

I wasn't happy having Phil around as a bad influence on Deborah and that caused more tension between Jerry and me. Our marriage was quickly deteriorating, worn down under the strain of an explosive atmosphere that could detonate unpredictably, like the evening I walked in on Deborah and Phil playing chess on the kitchen table. Deborah was a proficient player (she'd majored in chess at the New School in New York), so I wasn't surprised when she won, but Phil, drunk and disgusted that Deborah beat him, swept his hand across the board, spilling game pieces all over the floor!

In the Middle of the Brook

Things were changing drastically for Jerry and me.

Jerry was unhappy and he was stuffing down his unhappiness even though one of the rules of the road for our marriage was to stay on track and not live a lie. If one of us was unhappy, we promised that we would tell the other and not borrow something else to talk about. Neither one of us honored that contract. Jerry drank and worked to escape. I coped by rebelling against him in small ways—like the time I disobeyed over a television.

When Deborah graduated I didn't have the same life anymore. My suburban sanctuary became an empty nest and I filled the vacuum by watching television, sitting for hours glued to the screen of our crummy TV. I told Jerry we needed a new set, but he wouldn't listen. "You don't want to be watching television. God, you could use that time to study and practice, blah, blah, blah, blah, blah." Defiant, I took some of my savings and bought a $400 Mitsubishi big-screen TV, the first year that model came out. Jerry was speechless when he got home and saw a large TV box sitting in our living room. I wasn't naive enough to think he would be glad for me, but it didn't matter. That television was for me! I was glad for myself, but the sour side of my victory was having to defy Jerry to get it. Why did I feel it necessary to do that? My state of mind was a puzzle to me and I needed some answers. That's when I started visiting the brook.

The prominent landmarks in our neighborhood were trees, a dirt road, and the brook of Bear Brook Road. The brook wasn't deep or very wide. It ran between our house and the Phillips's place and was used by all four of us as a convenient shortcut. I was the only one who thought of it as a personal space.

Whenever I was blue and needed to be alone, I'd hike up my skirt and wade out in my bare feet to sit on a rock that was at the highest point of the brook so hikers passing by couldn't see me. One time sticks in my mind. On my rock in the middle of the brook, with the cool water running over my feet, I started crying my eyes out. I didn't know why. I still was convinced that I had the perfect marriage. Hell, why stop there: I had the perfect house, the perfect husband, the perfect daughter, and when I worked with Ruby Braff, the perfect rhythm section. All that perfection and I was unhappy? I didn't deserve to be unhappy. Obviously, I was being selfish and needed a good talking to!

Bawling myself out was liberating. My emotions spent, I had a flash of inspiration: When I thought I was being selfish I was actually feeling an intense need for survival, a need to survive by playing my own music for the rest of my life. Music was such a major part of my life, and I just wasn't playing enough.

Especially with A-team musicians. Boy, did I miss that! I wanted to play with giants of the music all the time, but it seemed an impossible dream. I mean, I didn't think I even measured up to Jerry—I still thought of him as the teacher and I was still the student—so maybe I wasn't good enough to get any more than I was getting.

I can't deny that when I first started playing those gigs with some of the founding fathers, like Vic Dickenson and Wild Bill, I was lapping it up, having a ball; but after a while I felt sidelined by that historical style. Especially in contrast to the modern masters Jerry was working with, like Oliver Nelson, Quincy Jones, and Thad Jones. I also felt handcuffed in all-woman bands. Promoters and club owners would jump on that bandwagon like crazy, but since so many women at that time were not serious about playing it was usually a gimmick, a hook—"All women, Ta-Da! Freako, Freako!" Overall, my big-picture takeaway was that the caliber of what I'd been getting wasn't enough. It just wasn't enough, and that made the tears start flowing all over again.

I was on that rock a long while—long enough to get a fresh take on Jerry and me—and it was the height of simplicity. Jerry, on his own, touring with his fine bunch of musicians, left me high and dry. I was going to have to be on my own. I had a right to follow my own path—Jerry was—but the hitch in my get-along was that I wasn't playing; there was no work for me. I didn't know what to do. The clouds parted when Richie Cole showed up.

Jerry and I had known alto saxophonist Richie Cole for a while; he had been one of Phil Woods's students. One day, when I was at my lowest, Richie arrived out of the blue for a visit, and soon he was living in his Volkswagen bus parked in our driveway. From the first, Richie got me out of the house. He invited me on weekdays to join him sitting in at Gulliver's, a landmark Jersey club one city over in West Paterson, followed by the occasional one-nighter at the Three Sisters, another tavern with the same jazz policy in the same town.

Eventually, the jobs got steadier and expanded to venues in Trenton and Long Island. Sometimes we'd crash overnight in Richie's bus, but most of the time we'd stay over at somebody's house and work the jobs that he'd dug up. I really depended on Richie; I would never have gone to those clubs by myself, much less had his go-getter spirit.

Richie shored up my sanity and my confidence, too, because he believed in me and knew my reputation. As he put it, "Dottie was unusual. I mean she was totally accepted by all the guys in New York. . . . Everybody loved playing with Dottie because she could swing. . . . She was one of the first calls. . . . Plus she was cool. Ain't nobody cooler than Dottie Dodgion."

After a few months paying our dues in the Jersey/New York metropolitan area, we piled into Richie's Dodge van—"I graduated to a little better place to live," he said—and went down to DC to play weekends at Harold's Rogue and Jar club. We called it "Harold's House of Jazz," because Richie was really good friends with the owners, Harold and Sue Kaufman; after we started playing there regularly, we stayed in their beautiful apartment.

I made a lot of friends during our trips to the Rogue and Jar and two of them paid huge dividends a few years later. One was Jean Pierre, who ran a DC beauty salon, "The Cut Above." The other was Harold Kaufman, who, in addition to being the club owner, was a lawyer, psychiatrist, and piano player. Harold was impressed by the reputation I had built in New York and all the musicians I knew. Once in a while we'd talk business, and I'd give him some suggestions for running his shop, presaging our future relationship.

Those jams with Richie steadily revived my career. Over the next few years I worked no less than sixteen weekend gigs at the Three Sisters alone, some with Richie but also with a parade of other good musicians, such as Bob Cranshaw, Kenny Barron, Al and Zoot, Ron Carter, Tommy Flanagan, and Frank Foster. I felt like a phoenix!

Two of the gigs at the Three Sisters club were quartets that included Jerry, and as things turned out, they were a lead-up of sorts to an opportunity that Jerry and I would soon have to work together with our own handpicked band on an extended booking in a European club..

It was July 1974, and Jerry, with Deborah and me in tow, was off to Perugia, in central Italy, with the Thad Jones/Mel Lewis Orchestra. Deborah was on holiday, but I went along because Jerry and I had a weeklong gig with our quartet the following month at the Jazz Domicile in Munich. Our band included two veterans of the Thad Jones/Mel Lewis Orchestra: pianist, Walter Norris; and our close associate, bassist, George Mraz. Mraz, who was friends with the owner of the Jazz Domicile, got us the Munich gig.

My one memory of Perugia was the hilarity one afternoon when my standing as a drummer was summarily revoked by one of the sons of the famous Italian movie director, Vittorio De Sica.[1] "Jerry, Jerry, how are you?" the younger De Sica asked as he walked up to us in the lobby of our hotel, adding "I want you to hear this drummer I've found!" Jerry didn't miss a beat. Pointing at me he countered with, "Well, you know my wife's a drummer." De Sica, aware of my presence for the first time, shot me a glance and took pains to clarify, "No, no, this guy's a real drummer!" Jerry and I just howled, effectively ending the conversation. I had been through enough comedies like that in the States so I didn't take offense, but that's a good example of how I was a pioneer. Plain and simple, a woman didn't play drums in those days.

At the end of the Perugia gig with Thad and Mel, our spin-off quartet rented two Fiats for the drive north along the Adriatic coast to Munich. Mraz and Walter Norris took one car; Jerry, Deborah, and I drove the other. We had a good time, leisurely stopping in different towns and staying at a few hotels on the beach. During the first leg of the trip, as Mraz recalls, he got a speeding ticket in a small Italian village: "About five cars passed me . . . very good cars, and they're going three times as fast as me. So, the policeman stopped me. I said, 'Well, what about these other guys who just passed me?' He said, 'They're too hard to catch!'"

Our two-car caravan made an overnight stop in Venice that has blistered my memory. It began innocently enough: We parked the car on the mainland and took a public ferry across the lagoon to the Venetian shore. Hitting the wharf, we headed straight to Harry's Bar, a world-class watering-hole and a favorite of such celebrities as Charlie Chaplin, Ernest Hemingway, Alfred Hitchcock, and Orson Welles. After a few of Harry's delicious peach fizz cocktails, the guys went back to the mainland to get our instruments out of the cars and onto a boat to the hotel.

Since there were too many instruments for them to handle at one time, Mraz's bass, which coincidentally was built in Venice in 1803, had to be left until the next trip. George remembers what happened as he and Jerry got on the boat: "I asked Walter to watch the bass. And as the boat started pulling off, he just got up and completely forgot and walked away and left the bass there. And I'm screaming and, of course, he couldn't hear me. There's like four old men who are trying to have a little competition trying to spit on the bass from like ten yards away. It's sitting on a bench. . . . It was covered, but still."

In the meantime, despite feeling a bit under the weather, I decided to take Deborah shopping in the Piazza San Marco. It was oppressive. Hawkers filled the piazza, many of them young, good looking, and very Italian, yelling to get our attention: "Hey, hey, over here!" We tried in vain to window shop, but the "Italian Stallions," eyeing Deborah up and down, crowded us until we had to flee, our flight stirring up flocks of birds so thick we could hardly make our way across the square.

I felt much worse that evening. Sweating profusely at dinner, my skin began tingling and my face turned blood red. When my throat closed up I had to leave the restaurant. Propped up by Jerry and Deborah, I trudged through the narrow streets and collapsed on my bed. I felt deathly ill. As I laid there, feverish, I heard music and hallucinated that someone was serenading me. Jolted upright by two loud booms, I saw the door to my room crack open and Mraz peering in. Seeing me stir, he pulled the door wide and stood proudly holding his precious Italian bass, successfully retrieved from the spittle tournament on the wharf.

He told me that the bass sounded so good when he took it out of its case that he skipped dinner and played it for several hours. I had heard every note serenading me through the thin hotel walls! "Dottie, Dottie, listen!" and he pulled that booming low note again. He was thrilled because never, ever before had he been able to get that note out of that bass. Not until it was back home in Venice!

Cool as it was, the sound of Mraz's bass did nothing for my temperature. At 104, Jerry bundled me like a sausage and we hiked to a doctor. Inside the doctor's house it was so dark we could barely make out the stairs in front of us. As our eyes adjusted we glimpsed a figure on the landing, illuminated by a small light with a long string hanging down. It was the doctor, smoking a cigarette next to a sign that read "No Fumare." Giggling, Jerry and I braved the stairs to the examination room where the doctor gave me a pill that seemed at first to have little effect. Back at the hotel, with chills setting in, I fell asleep feeling pretty bad, but the next morning all the symptoms were gone! I was the old Dot again!

Looking back, it strikes me that Venice gave me a warning. I had been perfectly fine all the way from Perugia to the public lot across the water from Venice, but I felt feverish as soon as I stepped off the ferry and put my foot down in that floating city. That is grounds enough for me to conclude that my illness was caused by bad karma from a previous life in Venice. Without trying to sound dramatic, my instincts tell me—and I've always trusted my instincts—that there are certain places, Mexico and New Orleans among them, where I have been killed in past lives. This time around I would not dare go to those places; nor would I risk a return to Venice. It would be gambling with my life.

On the road again, we headed to Innsbruck, Austria, then crossed the German border. Throughout the roughly one-hundred-mile trip to Munich, Walter drove the Fiat and Mraz rode in the trunk. He was afraid he'd be stopped and taken back to Czechoslovakia, which was still under totalitarian rule, but we made it without incident to our final destination. Our quartet played the Jazz Domicile from August fifth through the eleventh.

The club was nondescript and the German audiences were attentive but reserved. Their reticence and my not speaking the language meant no mingling with the crowd during the short intermissions each night. Instead, I sat alone with a drink while Jerry hung with Mraz and the club owner. Walter, in another part of the room, silently did his thing, practicing piano with his fingertips on a table top. But the blahs and the boy's club were a small price to pay for the music we played. The band really hit, I had a ball on the bandstand, and that made for a marvelous time in Munich, spoiled only by Jerry's drinking.

When we got to Munich, he was drinking heavily, and there was one particularly ugly scene when he returned wasted to our hotel room and wanted to make love. The repugnant memories of Ed Jensen and a priest tipsy on sacramental wine put me off, so I said point blank, "Jerry, what makes you think I want to make love to a drunk?" He complained, "Maybe if you gave it up, I wouldn't be a drunk!" So, this was my fault? He was getting drunk because I didn't give him enough? That was a real slap in the face because I couldn't remember a single time before when I'd turned Jerry down.

Back in the States, I got back on the circuit. Over the Labor Day weekend in 1974, I worked the famed annual Dick Gibson Jazz Party, hosted by the Broadmoor Hotel in Colorado Springs. Zoot got me the gig, I know he did. God love him! Zoot, his wife, Louise, and the Gibsons were tight; Dick revered Zoot so he listened when Zoot told him, "You oughta have Dottie." I remember mentioning my invitation to Marian McPartland who had been the first woman to play the party. Marian's wry reply was, "Oh, so you're the token this year. Good luck, I was the token last year."

The party took place in a huge ballroom. An audience of maybe a hundred, who had paid through the nose for reservations, enjoyed nonstop jam sessions from early afternoon until late at night, swung by seventy all-star musicians. I did two or three sets a day with various combinations of rhythm sections and front lines so I got exposure like crazy.

Back in New York, Zoot did me another favor: A chance to play with one of the greatest violinists in the world, Joe Venuti. The first time I met Joe was when Zoot hired me for a private party on a Sunday afternoon in Queens and Joe was on that band. Joe, Zoot, and I had so much musical fun that day—boy did we fit! When the gig was finished Joe went up to Zoot and told him, "Yeah, you really picked her right, Zoot! Yep, yep!" So that's why Joe hired me, because of that one job with Zoot, and I worked with him off and on for about a year after that. Joe always had fine musicians, great rhythm sections, and was known as "Maestro" wherever we went. Between jobs we'd sometimes stay at his house, in rural upstate New York, and rehearse.

When I played with Joe, he was in his early seventies but his chops hadn't declined. He could play jazz like no other violinist—never mind Stephane Grappelli—and boy he was fast! As fast as Benny Goodman on the clarinet, if not faster. I remember a six-day engagement in June, 1975, at the Colonial Tavern in Toronto (the same place I'd been earlier with Wild Bill). We had Major "Mule" Holley on bass, and because our regular pianist couldn't make it, Joe hired Mike Longo, formerly Dizzy Gillespie's piano player. Mike had never played with Joe before, so during our first afternoon soundcheck, Mike, trying to get his sea legs, asked Joe, "Do you want to rehearse, Mr. Venuti?" "No," said Joe. "Well, are there any special charts?" Mike wondered. "No, you'll know 'em," was Joe's nonchalant response. "We hit at eight," were Joe's parting words as he left the club, and boom, that was that.

As we were setting up that night, a more confident Mike whispered to me, "This is gonna be a snap." "Yeah, sure it is," I told him, trying to give him the benefit of the doubt that maybe, somehow, he was prepared to keep up with Joe. He wasn't. The first number Joe called was the jazz standard, "Cherokee,"[2] at a furious tempo. Joe whipped off chorus after chorus at breakneck speed and ran Mike, not to mention the rest of us, ragged. "Oh, my God!" Mike said after we finished. I had to laugh. He'd expected easy tempos, sweet violin stuff. That was definitely not Joe; the violin flew when he played.

Joe loved me, but my association with him ended unhappily not long after the job in Canada. Just previous, everything looked rosy; Joe had lined up a lot of gigs in Europe and he intended to take me, the only stateside member of his band, with him. He would pick up the rest of the band over there. Joe even had the itinerary worked out: At each stop, we would stay at palaces and villas surrounded by beautiful countrysides that were owned by counts and countesses he knew. "And wait 'til we hit Italy! Oh, they're gonna love you in Rome," he enthused. I was so excited, but it never happened. Joe's manager stepped in and talked Joe out of taking me. "You're Joe Venuti," he argued, "you don't need her. You can get any male drummer you want and then I won't have the inconvenience of booking a woman."

I could have killed the bastard! Maybe he was afraid I would take attention away from Joe because I'm a woman drummer, and a good one, but Joe didn't think that way about me; he didn't mind sharing the spotlight with me at all. Besides, nobody but nobody could have taken Joe's fame away. God, I was disappointed, and I was disappointed in Joe for allowing it to happen.

On May 27, 1975, not long before I left Joe, I played sessions with Vic Dickenson and Ruby at Eddie Condon's.[3] That closed one chapter of my professional life in New York. A chapter of my personal life closed when Jerry and I separated.

It was hard; I had gladly given plenty in that marriage, but I wasn't giving it gladly anymore. When I'm in a difficult situation I have a way to measure my stress level. If my hand goes to my décolletage I can tolerate it, but if my hand goes to my neck that means the stress is cutting off my windpipe and I can't breathe. That's how far it went with Jerry. When things get that critical, I have to do whatever is necessary to survive.

There was no talk of divorce yet, but after we broke up I had to get out of New York. The city was too small for both of us to stay, knowing as we did everybody in pretty much the same circle. And for me at least, having worked with the cats with the names, I was ready for a major readjustment in my life.

My chance arrived courtesy of The Merv Griffin Show. I had known several of the guys in Griffin's band before he moved his show from New York to Los Angeles in 1970. Around the time Jerry and I were parting company, a couple of the guys were back in the city for a spell, and they filled me in about a band they had put together with gigs lined up in Los Angeles. Only problem was they didn't have a drummer. "Boy, we want you on this band, Dottie, you'd be perfect for it," they told me. "You know I don't read," I said. "Oh, you'll have the charts down, we're not worried about that. So, if you come out, you've got the gig."

It was an attractive offer, especially after Jerry took a girlfriend and things got increasingly unpleasant. "Now's the time to go," I decided. Before I left, I helped Jerry load up both our cars and move his new flame into the Park Ridge house. As hysterical as that may sound, it was self-serving; a parting gesture that helped me let go.

It was the summer of 1975 and I was free! Deborah and I packed our bags and headed way out west.

Harold's Rogue and Jar

We made it to Los Angeles on an American Express card only to find that the job fell through! The band already had a drummer and the guys who encouraged me to come out had nothing to say about it. It was my own dumb fault for taking their word that I should pick up and move.

Deborah and I took a cheap apartment in West Hollywood off Sunset Strip, just up from Evel Knievel's place, right behind the ritzy Chateau Marmont hotel. The apartment complex had a half-pint pool and our room had stick furniture—we had to be careful sitting down. I asked Grandmother Giaimo for a few utensils and some clean bedding, but she wouldn't give us anything. That hurt. She was stingy, but, c'mon, I was her only granddaughter.

Both of us badly needed jobs to get back on our feet. We tried to win some easy money as contestants on the television game show, "High Rollers," but feeling so glum I guess we didn't ooze enough personality during the interview to get on the air. The two of us finally landed a job, but in both cases there was a dark cloud crowding the silver lining. I found a steady gig in a trio with two other girls who weren't very good musicians at all. We worked in Army bases, driving in trucks to get there, me lugging my drums, and the guys hitting on us all the time. I hated that job. It was lousy; it was just lousy.

Deborah made good money waiting tables at the famous Rainbow Bar and Grill. The Rainbow was a celebrity watering hole and Deborah got some pretty big tips—after all, she could open twelve bottles of champagne in a minute and those big spenders drank champagne all night—but to get those tips she had to stomach the nastiness of the Hollywood crowd that handed them out. After a couple months Deborah had enough of selling her soul for a buck. She came home, threw a $100 bill on the chesterfield sofa, and told me that was her last tip. Deborah had quit that night.

We were miserable. I got so depressed I contemplated pills as a way out—my old nemesis, "Death Valley," back for the kill! Suddenly, I got the crazy idea—maybe the dumps made me creative—to call Ron Rose, the organist at the Top of the Wheel room at Harvey's Casino Resort in Lake Tahoe. I had played with Ron one time before when Jerry worked with Red Norvo at Harrah's. Ron made no secret back then that he'd love to have me join him on a permanent basis. Reminding him of that on the phone, I said, "Ron, you don't happen to have an opening for a drummer, do you?" "As a matter of fact I do, he replied. "All right!" I shouted.

I was all but out the door, but Deborah had different ideas. She was at a turning point in her life, wanting to leave dead-end entry-level service jobs for something more skilled and permanent. As soon as she heard about my pending move to Tahoe, she phoned my Mom and pleaded: "I don't want to be a waitress, I want a profession. I want to come home so you can put me through beauty school!" Of course, Mom and Bob couldn't wait to get Deborah back; they were missing her like crazy. "You come home to us," Mom said, "and we'll put you in any business you want!" She sent us traveling money, and the next day Deborah was off for my Mom's in Sacramento to study at Lyles School of Beauty. I headed east across the state line to Nevada.

My gig with Ron started in the Fall of 1975. The first day, when we rehearsed some cha-cha's for the evening performance, I told him, "Ron, if you keep playing this shit I won't be able to fill the ad." That was a powerful bit of forecasting on my part because the same red flag waved ten months later when I quit. But, boy, between times we had a ball!

The marquee outside Harvey's said, "Ron Rose and Lady D." Ron used all the stops on the organ and the two of us cooked just like we were Basie's big band! Playing with Ron was great and so was the money, and when Deborah graduated from Lyles she moved into my apartment in the woods on Ski Run Boulevard and worked as a hairdresser's apprentice in a local salon, Shampoo.

The only dissonant note was crudely struck. One night at Harvey's Top of the Wheel I was in the middle of a solo when a guy walked up to the bandstand and very curtly asked, "Are you Dottie Dodgion?" "Yeah," I said.

"You've been served," he declared and dropped divorce papers smack on my tom tom! "Oh, that's cold," I told Ron. "This has got to be a first for anybody!"

It was a total surprise. Jerry and I used to talk about how at some point we might have to let go of one another, but he promised me that if we ever did we'd always get back together, no matter what. I really did believe that. Another dream shattered. The divorce was finalized and twenty years of marriage went down the drain.

Not long after I quit Harvey's. All because of a silly pop tune that set off another red flag. Ron and I played jazz night after night at Harvey's. Except when Ron got insecure about something, like maybe the place wasn't quite full enough. Then he'd call for that one damn tune, "Tie A Yellow Ribbon 'Round the Ole Oak Tree,"[1] his "thumb-sucking tune" for all the corny people in the club. Worse yet, he'd play the melody straight, like Lawrence Welk. Ron was insecure a lot, so we played that trifle so many times I got to hate it. Finally, I reached my limit. "You play that tune one more time," I warned him, "and I'm quitting." Ron laughed it off and a few nights later he played it again! If he was pulling my leg it backfired, because when we finished for the night I looked right at him, smiled, and said, "You've got my notice, Ron."

I can't lay all the blame at the feet of that silly tune. There was also the isolation Deborah and I felt in Lake Tahoe. The grinding halt of winter was not conducive to meeting people. Summer it was a town of transients; if you found a boyfriend, come winter he was gone. Tahoe had been good as a layover to catch our breaths, but it was time to leave and I wanted out. Fortunately, I had a lifeline: Jean Pierre.

Jean Pierre was the beautiful Frenchman I had met at the Rogue and Jar in DC where he owned a beauty salon, "A Cut Above." Back then we clicked as acquaintances, but he took our friendship more seriously. A few months after I opened with Ron, Jean Pierre started sending me the most beautiful love letters. Several times in those letters he urged me to come back to Washington if I wasn't happy in Lake Tahoe, even offering his apartment to Deborah and me as a place to land for a couple of weeks while we got ourselves together. It was an attractive offer, to move to a city where a lot of jazz was happening, but the problem was that neither Deborah nor I had any work lined up.

That problem lightened when Richie Cole also encouraged me to return to DC, with the assurance that Harold, the owner of the Rogue and Jar, would give me a couple of nights to start off. The problem disappeared when, after I told Jean Pierre that Deborah had her cosmetology license, he invited her to work at his exclusive salon. With the puzzle parts in place, I had the confidence to leave Lake Tahoe in such a bold manner.

In the end, my departure worked great with no hard feelings. Ron and the staff at Harvey's gave me a going-away party and the girls chipped in to get me a brand new outfit with some travel accessories. Ron caught me alone and admitted that he loved my chutzpah, that I could say, "that's it!" and go.[2] And the next morning Deborah and I did just that.

I had saved about $2500 so we went easy and made it glamorous: We stopped every day at five o'clock to find a motel with a pool where I had my martinis. We got to DC in early September, 1976, and went straight to Jean Pierre's apartment, which was across the bridge in Arlington, Virginia. The first few months of my return, Jean Pierre and I got even closer, but the romance fizzled when I learned he was married. Nevertheless, we remained good friends, and when Jean Pierre returned to France for an extended stay, Deborah and I lived in his apartment for several months, rent free.

I was glad to be back east and close to New York City, but trying to crack Washington for a second time was slow at first. I worked the occasional gig at Harold's and eventually hooked up with established locals like pianist Ellsworth Gibson and bassist James King for trio jobs at other DC area clubs such as Manuel's and the Top O'Foolery. Finally, after weeks of scrambling, I found myself at the intersection of the right place and the right time.

Harold Kaufman, the owner of the Rogue and Jar, had a dispute with the woman managing his club. To be honest, I saw that coming, so when she left I was ready. I don't know if Harold remembered suggestions I'd made about running his place when Richie Cole and I played that cellar club a few years before. If he did, maybe a notion of my business savvy had been planted in his head.

In any case, I told him straight away that I could book some of the most famous musicians in the world for his club if he would trust me to handle the details. Then I proposed a schedule that would benefit both of us: I'd get Tuesdays, Wednesdays, and Thursdays to work my own trio as the house band, and Harold, who moonlighted as a jazz pianist, would get Mondays to lead his group. On Friday and Saturday nights I'd bring down top musicians from New York City, but only on the condition that we treated them with the respect they deserved—most club owners took advantage of jazz musicians because they enjoyed playing so much.

I pitched that on Friday and Saturday nights we'd pay $150 for the leader and $100 for the sidemen, plus an allowance for transportation by car, complimentary first-class accommodations, free food and booze, and the musicians could bring their ladies along. Lo and behold, Harold agreed to the whole package! I was elated knowing that the New York cats would love it. Most of them had been on the road for a lot less, plus they had to pay for their room and food, so this was a vacation for them. A fully paid one at that.

Harold's Rogue and Jar was in a very chic neighborhood, on N Street Northwest, off Connecticut Avenue, right around the corner from the Palms Restaurant that served the Washington elite. Rumor had it that in earlier years the upstairs was a church, and the downstairs, where music poured through the walls, was a whorehouse!

When Harold hired me, his club was in the red. Getting it solvent was a challenge, but I was a good businesswoman and I had a ball doing it. As the club's booking agent, I had my list of musicians that I would hire from New York; I brought them down because if Harold tried to get them it never would have happened. As Richie Cole observed, "All the guys did it as a favor for Dottie because everybody loved Dottie Dodgion." Harold was very happy with the musicians I got. He didn't show up at the club too often—most of the musicians didn't even know he existed—but the steady stream of world-class players gave him prestige, a lot of prestige.[3]

I was thrilled that so many musicians answered my ad. When I booked them, I took into account the long drive from New York to DC. A straight shot took at least four to five hours and delays on those congested highways were not uncommon. Since I knew what it was like to panic if you're running late, I purposely adjusted the terms of every musician's contract to protect them and me. A memorable example is when I booked the Roy Haynes Quintet.

I first met Roy Haynes when I sat in with his band in the early 1960s at New York's famed Five Spot Cafe; it was in the East Village on the Bowery and it was rough. I was by myself that night, but I wasn't afraid to go anyplace in New York. When I walked in, Roy knew who I was and that I had been playing with the big guns. Between sets he approached me at the bar, "Good to see you, Dottie. Still playing drums?" "Oh, yes," I replied. "Want to sit in?" he asked, sounding halfhearted—I bet he thought I'd be too scared to do it.

I ignored that vibe and cheerily said, "Okay." Well, when he went backstage and told his guys that I was going to sit in they were irked, and as I climbed on the stand to get behind Roy's drums they continued to grumble. But I wasn't intimidated; once again I remembered Eugene's words: "Jump in where the water's deepest and show them what you've got." Well, when we finished the first tune everybody in the Five Spot was clapping really loud and the musicians who didn't want me up there in the first place were hugging me. The finishing touch was when Roy put his arms around me and said, "All right, Baby, swinging!"

Roy and I had that bit of history when I called him about a date at the Rogue and Jar. I told him the arrangements and asked, "Are you interested?" "Damn right!" he said, and I promptly sent him a contract for a Friday-Saturday engagement from nine to one both nights. Well, on the first night Roy came dragging in at quarter to ten. I could tell he was a bit sheepish about being late, so instead of lecturing him: "Oh, God, you're late!" I was collected. "Hey, Roy, what's up?" "Aw, Dottie, there was traffic and everything," and he turned to hurry his band, "You guys start setting up right now!" That was my cue to cool things out: "That's alright, man, put your instruments down, relax, have a taste, then go on." I was easy because in truth he wasn't late. The actual contracted time for the gig was from ten to one, but he didn't see that copy. I had learned how to show the musicians respect and protect the club at the same time.

Many of the musicians I booked, like Roy Haynes, came with their own rhythm sections. When a horn player came down by himself I might climb behind the drums—like when I backed Pepper Adams with my dear friend John Marabuto at the piano—or, as an alternative, I'd get drummer, Bernard Sweetney, and then pick up other local talent to complete the band. My own nights went smoothly, too; sometimes local favorites would sit in, like nationally acclaimed tenor saxophonist, Buck Hill. On bass I'd have either Keter Betts when he was available (he was Ella Fitzgerald's longtime accompanist) or Marshall Hawkins.

My steady pianist was Reuben Brown; his style was like a DC version of Kenny Barron. Reuben and I didn't hit it off immediately. When I knew him, he was pretty prejudiced against white people, but he took the gig and we really cooked. One night we swung so hard that at the close of the evening when I walked off the stand Reuben looked straight at me and said, "You know, you better check your roots." He meant I was passing for white. I thought that was the greatest compliment!

What I made at Harold's didn't meet my expenses so I supplemented it with a variety of jobs in Washington, Virginia, Maryland, and on occasion back in New York. I also took short leaves from the club to play special events. My second year at the Rogue and Jar I worked a Kennedy Center gig with Zoot and Al, backed by Jimmy Rowles at the piano and bassist, Steve Novosel, who was married to renowned soul singer, Roberta Flack. When Zoot was putting the band together, he remembered that I was already down there in DC, so he thought: "Why bring a drummer? Let's have Dottie." Returning the favor, I had Zoot in for two nights at Harold's.

The next year, Marian McPartland invited me to join an all-female group for a guest spot on NBC's Today Show. Marian organized the band because, as she told Hatley N. Mason III in an interview for the Sacramento Bee, "I was getting sort of annoyed at promoters always saying that there weren't enough good women players, so I put together a women's group, to show them."[4] Aside from Marian and me, the band included guitarist, Mary Osborne; alto saxophonist, Vi Redd; and Lynn Milano at the bass. Three months later, Marian booked us into the Rountowner Motel in Rochester, NY, where we did a taping for the PBS-TV jazz series, "At the Top," and played three nights in the Monticello Room. A live recording, "Now's the Time,"[5] was made during our engagement at the Rountowner and released on Marian's Halcyon label.

The Rountowner gig had some excitement of the wrong kind. The day after we finished the album, we had an afternoon rehearsal for that night's performance. As we were working out an arrangement I saw big tears coming down Lynn Milano's face. I leaned over, and so as not to get Marian's attention, quietly asked, "What's the matter, Lynn?" but she wouldn't talk to me.

Later, on a break in the lobby, Lynn stood beside me, and, still teary, confided how she felt that all of us in the band were being "used" by local and national media. A lot of hoopla was being stirred up because we were women, not because we were great musicians. "We're being used and I'm not going to let that happen to me," she said. I told her, "Of course we're being used, but we're using them, too. Look at it that way." There was no consoling her; she didn't get it at all. She told me she wasn't going on that night, she was going to pack up her bass and take a train back to New York. I advised her to tell Marian right away, but she walked away, giving me the impression that was it.

I felt caught in the middle. I didn't want to run to Marian; it wasn't my style and it wasn't my band, but I also wanted to save the day. At that time, an all-female band, made up of women who could really play, was very, very,

very rare and the bass player was the hardest to find—women didn't want to get calluses on their hands. So, I told Marian what Lynn had said and she exploded: "Well, fuck her! I'm not going to put up with that shit! We'll get a man!" Marian was still fuming when, after the break, she called the band into her room to hear a playback of what we'd recorded for the album. As we were all listening, Lynn, with a shy smile on her face, whispered to me, "Gee, we sound pretty good." "Yeah, Lynn!" I said.

Hearing that recording changed Lynn's mind; she decided to stay and play that night. Lynn, of course, hadn't said one word about any of this to anyone else, including Marian, so Marian naturally thought the worst about me. All of a sudden, I was the bad guy—Marian gave me the dirtiest look and read me the riot act: "What the hell is this all about, Dottie? Why are you making trouble?" That was a real prima-donna thing for Lynn Milano to do, and I've never forgiven her for it, never, ever, ever!

That backstage brouhaha was balanced out by an honor I never expected to get. Late in 1977, I was tapped to replace Mel Lewis in the Thad Jones/Mel Lewis Orchestra! Mel was sick and the band needed a replacement drummer for one night at the Village Vanguard. Thad told me he asked bassist, George Mraz, who he wanted to sub in the rhythm section and Mraz said, "Get Dottie, she knows the charts backwards and forwards." That was true, I did. Because Jerry had been with Thad since the birth of the Orchestra, I had heard that band almost every Monday night for a decade. So, Mraz, knowing I would be comfortable the moment I sat down, was relieved that he wouldn't have to break in a new drummer for just one night! That was the hottest band happening at the time—Thad was the new Ellington, he was really making waves. There were so many other drummers available in New York, I was honored to be asked.

I played that whole Monday night behind Mel's drums and it was a real trip to work my only time at the Vanguard. That club had the smallest bandstand I'd ever seen, but everybody fit because of the different levels they were on. The band was in a semicircle with the different sections stepped into tiers; that arrangement was beautiful for sound. It was extremely compact, like being in a womb, so all the guys could clearly hear each other. It was great for me because everybody in the band could hear the hi-hat. In an ensemble of that size, the clap of the cymbals has to be so distinct and crisp that there's no question about where you're bringing it down on two and four. That's what musicians listen for, where two and four are coming in.

When we finished that night, guys in the band told me I did a good job. I wasn't thrown when Thad brought in a composition that I hadn't heard before. I'd listened to so many big bands that I could anticipate the writing for the different sections in that new piece, and when accents came up I could sense them breathing beforehand. I couldn't sight-read, but I had good intuition, and my ears went out there a little bit more. Besides, when an arranger writes a big-band chart there are usually phrases that have been played many times on other bands. Once you're into the first chorus you pretty much know that a particular strain or lick is going to go through a certain set of repeats and variations. It's an insider's knowledge of a band.

Another cherished memory from that period of my life is playing on one of the headliner bands at the historic Women's Jazz Festival in 1978. The three-day celebration began on Friday, March 17, with clinics and jams at clubs and halls in Kansas City, Missouri. For the main event on Sunday evening, the Festival moved across the Missouri River to Memorial Hall in Kansas City, Kansas.

The five-hour program was emceed by jazz critic, Leonard Feather. The last set before intermission featured "The Women's Jazz Festival All-Stars." A sextet, assembled and led by Marian, it included, other than Marian and me, two other musicians from the Rochester band: guitarist, Mary Osborne, and bassist, Lynn Milano; plus Janice Robinson at the trombone, and reed player, Mary Fettig. The festival was covered by national and international press: Our All-Star jam reportedly "drew great applause,"[6] and "offered spirited readings of 'Now Is the Time,' 'Autumn Leaves,' and 'Straight No Chaser.'"[7]

I returned to DC basking in the excitement of the Kansas City festival. That appearance, not to mention the chance I had earlier to sit in Mel Lewis's drum chair, in conjunction with my job as music director at Harold's, kept my visibility and reputation afloat. Ten months later my fortunes sank.

I had been successful at the Rogue and Jar precisely because I demanded that top jazz players get the respect they deserved. The payback was that I took that club out of the red and put it back in the black. But that mattered little in January, 1979, when Harold sold the Rogue and Jar to a bunch of lawyers and the building was torn down.

I spent the next year-and-a-half cooling my heels in the DC area, working one-nighters and more extended jobs when I could find them, like four weeks with my quartet at Hogates Seafood Restaurant in the Marriott. The only highlights that year were an article about me that appeared in the *Washington Post*,[8] and playing in Mary Osborne's quintet at a Women's Jazz Festival. A two-day event, the concerts were part of the annual Festival of Wheels celebration, in Dearborn, Michigan.[9] Our group performed Saturday evening, May 12, in a tent on the lawn of the Hyatt Regency Dearborn Hotel.[10] Working with Mary, the brilliant "Queen of the Jazz Guitar," was always sublime, but what happened the night before really caught my attention.

We arrived early enough on Friday for me to check out some of the bands billed for that evening. I wasn't prepared for what I heard when I walked into the tent show that featured a thirteen-year old drummer named Terri Lyne Carrington.[11] I couldn't get over how great she was! Her time was impeccable. I waited until Terri Lyne got off the stand and then said to her, "Am I going to have to break your fingers?" She smiled, because she knew that was the biggest compliment you can give a drummer.

In DC I was back to scraping by, but Deborah was full steam ahead. She had left A Cut Above to work at a day spa, Lillian Laurence, Ltd, where she picked up the skills to be an aesthetician[12] and was making good money doing facials. I contributed what I could to put food on our table and pay the rent—we had long since left Jean Pierre's Arlington apartment—but over the dark stretch of those sixteen months I was becoming a dead weight.

Then, gloriously, my angels took another encore, this time in the form of Cobi Narita, a New York–based philanthropist and jazz concert producer. Cobi was a champion of the eminent band leader and composer/arranger, trombonist Melba Liston. Cobi called me in DC and said that Melba was organizing an all-woman septet, "Melba Liston and Company" and they needed a drummer. When I talked with Melba about it, she told me that Cobi was arranging tours of Europe and Asia. "We're going to be world ambassadors!" Melba declared.

When Cobi guaranteed me some money to make the move back to New York, that clinched it. It was "Goodbye DC, Hello Brooklyn!"

Melba Liston and Company

I didn't move immediately.

The first few weeks I took the train or flew back and forth from DC to New York. Then, in early spring 1980, Melba needed me to make the move permanently so I left Deborah in our apartment in DC. We wouldn't be roommates again for almost a decade.

I quickly found a place in Brooklyn and was on deck as the band prepped for overseas in a Chelsea rehearsal hall, Black Bean Studios, owned by the Brazilian percussionist, Dom Um Romão. When I joined Melba, the band members were electric bassist, Carline Ray; tenor saxophonist, Erica Lindsay; alto saxophonist, Jean Fineberg; a second trombonist, Lolly Bienenfeld (Melba was in front most of the time, leading the band); and pianist, Sharon Freeman, who doubled on French horn. The band rehearsed several days a week for probably a month at Black Bean.

At one point, when Sharon Freeman took sick and was in the hospital for two weeks, she was replaced during rehearsals by a close friend of Melba's, a key figure in twentieth-century music, pianist/composer, Mary Lou Williams. During a break in one of our rehearsals, I overheard a conversation that unsettled me. I was within earshot when Melba and Mary Lou started talking about a forthcoming concert, "blah, blah, blah, and Marian McPartland's going to be there," one of them said. "Yeah, the whitey one, she can't swing," was the reply as the first one snickered. Well, that got my ire up. I strolled into the room and told them, "You know, I've worked with Marian and really respect her and neither of you have, so I don't think that's a very charitable, or, for that matter, accurate thing to say." I was indignant for

Marian. (Now, looking back, maybe I had no business saying those things because Melba and Mary Lou were crackerjack musicians. At the same time, I still don't like the "whitey" part and that they were putting Marian down. They didn't give her credit for being the musician she was. Marian swung in her own right, it was just a different feel.)

Aside from Melba, the only one in the band that I knew was Carline Ray, a helluva bass player who could stomp and make her electric axe talk like it was acoustic. Melba, Carline, and I were seasoned professionals, all of us in our early-to-mid fifties. The rest of the players were unfamiliar to me, including Sharon, who was an accomplished musician when she came on the band. The others were young and unseasoned; they were sweet girls who were doing their best, but they were of a different age. They didn't have anybody showing them how to listen, how to adjust, so they didn't know how to play with anybody else, sorry to say.

My apartment was in Fort Greene, at that time a rough, poor neighborhood of Brooklyn. When I first got back to New York, I remember driving over the Brooklyn Bridge and seeing on the right the high-rise buildings of upscale Brooklyn Heights and on the left Fort Greene, a hotbed of bums and winos and broken glass. That was my new home, where people threw bottles out their windows. The first time I walked into my ground floor apartment I got my usual New York City welcome: checking out my bedroom I looked up and saw a rat's ass poking out of a three-inch hole in the twelve-foot ceiling! My other roommates were Erica Lindsay, and a pianist friend of hers, Francesca Tanksley, both in their twenties.

During rehearsals, Melba decided we should all wear a band uniform. As Sharon Freeman remembers it: "Melba had a friend, Jodora—she called her Jo—who lived in Lennox Terrace, an apartment complex in Harlem, and this woman made the uniforms for us to wear. They were slacks and tops. . . . We might have even done some rehearsing at Jo's apartment. We would go over there, she would cook, and it was like we were getting to know each other. Cobi Narita was there too. And Melba was saying how important this was; it was like we were all getting ready to have this great adventure."

Before we set out for Europe, the band did a trial run playing a weeklong gig at the Tiber Pub, a hotel lounge in Washington, DC. Sharon Freeman recently reminded me of an incident that occurred during our stay in DC, an incident that brings home how deeply I had been affected by my divorce from Jerry. One evening all of us in the band were waiting to be picked up and returned to our hotel in Maryland. Suddenly, Sharon said to the group "Wow, I'm really tired and I'm really hungry" and I lashed out at her: "Little girl, everybody's tired, shut up!"

Sharon had respect for me so she didn't fire back, but she knew that I had some kind of problem. A few days later when I told her about my divorce, I think we both could see that it was Sharon's resemblance to Jerry's young African-American wife that had upset me. Sharon, who had just been divorced herself could see that I was "very hurt, very, very hurt."

Melba Liston and Company left in early July 1980 for its first international tour. Cobi booked us to play five European cities starting in Munich (July 9); this was followed by concerts in The Hague (July 11) where we headlined the Northsea Jazz Festival in Rotterdam; Pori, Finland (July 12); Nimes in southern France (July 13); and the next day in Nice as part of the Grande Parade du Jazz at the Cimiez Arenas.

Nice was the most memorable stop of the tour. Imagine having breakfast every day in the company of blue-chip jazz players—Carmen McRae at one table, Lee Konitz or Clark Terry at another—then everyone leaving to work or listen at the different fairground stages where every effort had been made to accommodate the musicians. Rhythm section instruments were on each bandstand, drums set up alongside a piano, and a bass was ready if you didn't bring your own. All drummers had to do was adjust the cymbals and throne for their own height, which brings to mind another amusing anecdote about Roy Haynes.

One evening at the festival, I listened to a band with a really tall drummer who had the throne and cymbals set way up high to suit his long torso. I stayed in the audience through to the next set, which featured Roy's band. Just before the band was set to hit, I could see that the adjustments on the drum set hadn't been changed. A stagehand saw the same thing. He asked Roy, who at five-foot-four was about a foot shorter than the previous drummer, if he wanted the throne and cymbal lowered. "Nah, nah," Roy said, "I can play 'em." Roy didn't even ask for a pillow to raise him up a bit. Instead, he played the entire set standing straight up, the back of his legs braced against the seat so he didn't topple over, with his left foot on the hi-hat and his right on the bass drum. Roy had a thing about being short. He drove a great big white Cadillac, I mean it was huge, and when he passed by you could just barely see his head over the door. Even in his car he didn't use a pillow!

The Grande Parade festival was produced by jazz impresario, George Wein, and for the 1980 edition he rented two major hotels, the Hotel Mercure Nice and the Mercure Nice Promenade des Anglais. He rented out both hotels so there was nothing but musicians in them, three-to-four hundred of the best jazz players in the world. I stayed in the Hotel Mercure Nice. I could take the elevator to any floor in that hotel and it'd be jumping, doors swung open up and down every corridor, rooms full of musicians spilling into the hallways, talking, laughing, waving: "Hey, Baby, what's happening" and "Oh, man! I haven't seen you in a hundred years."

On my floor, Melba's room was at the end of the first corridor and mine was past hers, around the corner on the other side from the elevator. My first afternoon there, as I was heading to my room, I passed Melba's open door and Dizzy Gillespie, who was visiting Melba, spotted me. "Hey, Dottie!" he shouted, and waved me in. "How you doin', Diz," I said, as I took in the wild T-shirt he had on. "Wow, that's a beautiful shirt, Diz!" "You want it?" he asked, and I was thrown back on my heels as he took it off and handed it to me. Dizzy Gillespie literally gave me the shirt off his back! That for years was my proudest possession. I used to sleep in it; it was my nightgown until it went to rags.

A few minutes later, Freddie Hubbard came into Melba's room and spied me—I was hard to miss draped in Dizzy's oversized shirt. "Hey, Dottie, I need to talk to you," he said sort of urgently. "It's only five-o-clock and nobody's gotten off yet from the afternoon concerts, but the management wants some music and I want to play the first set so I'm grabbing some guys. You still playing drums?" Before I could reply, Dizzy interrupted with, "I guess so!" Encouraged, Freddie turned to me, "Want to come down and play the first set?" "You bet!" I exclaimed, figuring that Freddie's rhythm section would have great musicians.

Wired, I got dressed, went downstairs, and though there was hardly anyone in the bar, we started playing. The piano player was terrible. Freddie was appalled; he'd never played with him but he'd never played with the bass player either, and he was worse than the piano player. I think both of them were local, and, of course, they weren't used to somebody like Freddie, where every note is precise and perfect. Freddie and I persevered; it wasn't easy but we were professionals.

Just as we were finishing up the third number, a bunch of musicians came into the bar. Immediately, Freddie cut the tune off. In quick succession, he replaced the lousy piano player with someone who had just walked in, and then he pressed Basie's bassist, Eddie Jones, to come up and play even though Eddie had just finished a heavy set with the band and was kind of tired. Reluctantly, he said, "Oh, okay," and picked up the bass. Then, seeing a drummer he knew Freddie yelled, "Hey, c'mon over and play right now!" Well, that was flat out insulting! We hadn't even played a full set and Freddie wanted me off the bandstand!

I had helped Freddie hold the tempo together, but he didn't give me that respect at all. I knew that he didn't have that much respect for me in general, so when the Basie band came in he wanted to get rid of me just as much as he had wanted to dump the bass player and pianist. I mean, he might as well have said out loud, "Thank God you guys arrived so I can ditch this whole rhythm section."

I don't know how the other guys felt, but being discarded like yesterday's newspaper really got my back up. When the other drummer approached the stand and Freddie told me to get off, I shot back: "No!" "What do you mean, no?" he demanded. "Freddie, I went through the worst," I said, "and now I deserve at least one good tune with Eddie." "Is that so?!" he cracked, but I held my ground, "Yeah, Freddie, that's how I feel about it."

Steaming, Freddie kicked off a tempo that was faster than Godspeed. Thankfully, my chops were up because I was determined not to let that tempo drop. I held steady even though the new piano player was straining to keep up and a weary Eddie was struggling. In the audience, Basie trumpet man, Joe Newman, saw that while I was keeping the tempo up Eddie was starting to lag, so Joe yelled: "Don't let her down, Eddie!"

What went around came around because Freddie had kicked it off so fast even he was having trouble with it! Trying to humiliate me, he had set a tempo he thought I couldn't possibly make, but as it turned out he did it to himself. As we finished the tune I played a press roll shout-out on my snare, handed my sticks to Freddie, and smugly told him, "now you can get your other drummer!"

The run-in with Freddie galled me but the episode was soon eclipsed by the success Melba Liston and Company enjoyed at the Grande Parade Festival! As Leonard Feather reported: "The Liston band . . . offered some of the Grande Parade's most invigorating new sounds." In the same article, he made reference to "Dottie Dodgion's propulsive drums" and said that our group was "the principal surprise at Nice."[1]

George Wein changed up Festival offerings by organizing impromptu jams each night, combining musicians pulled from different name bands. I couldn't understand why George didn't choose Melba to play one of those spontaneous sessions—and she was madder than hell about it—so I was floored when he picked me for one of them! It was a septet jam with an awesome frontline: Clark Terry on trumpet; my contrary buddy, Ruby Braff, on cornet; trombonist, Benny Powell out of Basie's band; and Lee Konitz playing alto sax.

My rhythm section partners for the jam were pianist John Lewis, leader of the world-renowned Modern Jazz Quartet, and a young Swedish bass player. At that time, a handful of European bass players had become so popular that having one in your band was considered the au courant thing to do. So instead of drawing Milt Hinton or Mraz—bassists who stood heads above the European crop—Wein's musical lottery pinched a Scandinavian kid who was brand new to me (and I've never seen his name since) and very difficult to play with. He had no flow, and worse yet, I could barely hear him! John, too, was playing so soft, it was like a flea tickling the keys.

I wasn't getting support from either of them so I turned my attention to the front line and where the horn players were playing within the tempo. Each of them had a little different spot. I listened closely to the overall sound and played right in the middle, just under all of them, never getting in their way or being heard first, and it turned out okay. The horns and I, we had a ball, but what Wein did, mixing rhythm players who didn't fit, was cold. Still, I'm not complaining; that session showed off one of my strengths—my ability to adapt and work with a variety of musicians.

Melba Liston and Company returned to the states in late July and, before we left that October for a tour of the Far East and South Pacific, Melba made two replacements: Ted Kelly joined us on trombone and Luther Francois on alto sax. Cobi Narita once again was instrumental, setting up the tour through the U.S. government, getting it sanctioned by the State Department and funded by the National Endowment for the Humanities. She got all the necessary permits and accompanied us on the trip as tour manager.

Our first stop was a week in Malaysia. It was the quietest part of the trip since we gave only two performances and because Melba, who had a taste for hard liquor, was on her best behavior. We rode in a Jeep from the airport to downtown Kuala Lumpur, passing herds of animals like we were on a safari. The band stayed at an American Holiday Inn, which I thought was pretty funny, except the food was terrible. Barbara Watson, the U.S. Ambassador to Malaysia, was our host; early in our visit we went out to her plantation for a lunch on her lawn, which was a big affair because, not to put too fine a point on it, we, too, were ambassadors. Barbara gave each of us a sari[2] to wear when we played a concert in her home; I can laugh now about the fits I had trying to play my hi-hat and bass drum with several yards of drape coiled around my legs!

Our next destination was Taiwan for two weeks where we played mostly at different schools, traveling by bus or a passenger boat down the river. When we were off the stand, Melba wanted a buddy to hang out with and drink. I tried to run from her—I didn't want to be sucked into binges and have Melba blather at me all night long—but it was no use. She knew I was one of the guys so she regularly pulled me aside whether I wanted a drink or not. Melba would say to me, "Come on, Dottie, let's go get some kick-a-poo juice!" That meant gin, but because American gin in Taiwan at that time cost $8 a shot we settled for the Taiwanese version. A white juice in a beautiful blue bottle, it looked mellow enough but the first sip left no doubt that, boy, it was kick-a-poo juice!

The final stop of our tour was Fiji, five thousand miles across the South Pacific. We landed at Nandi International Airport on the western coast of the Melanesian island of Viti Levu and changed planes to a ten-seater. It was a white-knuckle flight for me on that small airplane, hurtling over volcanoes as we skirted the island's southern border east to Suva, the capital of Fiji. Everybody was exhausted when we landed. "It seemed like we were flying forever," Sharon Freeman remembered. So we weren't exactly thrilled about having to walk up and down the air stairs several times so that all the photographers and media people gathered beneath the plane could get pictures of our arrival. Then, because the restaurant was closed by the time we got to our hotel, we had to scrounge among ourselves for a supper of candy bars, cookies, and chips. All was forgiven the next morning, though, when we opened the blinds and saw the extraordinary beauty of that port city. "Oh, my God! We're in Heaven!" is how Sharon described it.

We were on the island for eight days, staying at the Palace Hotel. The rooms were very sparse, with wicker furniture and lumbering Casablanca ceiling fans. Every night we'd dine out and every restaurant was staffed with huge waiters, naked above the waist with a wide sash around their hips and a bolo slung at their sides. Our second night on the town one of those hulking waiters in a particularly fine restaurant took a fancy to me. The girls in our band gleefully teased me, "Look out, Dot, look out!" But I sloughed it off, "Yeah, yeah, yeah." After we finished our main course and were drinking coffee, that very same waiter sidled up to me, and with the house orchestra in accompaniment, he sang "I'm in the Mood for Love."[3] He sang the whole damned thing only for me! I was mortified.

The adventure continued that night when the orchestra broke for intermission. I guess word had gotten out that I was the drummer in the visiting band from the states, so I was escorted by several of my Fijian counterparts to see their Lali drums in a lanai adjacent to the restaurant. We entered through large French glass doors and there, arrayed across the floor, was an imposing assortment of logs of different sizes and different lengths, all of them with a slit in the middle, all of them played with a huge mallet or stick. Excited to give it a try, I grabbed a mallet and started circling the logs, at times almost running from one to the next, sampling all the different sounds as if each log were a bar on a vibraphone.

We gave four performances during our stay in Fiji, all of them at the Ambassador's country club. Our first night, as we were getting ready to leave the hotel for our debut concert, Melba said, "I want some kick-a-poo juice to take along." What we got this time was in a pink jug, and, just like its Taiwanese cousin, it was powerful. We had some sips en route and Melba kept drinking in the dressing room. I tried to talk her out of it: "Honey, we're almost on the edge now," but I was wasting my breath. I watched in disbelief as Melba commenced to taking big swigs right out of the jug and then handing it to me. I don't think she knew, but I didn't dare take as many gulps as she did. I was used to drinking with the guys in New York, but I couldn't keep up with Melba, not if I intended to remain sensible and play that night. And, as Melba kept lifting the jug I got concerned about her making it. She had hurt her leg years before and relied on a cane, so even without the booze Melba was wobbly.

Somehow, together, we managed to get to the bandstand. It was beautifully decorated, backed with velvet drapes and carpeted with plush red pile—a classic intimate "Nat Cole room."[4] As the band was setting up, I watched from behind my drums as Melba checked out the stool left for her to sit on. She picked up her trombone and using her cane for support she eased herself up on the seat and then slid part way off until her feet touched the brace at the base of the stool. That gave her enough space to work the full extension of the slide. Then, with the band ready, Melba kicked off the first tune, "Shafi."[5] "One, two, three, four!" she counted, and at the same time she bent her body backward to pull up the slide to the pitch position for the opening note. Trouble is, she got stuck in reverse! Back, back, back went Melba, like a slow-motion slapstick, until she tumbled completely over onto the floor. The audience and most of the band turned silent; only Carline and I kept playing. Happily, she wasn't hurt. The heavy carpet cushioned her fall, but she was a sight, laying on the floor yelling at the band, "Don't stop playing, for Christ's sake!"

After we got back to New York, Melba reorganized her septet. Carline, Erica, and I stayed, but Larry Smith from Chicago was our new alto saxophonist and Britt Woodman, best known for his decade-long stint in Duke Ellington's band, took the second trombone chair. Then, when pianist Sharon Freeman departed the band, I took a rehearsal tape of my roomie, Francesca Tanksley, to Melba. "You've got to hear her," I said, and Francesca was hired. ("It was through Dottie that I got the job, so I'm indebted to her," Francesca said.)

At times, Melba augmented the band by adding baritone saxophonist, Fostina Dixon; she took that particular octet into Sweet Basil on January 12, 1981, to start a series of Monday night concerts that lasted a few months. The presence of Smith and Woodman in the otherwise female lineup at Sweet Basil got the attention of *New York Times* columnist, C. Gerald Fraser, who wrote that Melba Liston and Company was "the nation's most prominent male-female jazz band."[6]

While I was working Melba's bands and occasional combo gigs that Cobi Narita lined up, I still had to freelance to barely survive. Starting in 1980, for maybe eight to ten weekends a year, I began driving to the Delaware Water Gap to join pianist, John Coates Jr., and his bassist DeWitt Kay, at the Deer Head Inn. That drive took two hours at least one way, but it was worth it to play with John.

I stayed five miles up the road at the Lamplighter Motel in Stroudsburg; I would have preferred staying at the Deer Head Inn but the rooms were always booked. There was a little two-room apartment upstairs that I'd had my eye on for some time. The bedroom had a snug nooklike recess and a chesterfield sofa; the kitchen was about fifteen feet wide and included a tiny two-burner stove with a small refrigerator beneath. It was the perfect Lilliputian retreat for me, but with a long waiting list it was always out of reach.

One of the more colorful non-jazz jobs I took at that time was in an off-Broadway production, "Jerry's Girls,"[7] a revue of songs written by Jerry Herman of "Hello, Dolly!" and "Mame" fame. The first production of "Jerry's

Girls" premiered on August 17, 1981, and ran for three months at Onstage, a modest cabaret on West 46th Street in midtown Manhattan. It was an all-female show and I was part of a female trio that provided the instrumental accompaniment. My band mates were Carline Ray on electric bass and pianist, Cheryl Hardwick, who had been a keyboard player in the Saturday Night Live band and composed songs for the children's television series, Sesame Street.

Jerry Herman hired Cheryl as musical director and told her to fill out the trio with ladies who could play. The only condition was that he didn't want jazz musicians, but Jerry's idea of jazz was very narrow. He'd heard bebop, hated it, and thought all jazz music sounded that way. So, Cheryl shrewdly hired Carline and me to join her in a mainstream trio. We played Swing, a style of jazz that preceded the Bebop era, but she warned us never to let on that we were jazz musicians, to never let drop that we'd even so much as played with jazz musicians! It worked out beautifully. Our group, sitting on the back part of the stage, accompanied the singers and dancers with flowing Swing-style rhythm. Jerry was knocked out by what we did, but what he didn't know was that the flow we swung was jazz!

In 1983, "Jerry's Girls" was revived, starring actress and comedienne, Jo Anne Worley. I rejoined Carline and Cheryl in October of that year for a three-week tour of the show in upstate New York. We were together again in 1984 when an expanded version of "Jerry's Girls," starring iconic stage performer, Carol Channing and actress/singer, Leslie Uggams, went into rehearsals for an extended pre-Broadway tour at the Royal Poinciana Playhouse in Palm Beach, Florida. I lasted a week with that version.

During the first days of rehearsal our trio, as usual, sat on stage to accompany the performers, and Carol Channing loved my drumming, the way I caught all her moves: "Oh, Dottie, nobody else catches those bumps!" she told me (this was good return for all those Borscht Belt dance-team gigs I suffered in the sixties). Carol's endorsement meant a lot, but it couldn't protect me when the conductor for the show rewrote the charts and added tympani parts. Since I didn't play timpani they had to let me go, but I remember that Carol wasn't happy about it.

My last day with the show, as I was packing and waiting for the new drummer to arrive, I overheard Carol Channing ask, "Where's Dottie?" Somebody answered, "She doesn't play timpani." "I don't want timpani, I want Dottie!" a distressed Carol Channing hollered.

Fazee Cakes

By late 1981, I was weary of living in Fort Greene, tired of driving on glass, hearing rats running in the walls, looking at weeds in the backyard as tall as the windows. Today, Fort Greene is a rich man's paradise, cleaned up and gentrified, but back then it was a slum area, man. Fort Greene was depressed and so was I, and in quiet moments my state of mind was even lower because I was lonely for Deborah who was still in DC. It was such a down time. Then my car got "raped."

I was at Bradley's, a popular jazz joint in the Village, drinking in the wee hours with Danny Moore, the trumpet player I used at Eddie Condon's. Danny and I were the last ones to leave that night—shortly before closing time at 4 A.M.—and when we walked out to the street my car was gone. It had been hot-wired and stolen right in front of Bradley's! I almost went to pieces.

"What'll I do?" I asked Danny. He surprised me by saying, "Let's go to the police station in Fort Greene where you live." Danny was street smart, and as things turned out, maybe a touch clairvoyant because his hunch was dead on: The police found my car stripped and abandoned a few blocks from where I lived! Hooligans had gutted it. Engine, wheels, head, and taillights, even the upholstery had been removed. What a sad thing that was; it was the worst of times for me.

I might have coped better if at least the music in my life was happening, but frankly, even though it was Melba Liston, the band by that time wasn't together. It didn't swing; anybody who heard us at a rehearsal knew it was ragged. Then Melba put us through hell when she brought in a new alto player. He was at least fifteen years younger than Melba and he was knocked out by her and kind of shined up to her—he wanted the gig really bad—but he was an awful player! That made me mad and Carline was none too happy either. At one rehearsal I said to her, "I hope he's taking care of business someplace else 'cause he sure isn't doing it on the bandstand."

Our sagging morale wasn't helped by not having enough work. To survive, I took casuals in New York or wherever I could, but the handwriting was on the wall. The band was falling apart so I got out. (The band folded in 1983; Melba stopped playing in 1985 after suffering a stroke.)

After Melba, I hit the skids. Out of work and forced to quit my apartment, I was homeless, skirting poverty, and generally in a prison of hard knocks. I leaned on friends for a while, but my get out of jail card was the Deer Head Inn.

The proprietors of the Deer Head were Bob and Faye Lehr (John Coates nicknamed Faye, "Fazee Cakes"). I had been calling Fazee Cakes periodically to check, fingers crossed, if my special room with the nook and the chesterfield was available, and one night when I really had the blues I hit the jackpot: "It just so happens that the tenants in that room are moving out and you got it!" Fazee Cakes declared.

Living at the Deer Head saved my life. The rent was a bargain and that was a blessing, because at fifty-two I wasn't old enough to go on Social Security. I could pretty much cover my rent by playing with the house band at the Inn, supplemented with income from other gigs working with musicians I knew from New York City who lived in the Delaware Water Gap area. As the crowning touch, I was in jazz Shangri-la, playing with the revered John Coates Jr. (who had been hired as house pianist at the Deer Head in 1962) in his trio that included bassist, DeWitt Kay. When it was time to work, it didn't matter if a blizzard had rolled in; I just opened my door and walked downstairs to the club where my drums were set up all the time. After a few weeks, manna dropped again on my doorstep: I was hired as the permanent house drummer at the Deer Head.

John Coates explained why I got the job: "There hadn't been a drummer who was hired in my memory since the early '60s. . . . What prompted us to want her more than anything was she was a swinger; things just felt rhythmically great when she played with us. . . . I sincerely feel that many of the Deer Head's best toe-tapping or finger-snapping moments came when Dottie was the drummer. . . . Also she was very outgoing and happy as a person.

. . . Dottie's ebullience engaged the crowd, lifted the group and affected the energy of the performances. I think of Dottie as a big smile."

Playing with John would have been difficult for a lot of drummers. He played fast, he played a lot of notes and he played mostly his own compositions, taking charge from note one to the very end, hardly leaving room for anything else. DeWitt would play real light so he never got in John's way, and that's how I had to play with John, too. I played the underneath and made it wide, my brushes just easy. It was really a challenge. Although I didn't sing at the Deer Head, my experience as a vocalist played no small part in why we fit together so well. "I thought she was very good with the brushes and she liked playing ballads," John said. "And also being that she's such a good singer," he continued, "I felt that in the ballads she was singing even though it was not audible. She had a real melodic sense."[1]

I stayed at the Deer Head for about three years. The trio worked year-round, but when winter came we did only Saturday nights so I was strapped a chunk of the year. That really hurt when my mother, aged seventy, died on January 15, 1982, and I didn't have enough money to go to her funeral in Sacramento. My stepdad, Bob, who stayed on as caretaker of the double-wide, said he understood, but I was heartsick. At least Deborah was able to go and represent us. She was much more flush than I was at that time, pulling in a good salary at one of the DC beauty salons.

To earn extra money, I took a day job working in an office five days a week selling shares for Pocono land deals. I'd get people's attention on the phone by telling them that they'd won a trip. A lot of my older clients would be blown away by the offer. "Did I really win?" they'd ask incredulously, "and I don't have to buy anything?" "Right on both counts," I'd reassure them, and they couldn't believe it.

I thought the whole thing was legit, so I enjoyed making all those seniors happy. Plus, there were incentives. The operator who sold the most invitations each week won a prize. Well, my enthusiasm for the job paid off because I won the prize every time! But, sad to say, my attitude did an about-face once I found out what my clients were subjected to when they arrived to claim their trip—a four-hour lecture and other hoops to jump through. Then, when I learned that the whole operation was a con game, I quit. I had lasted three months.

The end of my telemarketing career really dented my pocketbook. Over the next several years I had no choice but to travel a lot, on the road doing one-nighters or taking extended gigs on leave from the Deer Head (like I did with "Jerry's Girls") to earn extra cash. I worked jobs in the Poconos and Catskills with a variety of bands (including my own quartet[2]), and I did "B-Joint" and second-string gigs in the New York area that usually paid $50 or $60—but I'd get $75 because I drove all the way from Delaware Water Gap.

Sometimes that gig you drive a long way to make can bear unexpected fruit. In 1982, I played the Village jazz club, Lush Life, accompanying gospel, blues, and jazz vocalist, Sandra Reaves-Phillips.[3] Seventy-four-year-old virtuoso trumpeter Jabbo Smith was also on that band. Smith was in the midst of a late-life comeback, having established himself as a brilliant instrumentalist in the 1920s and 1930s. It was a fun date, working with yet another important early jazz figure.

That was the first time I'd met Sandra, and I guess I must have made an impression because six months later she called me about another job, an overseas engagement that was lined up for the following spring. She was taking a tribute show she had created, "The Late, Great, Ladies of Blues and Jazz," to Bern, Switzerland, and was putting together her back-up band. Sandra had decided on an all-woman band that included my old friend, bassist, Carline Ray, plus Lillette Jenkins at the piano, and tenor player, Willene Barton, who sounded like saxophone icon, Ben Webster. That was an impressive group of musicians, so I grabbed the chance when Sandra asked if I'd like to go along.

In Bern, we stayed across the street from the train station at the Hotel Schweizerhof and played downstairs in a great little room, Jaylin's Club. The show opened on April 23, 1983. Sandra's a belter, and when she sang the blues I leaned on the back beat a little bit more, or as Sandra put it: "The way she played for us, you couldn't tell if it was a man or a woman because she played the hell out of those drums." Sandra had this to say about our bandstand rapport: "She kept her eyes on me so everything I did she was right there with me. . . . She never left me, she never got off on her own journey. . . . When Dottie was on that stage she listened, she breathed with me, she knew just where to go and when to go and she knew when to pull back. That's what a consummate pro is."

We were back home in early May, and I resumed my double jazz life: house drummer at the Deer Head spelled by commutes to freelance gigs in the environs of the Gap and NYC. In November, a month after I did the upstate New York tour of "Jerry's Girls" mentioned earlier, I worked another

Off-Broadway show, "Peggy Hewett's New Tropical Revue," a musical parody staged at the Ballroom cabaret on West 28th Street, where jazz songbird, Blossom Dearie, used to play. Cheryl Hardwick, my pal from "Jerry's Girls," got me the job and also a place to stay for the six-week run. Once again, Cheryl and I were part of an all-female unit that included reeds player, Martha Hyde, and cellist, Faun Stacy. One critic wrote that our band gave Hewett "topnotch support"[4] and described me as "a dynamite drummer."

In 1981, when I was hired as the house drummer at the Deer Head Inn, my ambition was to work there forever, and by my third year in the trio I was a fixture on the local Delaware Water Gap/Stroudsburg jazz scene. My claim on local celebrity was enhanced by appearances in three COTA Jazz Festivals[5] and profiles published in new books about jazz women by, respectively, Sally Placksin[6] and Linda Dahl.[7]

My optimism sagged in the mid-1980s. John Coates's appearances at the Deer Head began to decline due to bouts of bad health. That was hard enough, but when John left for good, nobody could replace him so the group disbanded. I tried to hang on for a time, but it was dicey. Nothing was happening musically for me—the Deer Head without Coates, it wasn't the same—and although I was drawing unemployment, it wasn't enough. With my bread and butter seriously threatened, I started looking for another day gig to stay afloat. My search was interrupted when I learned that my stepdad, Bob Musselman, had passed.[8]

With Bob gone, Deborah and I were the only heirs. I had to go back to California in 1985 for Mom's will to be admitted to probate. And that was okay with me; I needed a break from my post-Coates grind in the Gap. Figuring I'd sell the house trailer and go right back east, I called one of my local cronies to help pack what amounted to virtually all my belongings and put them in storage until I knew where I'd be living. Some of my stuff was valuable; really expensive, vintage ceramic Italian bowls and dishes that friends like Chan Parker had bought for me in Europe. By the time we finished packing, there were enough boxes to fill a warehouse, all awaiting my return.

They might as well have been "waiting for Godot" because I never went back to collect them.

PART III

CALIFORNIA REDUX

The Best Kept Secret in Town

"When I went back to
California I buried myself."
—Dottie Dodgion

I didn't intend to stay long in Sacramento, but when I learned that probate was going to take at least two years due to a crowded court calendar, my getaway was stalled. With no place else to go, I reluctantly unpacked in my Mom's mobile home. At first, I was very lonely and lost, but before long the arrangement started to have some appeal. Although I didn't much like Sacramento, my pocketbook was telling me to stay put in that double-wide with its very attractive $150 a month to rent the trailer space. And, as I acclimated I began to relish how my life calmed down. I had time to think, and with the perspective that 3,000 miles gave me, I started having second thoughts about the East and my place in it.

What would I be going back to? The snow? That romance was over; I'd had my fill of the cold. Was I returning to the embrace of a relationship? No, I was all by myself. The East is for couples, people who take care of each other; otherwise it can be very lonely, just awful lonely.

Would I be able to rebuild my career? Well, John Coates had moved on so if I lived in the Gap I would have been scuffling, running back and forth to New York trying to find gigs to play. Where would I fit in anyway? At 56, look out! Nobody in New York was going to hire an old broad on drums.

To top it all off, the New York jazz scene continued in free fall. The glory days of the 1960s were gone; rock was in and jazz was out. The jazz musician was no longer appreciated; both the prestige of the music and the aristocracy of jazz musicians were in steep decline. Die-hard New Yorkers, they're going to live in New York no matter what is happening; anyplace else would be below their status, but that wasn't me. The more I chewed on it, the less I wanted to go back.

My life was on hold, my career in limbo. Desperate for work, I made the rounds of Sacramento-area clubs and found that my reputation among musicians had preceded me. Before long, I was behind the drums playing dance music with local bands. Then Jimmy Rivers found out I was in town. Rivers was a western-swing, bebop guitarist who had played with my dad, but that didn't stop him from trying to make it with me back in 1947 when I was a vocalist with his band on a short tour of Louisiana. I hadn't seen Rivers since, so my transition to the drums was a surprise that kicked his sexism into high gear. He thought it was "the cutest thing," but ever so sweetly just had to ask: "Why do you play drums? "You don't want to play drums, do you? Maybe you'd like to sing?"

Rivers got his comeuppance a short time later when he needed a drummer for one of his gigs and he had to "settle" for me, a woman! What was unspoken, of course, was that I could play the right rhythm better than a lot of men. If they'd been able to find a guy drummer who swung as well as me they would have hired him. I needed the work so I swallowed my pride and took the gig in a little Western bar on the outskirts of the city.

In Rivers's band, I occasionally sang a tune from behind the drums, which back then was still a difficult thing to do. I had to hold the mic in one hand and play my cymbal with the other. (These days I have a microphone on a boom arm swung over and locked above my snare, freeing me to be a two-handed drummer while I sing.) I did the same balancing act with a mic and drumstick in a trio led by clarinet player, Dutch Schultz, at The Shot of Class, a beautiful, very-uptown Sacramento club. Pretty soon I was singing regularly behind the drums in the Sacramento area because I could work more.

Jimmy Rivers Jazz Band was a hardship post. Some of the places we played were utterly forgettable, like Straw Hat Pizza, Art of Pasta, and Laughs Unlimited, and his musicians, while their hearts were good, were definitely second string. Making matters worse were the bandstand politics. Now that Rivers had the chance to consider my older and filled-out body, he picked up where he'd left off in Louisiana: Trying to get me in bed with him.

Jimmy Rivers fancied himself a slick dude and he was insulted when I kept turning him down. To retaliate he turned cruel, making little digs on the stand that I was forced to accept, like making fun of my smile or my overbite. In a patronizing tone he'd say, "Look at her cute little buck teeth," but none of it was ever cute to me. There was no excuse for that kind of conduct as far as I was concerned, but it was no surprise either. At that time, women musicians on "male instruments" still were not accepted in California. I was a novelty, although sometimes that worked to my advantage getting gigs.

But solid gigs were hard to come by. The jazz scene was thin; there just wasn't much call for jazz musicians in Sacramento, so I started a push to get my name in wider circulation. I contacted many of the musicians I had known before my move East. One of them was drummer, Vince Lateano. I've known Vince for at least forty years; he has played a big part in my life, always recommending me to anybody who needed a drummer. Early in my return to the West Coast, he introduced me to one of my very favorite bassists, Scott Steed, who has played with pianist, Horace Silver; vibist, Bobby Hutcherson; and tenor saxophonist, Joe Henderson. Scott and I, along with guitarist, Steve Homan, formed a trio that played in Sacramento from roughly 1985 to 1990.

My vocals at the drums were a regular feature of that group. Here's Scott's description of my singing at that time: "Dottie is a beautiful phraser of a lyric. . . . When Dottie sang you would feel the song. And her drums were an accompaniment to her vocals. It's like a singer who finds a piano player who accompanies her in a way that supports her phrasing and makes it stronger. That's how Dottie played drums with her vocals."

My rebirth as a vocalist got another boost in late 1986 when Vince told jazz impresario and drummer, Sonny Buxton, that I was back in California. Sonny, who owned Milestones, a jazz club in San Francisco,[1] knew about me, but he hadn't heard me play or sing. Sonny brought me in for a night, and as he remembers it: "I am extremely critical about singers and I was just simply impressed. . . . She just had a great sense of time and rhythm and phrasing. . . . Certainly it was a lot different than what any singers in the Bay Area were doing at that time, stylistically."

After the road test, Sonny invited me to be an "artist-in-residence" for a couple of months at Milestones, working primarily as a vocalist. He said, "Let me hire a drummer and you stand and sing. Occasionally, you can sit behind the tubs if you like, but I really would just prefer to have you standing and singing." I was a bit hesitant at first, but after my comfort level increased I enjoyed the arrangement.

It was also a blessing because it freed me from having to decide which vocal format I preferred: singing from behind a drum set or standing at a mike, which are, for me at least, two very different things. The downside of singing at the drums is that it divides me. Part of me has to really concentrate on my right hand playing my "apple pie"—the precise way I pull my triplets together when I play on the cymbals. The part of me that sings likes a more relaxed approach to the beat; I'll lay back, let a bar-and-a half go by, and come in on maybe the end of two. That's where my phrasing is very, very different from conventional, "straight" singers.

The conflict I feel playing and singing from behind the drums is why I prefer standing at a mike. The downside is I don't get a lot of opportunity to do that because I must have the support of a very strong bassist and piano player who don't move the tempo. And they can be hard to find. All things considered, that's why these days I mostly do my vocals sitting down; I have much more control from behind the drums, and everybody can swing.

As the vocal artist-in-residence at Milestones, I was the headliner on the bill and also the host for special guests Sonny hired to work with me. When the residency ended I returned periodically for about a year to do weekend appearances at Milestones, commuting between Sacramento and San Francisco and staying in friends' apartments.

Sonny was very good to me. I had no name recognition with the public, but, all the same, he gave me extended top jazz gigs as a singer. I was grateful because I didn't appreciate being forgotten, although on the flip side I was tired of being "discovered" each time I performed. I remember one night standing with Sonny at the bar during intermission when some newly acquired fans of mine blurted out a sentiment that has stuck to me like a label on my forehead for much of the more than thirty years since I moved back to the West Coast: "Boy! You're the best kept secret in town!"

A Leader at Sixty-Five

In 1987, I got a call from bassist Buddy Jones.

Buddy and I had a history. In the mid-1960s we worked the Poconos with Jerry and Dave Frishberg and a decade later I hired him at the Rogue and Jar. Buddy's call was a life saver: "We need a drummer, Dottie."

Buddy was in a band working Monterey. It was led by flugelhornist Jackie Coon with Eddie Erickson on banjo and guitar, and they couldn't find a drummer they liked. So, when Buddy learned I was in Sacramento he called to make me an offer: "Look, we're playing the Monterey Beach Hotel and we can give you $100 a night, Friday, Saturday, and Sunday. We'll pay for your gas, plus you get free room, booze, and board." It was the same great deal I had offered Buddy at the Rogue and Jar.

I accepted a trial run, but after we played together the first time it was such a wonderful fit you couldn't have pried me away. Happily, the feeling was mutual. In an interview with the Monterey County Herald, Jackie said, "She's the icing on the cake. . . . With her on board the band's complete."[1]

Every weekend for the next six months I made the commute from Sacramento to Monterey, five hours each way. It's funny, living in the San Francisco Bay area all that time, I'd never been to Monterey before, so I had no idea how beautiful the Peninsula was. Spectacular, really, and so were my bandmates.

Jackie Coon was a genius on his horn. I'd pit him against any flugelhorn player in the world, including Clark Terry. Buddy Jones had played with Charlie Parker and many other bebop musicians at the famed Birdland jazz club in New York. I was impressed that banjoist Eddie Erickson didn't sound

Dixieland; his chord progressions were modern, and his fingering on the strings was so unique it made you think he was playing guitar. All in all, I couldn't have asked for anything better to reset my career than this first-rate quartet tucked away on a strip of California coast.

Jackie and the guys returned my bouquets by spreading the word about me,[2] and pretty soon the local press noticed that I was in town. It all helped; by the time the Monterey Beach Hotel job ended, my reputation had a tailwind and gigs materialized in places that stretched along the northern, central, and southern coastline of California. Written records I saved from 1989 detail one tour that kicked off in Oakland at Yoshi's with the Eugene Wright Quartet and then continued south, first to the Garden Stage at the Monterey Jazz Festival (with Jackie, Eddie, Buddy, and pianist Chris Calabrese), then to Los Angeles, playing with different groups during the Los Angeles Jazz Classic Festival.

One of the most important mentions I got from Jackie and Eddie was when they introduced me to a Monterey-based band that had been established in California since the late 1930s, "Papa Jake and the Abalone Stompers." (Papa Jake and His Abalone Stompers opened the first Monterey Jazz Festival in 1958, sharing the bill with Louis Armstrong and Dizzy Gillespie.) I had tremendous respect for the leader, alto saxophonist Papa Jake Stock. He was in his late-seventies when I met him. He'd drink his stuff, he was still one of the guys, and although he might sometimes be squeaking and squawking his time was good; he would be there. I subbed for the Stompers's regular drummer for two years until, in 1991, I got the call to be full-time with Papa Jake. I stayed in that drum chair until Jake Stock's death in 1995 and the band folded.

In the meantime, the probate process finished (my Mom's will proved valid) and Daddy reentered my life. The sting from our estrangement over Monty more than thirty years before stayed sharp, so I'd seen very little of him. His last year was tough, a downhill slide that began when he was mugged at the entrance to his hotel. He wasn't hurt, maybe lost $20, but it shook him to his core to a point I'd never seen. Too scared to leave his room, he couldn't work; he turned coward and lost all interest in life. My father who had lectured me "To do it yourself!" and preached how wonderful life is because of music, couldn't take what life threw at him. His collapse broke my heart.

I got him into a San Francisco retirement home, but he didn't like it, so on weekends for a while I tried bringing him up to the mobile home in

Sacramento. Pretty soon he was trying to finagle his way into moving in with me but I just wouldn't have it. He was having trouble handling his bowels and I sure as hell wasn't going to change his diapers. If I had any chance of playing my music I certainly couldn't spend time taking care of him. In that way, too, I guess, we were cut from the same cloth. Years before, when his parents were declining, they offered him $50K to take care of my Aunt Toni, his sister with polio. "Nope," he said, "I won't do it." He didn't intend to be tied down away from the bandstand any more than I did.

He sank lower, so I moved him into a beautiful nursing home in Yolo County, just outside Sacramento. But it was no use. He laid in bed looking straight ahead, never smiling, hardly talking. To punish me, he refused to be happy. Not long after, on May 7, 1988, my father died at eighty-one. With the box from the funeral home on the back seat, I drove out to the famous Cliff House Restaurant in San Francisco and parked near a rocky outcropping not far from the stretch of sand where he liked to sunbathe. I opened the box and put my hand in to find the urn. I realized too late it was Dad I was searching through—they had poured his ashes straight into the box and sealed it. I felt terrible but then started to laugh; I mean, it was just so ridiculous. I walked to his favorite spot, sprinkled his remains, and returned to the car. Before leaving I turned for a last goodbye and saw a dog peeing on Daddy.

I needed a bright spot and as if made to order, I got a call from Deborah: "You want a roommate?!" That was an offer I couldn't refuse, and ten years after I left her in DC we were reunited in a California-trailer lifestyle. When Deborah arrived in Sacramento our first order of business was to find her a job, and, in what seemed at first like a touch of lady luck, right across the street from the mobile park was a hairdresser shop where she interviewed and got hired immediately.

I hadn't paid attention to that place before, but with Deborah back and forth and telling me stories as she settled into the job, and me making occasional visits to drop something off, I gradually learned enough to get suspicious. First of all, I didn't like the owner; he looked shabby and shifty to me. Ditto for the "underworld characters" who hung around inside, but we needed the money and the job was so close that I ignored the alarms. At least until Deborah, her hormones up, began dating one of the owner's buddies on weekends when I'd go down to Monterey and leave her in the trailer park.

Her new suitor, a rough-looking character named Frank, started giving Deborah money and jewelry after a few dates, and that put us in a tight spot. Feeling as I did about him, it didn't seem right accepting those gifts, and what, I worried, did he want in return? We were really poor, so we couldn't pay for them or reciprocate, but Frank was blasé about it, telling Deborah: "You don't have to pay me back. Just a pleasure to be in your company." Yeah, we sure fell for that! Frank was a no-good bum, that was clear, but things took a turn for the worse when his buddy, Vince, showed up. Their first move was to try and get Deborah alone in a motel. "No, I gotta go home," she told them, and without missing a beat they replied, "Okay, let's meet your Mother."

I was glad of that. I needed the chance to size up those two gorillas and it didn't take long for me to figure out that both were deep into the rackets. So, they wouldn't think I was a snob, I went "back to the streets" to talk with them and it got them to open up about some bad deals and robberies they had pulled. One of them actually confessed that he had shot and killed somebody! Through it all, I didn't break my face.

After they left, I figured Deborah had gotten an earful, so I was astonished when she told me that the next time I was in Monterey they intended to take her on a holiday—to Saudi Arabia! "Absolutely not!" I shouted. "You're pretty, young, and blonde, and these guys, they're mean; they won't think twice about putting you on the block and selling you!" I knew right then what we had to do: "Hon, we're moving. We are moving!"

I also knew we couldn't be obvious about it, otherwise they might hurry up their plans to put a bag over Deborah's head and spirit her off to some godforsaken place in an Arab state. So, as I lined up our options, Deborah stayed on at the hairdressers, nonchalant but alert to any tricks and always busy in the face of invitations. Within a week, I sold the mobile home for 16K, found us an apartment in Monterey, and Sacramento was history. The angels were really with me that time because I think if we'd been there even one more day, those hoodlums would have taken her. I never would have seen Deborah again.

That bankroll of $16,000 wouldn't have lasted us two weeks in high-rent New York, but it staked us long-term on the Peninsula. Deborah wanted a place with a balcony, so I found a cracker-box apartment complex at 2000 David Avenue in Monterey. It had a pool the size of a quarter but we got two-bedrooms one flight up with a balcony. At $650 a month it was very cheap, but we got what we paid for. All the rooms had cardboard walls so we could hear everything the neighbors were doing, the screaming and the fights, which drove us crazy, but we stuck it out for four years and I fell in love with Monterey.

Monterey was a pocket edition of a city, but it was the right size for me. I was lonely when I arrived but the community opened its arms to this Big Apple refugee. The nerve center of my social life was Alfredo's Cantina, a bar on Pearl Street where musicians hung out with the regular clientele. Doug, who owned Alfredos, installed three of my CDs in his juke box and dubbed it "Dot's Spot." Alfredo's was my personal "Cheers," where everybody knew my name, and Monterey was my home. I knew then for certain that I'd never go back east.

The kidnapping threat goosed our move to Monterey, but it wasn't the sole reason I had for hightailing it south. The Sacramento music scene was uninspired, and San Francisco was by then too much like New York. Monterey, as Goldilocks said, was just right. The guys in Jackie Coon's band had saved my soul by calling me down to Monterey, and working with that dream quartet was stake enough for me to feel confident about taking the step. Over the next decade, the four of us worked places like the Sheraton Monterey, the Monterey Bay Club, Big Sur River Inn, and Shanty Malone's.

I turned sixty-five in 1994, marking my fiftieth year of survival as a working musician. Although I had played as a side person on a few records during those five decades, I made none as a leader. That was about to change.

By 1994, I'd also had the good fortune of working for close to seven years with Jackie Coon and Eddie Erickson, associations that once again dropped an unexpected bonus on my lap. Matt Domber, who owned Arbors Records, was a big fan of Jackie and Eddie, and on several occasions before I came on the scene he had rented out a Newport Beach studio to record them. Out of the blue one day, Jackie told me that Matt wanted to record *me*, out front as a vocalist!

We cut the recording over two sessions in that same Newport Beach studio. A marvelous small-jazz world coincidence is that the bassist on those sessions, David Stone, had not long before bought Jimmy Blanton's bass from Monty.[3] I was proud to use four arrangements from the batch of eight that Phil Woods had written for me a decade before. "Oh, I'm so happy," I told Jackie, but the air came out of my tires when I heard the tapes from the date. The mix was terrible! Determined to improve the production values, I listened, drank tequila, and made notes about things that were wrong. Eight times the tapes with my critical commentary went back and forth, but the final product, *Dottie Dodgion Sings*, was worth it. 🎵

Critics responded well to the disc.[4] In the liner notes for *Dottie Dodgion Sings*, Stuart Troup, *New York Newsday* jazz critic, nailed the hallmarks of my singing. He wrote that "Her approach is infectious and full of surprise. Instead of gratuitous filigree . . . Dottie changes lyric emphasis, taking little turns that not only are pleasing but apropos. . . .Like Anita O'Day, her rhythm is infectious and flawless. . . .Like Billie Holiday or Peggy Lee . . . she delivers inspired phrasing in a conversational tone. . . . Dottie changes emphasis by adding syllables (. . . You *Are* My Thrill,' instead of 'You're' . . .). It's not a new device, of course, but rarely has it been used with such musical intelligence. . . . Dottie Dodgion is a solid example of the principle that knowing how to sing has little to do with great chops. Knowing how to sing—how to phrase, how to enrich melody, how to capture emotion—requires the kind of special internal understanding that Dottie brings to each song."

But the feedback that meant the most to me was from two close friends who were very wise musically. "Now I'll find out how good this really is," I thought, as I mailed a copy to Chan Parker who was living in France at the time. Chan wrote back: "Dottie, I tried my best to find something wrong with this, but I couldn't find a thing." Feeling great about Chan's response, I mustered the courage to send the disc to the widow of tenor saxophonist, Al Cohn, pianist and vocalist, Flo Cohn. In a handwritten letter, dated October 28, 1994, Flo raved: "Dearest Dottie, Your album is so wonderful! Everything about it is good! . . . You've done it Dottie-O!"

The finishing touch was when Swiss Airlines excerpted "You Go to My Head" for their inflight playlist. I followed Ethel Waters!

Pacific Grove

In 1994, Deborah and I moved to Pacific Grove, a coastal city adjacent to Monterey on the Peninsula. We took the smaller apartment of a duplex on Sinex Avenue.

Even though my move from Monterey to Pacific Grove meant I was inching farther and farther away from the metropolitan East, my name occasionally rose to the surface. I was given several paragraphs in a book about contemporary women instrumentalists published in 1995,[1] and the following year I was invited to participate in the first "Mary Lou Williams Women in Jazz Festival" at the John F. Kennedy Center for the Performing Arts in Washington, DC.

I had appeared with Marian McPartland in 1978 at the first women's jazz festival at the Memorial Hall in Kansas City.[2] That was an unprecedented event. By comparison, the Mary Lou Williams Kennedy Center Festival, held almost twenty years later, was just copying. What appeared to have changed during those two decades was progress in both the quality of women musicians playing jazz and the recognition that they got in the music industry. Some sentiments at the time went so far as to consider female jazz musicians "the ticket"; if they could put a horn in their mouth they got hired by agents.

But things hadn't changed all that much. Although there were some very serious lady musicians who benefited from the attention, by and large women in jazz at that time were still a gimmick, and there still weren't that many really good women musicians.

The All-Star Ensemble I played in on that Tuesday night at the Kennedy Center was, for me at least, a case in point. Pianist and educator, Billy Taylor, was the Center's advisor on jazz. He organized the festival and I'm still miffed that he put me in with musicians I'd never met before. To put it bluntly, I didn't know how they played before we got on and as soon as we got off I never wanted to see them again!

As far as I was concerned, they weren't seasoned players. I was in my mid-sixties and a pro and it made me mad that they were there only because they were women! I got even more steamed when I saw that Marian appeared with her own trio and she used two guys! When I confronted Billy about teaming me up with those musicians he paid me what he thought was a compliment; that if something went wrong with the tempo he knew I could fix it! But, damn, the concert was hell. I told him, "You owe me, Billy, you really owe me!

That same year, 1996, I led a quartet with Jackie, Eddie, and Buddy for a six-month run in the lounge of Monterey's Casa Munras Hotel. The nice crowds we brought in got the attention of Suzy Christopher, a Japanese national and big-time New York promoter, who promptly took us under her wing. When Yasuhiko "Sima" Shimazaki, a businessman in Japan, who also happened to be a jazz fan, arrived in town, Suzy hauled him into the Casa Munras and he went berserk over the Dot! It didn't take long before Suzy, through Sima, had lined up other Japanese businessmen to sponsor my quartet for a two-week tour of four major cities (Tokyo, Osaka, Kobe, Kyoto) and a couple of golf resorts in Japan.

Japan loved me. God, I had no idea. Suzy had sent my CDs ahead of me and by the time we arrived, I was really big in Japan!

Nonagenarian

My return to the West Coast was a trade-off. New York and California are two entirely different ways of living. Leaving the East with its snow, sleet, and little bit of Spring for sunshine all the time was like moving to Nirvana. My wardrobe streamlined, my lifestyle relaxed, my troubles in seedy Fort Greene evaporated. I've been extremely happy even though my career moved out of the fast lane.

Compared to the New York jazz world, not too many extraordinary things have happened to me during my golden years in the Golden State. I haven't played with hardly anybody here who's famous. The music still cooks but it swings in a different way; it's wider, it isn't New York with Hank Jones and Milt Hinton. Those days were over for me and I couldn't keep crying. Besides, as I found out, there wasn't too much to be blue about playing with Jackie Coon and the guys. At least not until Buddy and Jackie were gone,[1] Eddie started getting work out of town, and the safe harbor of the quartet was a memory.

Easing into my mid-seventies I began to slow down. Fewer gigs made it difficult to keep a working band, and because musicians who fit me well weren't always available at a moment's notice I had to depend on unfamiliar subs. Subs of inconsistent quality, and the older I get the harder it is for me to deal with lesser musicianship. But I'm not blaming anybody. My musicians aren't unworthy; they're giving everything they know about—as Billy Mitchell would say with a big grin on his face, "It's easy when you know how."

Instead of squabbling with my bandmates, I try to support them without changing their conception, but I do it in a sly way. When I'm working with somebody I can't trust, I use certain little tricks. If they're not playing steady enough to make it happen, I might play more basic, not tip on them, not try to do any of the inside things that can really make it swing. Even so, I often have to shift gears a lot, placing my division differently to fit the crime. If we're in deep water where a bassist or piano player starts to turn the time around, I'll have him take his own first chorus to make him decide where he wants to settle. I don't want to take control, but if I have to be a little bit aggressive—well, it's my job to make us all fit. That's what I've taken away from listening to the professionals.

Better for my soul as I stepped through my eighties has been the support of close friends in the jazz world. Sonny Buxton, for one. In 2013, Sonny conducted a yearlong series of Sunday afternoon interviews for the Jazz Heritage Center in San Francisco. The theme was historical figures who helped shape the role of jazz in the Fillmore and San Francisco music scenes. As the featured guest on July 21, I did a videotaped conversation with Sonny, followed by a live performance by my trio, with pianist, Marty Headman, and bassist, Heath Proskin.[2]

Not long after, a string of yesterday's kisses called. First, my beautiful-soul bass player, Eddie Gomez, phoned to say that he missed playing with me, that he'd love to see me again and even record together. The fact that he remembered how we fit in Marian's rhythm section that many years ago blew me away! He was my boy. More recently, I was speechless when, in the midst of setting up for a hotel gig in Pebble Beach, who should walk up to me but Terri Lyne Carrington!

For almost forty years, the only connection I'd had with Terri Lyne were some comments she made about me during a 1989 interview in the Sacramento Bee—"Dottie has a really smooth style. . . . The last time I heard her, she carried the rhythm section; she really swung"[3]—but I hadn't actually seen Terri since she was thirteen![4] Now, there she was! In town for an appearance at the 2016 Monterey Jazz Festival (and accompanied by Tim Jackson, artistic director of the Festival), Terri Lyne wanted to touch base and give me tickets. We hugged and I asked, "Do you remember what I told you all those years ago in Dearborn, Michigan?" Grinning, she replied, "Yeah, you said you were going to break my fingers." Tim Jackson almost fell to the floor!

At ninety-one, I am on my last lap, the twilight, the autumn and beyond in my existence on this Earth. Faced with mortality, I want to make one more recording: A CD of me singing, out from behind the drums, with only a bass player. That way I could let all the melodic end out and put an emphasis on how I phrase the story. As I envision it, on the last number of that recording, when the bass player solos I'd give him some rhythm, play him some time, by playing brushes on a magazine. I can swing you into bad health on a magazine!

That's how I started out, filling-in for a drummer who was late, playing brushes on a magazine. On my last CD, I can go out the same way I started! That would be plenty for me; I don't have to go out on top. Humble beginnings is the story of my life and I'm leaving humbly, glad that I got what I got: The ultimate thrill of playing with the ultimate musicians.

Who could ask for anything more?

Postscript

Although Dottie Dodgion has languished in obscurity for years, when principals in our media culture do their homework, her name occasionally rises to the surface.

In addition to the aforementioned *Down Beat* column by Carol Sloane[1] and two books on the history of women in jazz published respectively in 1982[2] and 1984,[3] Dottie was interviewed in 1983 for an issue of *Modern Drummer* magazine.[4] In 1995, she was included in Leslie Gourse's book, *Madame Jazz,*[5] and in 1996 her work was briefly discussed in the book, *The Wildest One: The Life of Wild Bill Davison.*[6] That same year Dottie was ranked eighth among the "Top 100 Greatest Drummers" in "Female Drummer Newsletter."[7] Dottie was featured in a 1998 documentary, "The Music Makers,"[8] part of the Longtimers series that highlighted artists and musicians who worked on the Monterey Peninsula in the twentieth century.[9]

This modest, late-career uptick of attention continued in the twenty-first century with commentary on the Dot in six books: *Jazzwomen*[10]; *Jazz Journeys to Japan: The Heart Within*[11] (ten years later, the same author published an anecdotal blog post, "The Remarkable Dottie Dodgion"[12]); Marian McPartland's 2012 biography, *Shall We Play That One Together?*[13] which recounted both the Stroller's gig in the early 1960s and the "Now's the Time" all-woman band Marian organized in 1977[14]; *Women Drummers/A History from Rock and Jazz to Blues and Country*[15]; the ethnicity-driven *Bebop, Swing and Bella Musica; Jazz and the Italian American Experience,*[16] published in 2015; and in 2017, *Changing the Tune: The Kansas City Jazz Festival, 1978–1985.*[17] In 2012, Dottie was the subject of a short profile in *Tom Tom Magazine*[18] and included among "Drumming's Leading Ladies,"[19] in "*DRUM! Magazine.* She appeared in two documentary films, "The Girls in the Band"(2011), directed by Judy Chaikin, and "Lady Be Good/Instrumental Women in Jazz"(2014), produced and directed by Kay D. Ray. Dottie has also been featured twice in the National Public Radio documentary series, "Jazz Profiles," first in 2008 for "Jazz in Song: The Singing Instrumentalists"[20] ("singing drummers are rare," commented host and acclaimed vocalist, Nancy Wilson) and again in 2016 for part two of "Women in Jazz."[21]

Notes

Prefatory Notes

1. Two of the most prominent were Pola Roberts and Paula Hampton.

Introduction

1. Carol Sloane, "A Drum Is a Woman: The Swinging Dottie Dodgion," *Down Beat*, March 20, 1969, 41.

Scene Two: Spot

1. Famed big-band arranger, Pete Rugulo, wrote some arrangements for the band.

Scene Three: Eleanor Powell's Shoes

1. Eleanor Powell was a celebrated tap dancer in Hollywood musicals of the 1930s and 1940s.
2. A well-known Hollywood director of classic movie musicals.
3. Lopez led his dance band from the 1920s through the 1940s.

Behind the Scenes Two: The Tiptons

1. Antonio DeMarco and probably his wife, Renee.

Scene Six: Jail Bait

1. Composed by Duke Ellington.
2. In 1952 Nick Esposito made another version of "Empty Ballroom Blues" on Mercury Records under the supervision of Norman Granz. Personnel for that recording included Oscar Peterson (piano), Ray Brown (bass), Flip Phillips (tenor sax), Bennie Green (trombone), and J.C. Heard (drums).
3. "Lama, lama, lama" refers to idle small talk.

Scene Eight: Mingus

1. Thanks to Professor Jennifer Barnes, director of Vocal Jazz at the University of North Texas, for suggesting the term *vocalise* as used by Rachmaninoff "for his wordless vocal melody compositions."
2. Composed by Billy Reid; published in 1945.
3. Dr. Bob Sunenblick, booklet essay for recording, "Charles 'Baron' Mingus/West Coast 1945–49," 23; Uptown Records, 2000.
4. This long-forgotten session was unearthed thanks to the invaluable help of percussionist and jazz discographer Michael Weil.
5. 4-Star, founded in 1945, was a small Los Angeles label at the time that specialized in country music but also released jazz (Charles "Baron" Mingus recorded eight titles for them in 1946), blues, and Latin music sides.

Scene Nine: Apple Pie, Apple Pie, Apple Pie

1. Roscoe Ates started as a concert violinist and vaudeville comic. His movie career began in 1929 and included supporting roles in "The Champ" (1930), "Freaks" (1932), and "Alice in Wonderland" (1933).
2. "The Remarkable Dottie Dodgion," William Minor, Bill's Blog, January 13, 2014.
3. Additional observations by Mr. Coates about my approach to playing with brushes can be found in "Scene Thirty: Fazee Cakes."

Scene Eleven: The Drummer Was Always Late

1. A classic scam, it went something like this: Bob lined up three small empty turtle shells on the bar with a tiny pea under one of them. He then shuffled them around to confuse the sucker, but even if he managed to follow the correct shell, Bob, in the meantime, would have palmed the pea. So no matter which one the "mark" picked, he would have lost.
2. Jimbo Edwards died in 2000 at the age of 87.
3. Baton Rouge: Louisiana State University Press, 1991.
4. Another possibility is that Jimbo may have associated my last name with jazz vocalist, Betty Bennett, who was active at the time. Interestingly, Betty Bennett replaced Jackie Cain in Charlie Ventura's band. See "Scene Eight: Mingus."

Scene Thirteen: Jerry

1. *San Francisco Chronicle*, September 9, 1954, 14.
2. Ibid.
3. *Call Bulletin*, September 8, 1954.
4. R. J., *San Francisco Chronicle*, December 5, 1954, 143.
5. Hal (The Owl) Schaefer. *San Francisco Chronicle*, January 22, 1955, 11.
6. Published by Sanga Music, Inc.
7. Vernon Alley was in Nick Esposito's Boptette when we recorded with 4-Star records in 1949. See "Scene Eight: Mingus."

Behind the Scenes Three: Eugene's Lessons

1. In swing music, triplets might be considered the "currency" with which musicians interact. There are four main pulses per measure with three notes inside each pulse (hence "triplet"). It is one of the most commonly felt and unanimously interpreted rhythms in swing. A highly functioning jazz group will interpret this rhythm similarly, if not almost identically. (Courtesy of Chris C. Parker.)

2. *Pocket* refers to the overall pulse and triplet feel of the band. If someone plays out of the pocket, it will often result in the listener realizing that something is wrong. (Courtesy of Chris C. Parker.)

3. *Four on the bottom* or *four on the floor* refers to when a drummer gently plays the bass drum on all four pulses in a bar. This helps to support the bassist's walking line and propel the music forward. (Courtesy of Chris C. Parker.)

4. The hi-hat, commonly played on the second and fourth beats of the measure in swing, can effectively control the tempo of the music. (Courtesy of Chris C. Parker.)

5. Four beats/pulses per measure, three triplets per beat/pulse. (Courtesy of Chris C. Parker.)

6. Thanks to New York City–based drummer and educator, Jason Tiemann, for his insights on the subject of "tipping."

7. *Temperament* in this context refers to the force/volume that one plays the bass drum with—and that one should learn to control its dynamic across the entire spectrum from whisper soft to thunderously loud. (Courtesy of Chris C. Parker.)

Scene Fifteen: First Time in Vegas

1. Saturday, September 1, 1956.

2. Released as "Beauties of 1918," The Charlie Mariano and Jerry Dodgion Sextet; World Pacific Records, 1958.

Scene Sixteen: Followed by Myself in the Moonlight

1. See "Scene Fifteen: First Time in Vegas."

Scene Eighteen: Thunderbird

1. In 1937, Gladys Palmer waxed several vocal sides with Roy Eldridge and His Orchestra. She recorded her own composition, "Palmer's Boogie," released on the Miracle label in 1949; it can be heard on YouTube and as a digital download.

Scene Nineteen: 14 Drummers

1. Some of the other players I remember are: Red Norvo, vibes; Chuck Israels, bass; and, on the horns were Zoot Sims, Buddy Childers, Carl Fontana, and Jerry Dodgion.

2. John S. Wilson, "Benny Goodman Rediscovered," *New York Times*, March 11, 1961, 14.

3. Ibid.

4. One of my fondest memories of playing with the Goodman band was befriending Jimmy Rushing. It was a real milestone for me when Jimmy had Jerry and me over to his house for dinner and to meet his whole family.

5. At this writing, the "What's My Line" episode is available on YouTube. Search for the episode featuring celebrity guests, Gordon and Sheila MacRae (season 12, episode 32) that aired April 16, 1961. Dottie Dodgion's appearance begins at 22 mins.

6. March 20, 1961.

Scene Twenty: Mount Airy Lodge

1. Turning on with pot, using a pipe.

2. A honeymoon resort located in Mount Pocono, Pennsylvania. It closed in 2001.

3. Located in Delaware Water Gap, Pennsylvania, about 20 miles from Mount Airy Lodge, the Deer Head Inn is known as "The Home of Jazz in the Poconos."

4. A Romanian or Israeli circle dance.

Scene Twenty-One: Strollers

1. Founded by co-owners, Lenny Stea and Billy Phillips.

2. Billy Phillips and his wife Anne became good friends of ours. They play an important role later in my story (see "Scene Twenty-Four: Park Ridge").

3. A medley of "Better than Anything" (Wheat and Loughborough) and "Mr. Lucky" (Mancini); "How My Heart Sings" (Zindars); "Night Song" (Adams and Strouse); "Bluesette" (Thielemans); and "The Forward Look" (J. Dodgion).

4. Red Norvo recorded "The Forward Look" in 1957 for an LP of the same name.

5. Out of necessity, I backed myself on drums for the vocal.

6. The David Wheat / Bill Loughborough tune discussed in "Scene Thirteen: Jerry."

7. Iola Brubeck in a letter to Wayne Enstice, dated August 30, 2013.

8. Ibid.

9. Editors of *Esquire,* Commentary by James Poling, "You've Come a Long Way Baby." New York: Thomas Y. Crowell, 2012, 138.

10. The same musician who was on the phone with William Morris Jr. at his NYC talent agency. (See "Scene Nineteen: 14 Drummers.")

11. He had the band with a young Chick Corea as mentioned earlier in this chapter.

12. See "Scene Thirteen: Jerry."

Scene Twenty-Two: The Village Stompers

1. "Cookin' with Dottie Dodgion," Bill Bennett, c.1976; Radio Free Jazz, Washington, DC.

2. Hal Willard, *The Wildest One: The Life of Wild Bill Davison,* Monkton, MD: Avondale Press, 1996, 317.

3. Ibid.

4. Ibid., 318.

5. They include Zoot Sims and Al Cohn, Phil Woods, Kenny Barron, Bob Cranshaw,

Billy Mitchell, Al Grey, Louie Bellson, Eddie Gomez, and others discussed later in the book. such as Ruby Braff, Milt Hinton, Hank Jones, and Joe Venuti.

6. The exception was Bonnie Wetzel, a powerful upright bass player who died in 1965 at the age of 38.

7. She could really swing with power in the lower register of the bass.

Scene Twenty-Three: Eddie Condon's

1. Dave Frishberg, "How Bob Newman Brought Bebop to the Poconos," *The Note*, Spring, 2010, 9.

2. Composed by Kurt Weil with lyrics by Maxwell Anderson.

3. Composed by Nat King Cole and Irving Mills.

4. Zoot recorded his vocal rendition of "September Song" on the album, *The Waiting Game*, Impulse Records, 1966.

5. See "Scene Four: The Eight-Day Clock."

6. *Dottie Dodgion Sings*: Dottie Dodgion, vocals; Jackie Coon, flugelhorn; Eddie Erickson, guitar; Johnny Varro, piano; David Stone, bass; Gene Estes, drums, Arbors Records, 1994.

Behind the Scenes Four: Pearls to Swine

1. See "Scene Twenty-One: Strollers."

2. Similar to the preparation my mother gave me when I made bus trips to Berkeley. (See "Scene Two: Spot.")

3. From the song, "The Boxer," written by Paul Simon. From the album, *Bridge over Troubled Water*, Simon and Garfunkel, Columbia Records, 1970.

Scene Twenty-Four: Park Ridge

1. Anne Phillips wrote the Pepsi jingle, "Taste that beats the others cold, Pepsi pours it on" and arranged the sessions to record it with several jazz musicians, including Jerry Dodgion, Zoot Sims, and Clark Terry. The jingle aired in the mid-to-late 1960s.

2. Colloquial term for Benzedrine, a drug that acts as a stimulant, or "upper."

Scene Twenty-Five: Piano Party

1. Sloane, *A Drum Is a Woman*.

2. Ibid., 17.

3. During that period, Roland Hanna was the regular pianist in the Thad Jones/Mel Lewis Orchestra.

4. Wilson, "Jazz Stars Find Park Ridge Haven," Sunday, November 5, 1972.

5. A week earlier I had worked the Three Sisters club in West Paterson, NJ, with Tommy Flanagan and bassist, Bob Cranshaw.

6. *Sir Elf*, Choice Records; 1973. Side one was recorded at Nola Studio, NYC, in April, 1973; side two was recorded in the Dodgion home at Park Ridge, NJ, in May, 1973.

Behind the Scenes Five: Ruby

1. For more on Marshall Brown and his studio, see "Scene Twenty-Two: The Village Stompers."
2. Thomas P. Hustad, *Born to Play: The Ruby Braff Discography and Directory of Performances*. Lanham, Md.: Scarecrow Press, 2012, 251. Used with permission of the author.
3. Ibid.
4. Morgenstern, "New York Roundup," *Down Beat*, January 20, 1972, 15.
5. Hustad, *Born to Play*, 253–259.
6. Ibid, 256.
7. Ibid.
8. Ibid, 264.
9. Elwood, *San Francisco Examiner*, "All That Benny's Fans Could Have Wanted," Monday, August 14, 1972, 23.
10. Hustad, *Born to Play*, 264.
11. John S. Wilson, "Braff, Cornetist, Leads Clean Jazz," *New York Times*, Saturday, August 26, 1972.
12. Words and music by Sam Coslow, 1935.
13. Wilson, "Braff, Cornetist."
14. Ibid.
15. Hustad, *Born to Play*, 266, 267.
16. *Ruby Braff and His International Jazz Quartet Plus Three*, Chiaroscuro Records.
17. Hustad, *Born to Play*, 274.

Scene Twenty-Six: Suburban Housewife

1. Willard, *Wildest One*.
2. *Live at the Rainbow Room*, Chiaroscuro Records, 1973. Personnel included trombonist, Ed Hubble; clarinetist, Jerry Fuller; pianist, Claude Hopkins; bassist, George Duvivier; drummer, Cliff Leeman or Dottie Dodgion.
3. I believe "scored" is a typographical error and that the word "scared" should have been used.
4. "Jazzwomen Prove Strong on Rhythm," *New York Times*, November 9, 1973, 30.
5. Abern, "RIFFS," *Village* Voice, November 15, 1973, 53.

Scene Twenty-Seven: In the Middle of the Brook

1. It may have been Manuel De Sica since he collaborated with the orchestra at that time: *Thad Jones/Mel Lewis and The Jazz Orchestra Meets Manuel De Sica*, Pausa Records, recorded in London, 1973, and live in Perugia, 1974.
2. Composed by Ray Noble; 1938.
3. Hustad, *Born to Play*, 308–309.

Scene Twenty-Eight: Harold's Rogue and Jar

1. Written by Irwin Levine and L. Russell Brown, it was a best-selling single in 1973, performed by Tony Orlando and Dawn.

2. Ron and I remained friends over the years. I called him every year on his birthday until his death in 2013.

3. Among others, they included: Thad Jones, Tommy Flanagan, Zoot Sims, Al Cohn, Michael Brecker, Joe Newman, Lee Konitz, Jimmy Rowles, Herb Ellis, Frank Wess, Carol Sloane, Pepper Adams, Roland Hanna, Sal Nistico, John Faddis, James Moody, Marvin Stamm, Cecil Payne, Bob Cranshaw, Kenny Ascher, Harold Danko, and Chris White.

4. Hatley N. Mason III, "Drumming Up a Role in All That Jazz," *Sacramento Bee*, May 25, 1989, METRO FINAL ed., Section: Scene; SC 1.

5. Recorded in the Monticello Room of the Rountowner Motel, June 30, 1977, Halcyon 115.

6. Shifra Stein, "Women's Festival a Labor of Love," Entertainment Editor, *Kansas City Times*, Monday, March 20, 1978.

7. Chuck Berg, "Caught! International Premier of Women's Jazz Festival," *Down Beat*, August 10, 1978, 46.

8. Hollie I. West, "*A Different Drummer,* The Crisp Jazz Beat of Dottie Dodgion," *Washington Post*, May 8, 1979, B1, B13.

9. *Dearborn Times-Herald*, Thursday, May 10, 1979, 3-A.

10. Ibid, 7-C.

11. Ibid.

12. A skin-care specialist.

Scene Twenty-Nine: Melba Liston and Company

1. "A Festival of Jazz in Nice Style," *Los Angeles Times*, August 3, 1980.

2. Traditional Malaysian Indian woman's attire.

3. Written by Jimmy McHugh and Dorothy Fields, published in 1935.

4. Discussion of a Nat Cole room appears in "Scene Twenty-Five: Piano Party."

5. Thank you to Ahnee Sharon Freeman for remembering the tune "Shafi," co-composed by Mary Lou Williams and saxophonist, Shafi Hadi.

6. "Going Out Guide," Arts section, January 26, 1981.

7. Music and lyrics by Jerry Herman; directed by Larry Alford.

Scene Thirty: Fazee Cakes

1. For additional comments by John Coates about my use of brushes, see "Scene Nine: Apple Pie, Apple Pie, Apple Pie."

2. The Dottie Dodgion Quartet, with trombonist, Rick Chamberlain; guitarist, Spencer Reed; and bassist, Paul Rostock.

3. A few years later she would play the role of Buttercup in the movie, *Round Midnight*, which starred tenor saxophone giant, Dexter Gordon.

4. Madd, "Ballroom, N.Y.," *Variety*, Wednesday, November 23, 1983.

5. The Annual Delaware Water Gap "Celebration of the Arts" (COTA) Jazz Festival, cofounded in 1978 by alto saxophonist, Phil Woods, celebrated its 40th Anniversary in 2017.

6. Placksin, *American Women in Jazz, 1980 to the Present; Their Words, Lives, and Music*, New York: Seaview Books, 1982, 235–238.

7. Dahl, *Stormy Weather/The Music and Lives of a Century of Jazzwomen*, New York: Pantheon Books, 1984, 92,184, 218–224, 258.

8. June 28, 1985.

Scene Thirty-One: The Best Kept Secret in Town

1. Milestones closed in late Fall, 1989, after the Bay Area earthquake (the building was red-tagged, meaning no occupancy). Today, Sonny Buxton is a broadcaster on KCSM public radio and a lecturer in jazz at the Fromm Institute, University of San Francisco.

Scene Thirty-Two: A Leader at Sixty-Five

1. George Warren, "Take Five," *Sunday Herald*, November 18, 1990, Life and Leisure section, D 1, 30.

2. Their endorsements coincided with Marian McPartland's very complimentary words about my drumming, originally written for *Esquire* in 1976 (see page 163) and republished in her book, *All in Good Time*, New York: Oxford University Press, 1987, 14–15.

3. See "Scene Twelve: Monty" for the reference to Monty and Jimmy Blanton's bass.

4. Dick Neeld selected my recording as a Writer's Choice Award for 1995 in Toronto's jazz journal, *CODA Magazine* "Singing for the Sake of the Song"; (July/August 1996, issue 268). Neeld went on to say, "She has one of the friendliest voices in vocaldom. It's informal, relaxed, conversational, comfortable. . . . She maintains a swinging pulse throughout." Shirley Klett, writing in *Cadence Jazz Magazine* (April 1995, 91), described me as "a straightforward singer with a fine voice." Commenting on my vocal approach, Ms. Klett observed: "She treats the lyrics with great respect, her phrasing contributes to the emotional enhancement, and she glides over and around the time effortlessly. Ms. Dodgion is, in short, a delight."

Scene Thirty-Three: Pacific Grove

1. Leslie Gourse, *Madame Jazz: Contemporary Women Instrumentalists*, "Chapter Two, A Status Report: Part Two." New York: Oxford University Press, 1995, 19–21, 24.

2. See "Scene Twenty-Eight: Harold's Rogue and Jar. "

Scene Thirty-Four: Nonagenarian

1. Buddy Jones died in 2000; Jackie Coon died in 2007.

2. The proceedings of that Sunday afternoon, along with all the recorded material from that special series, have been archived at San Francisco State University.

3. Mason III, "Drumming Up a Role."

4. See "Scene Twenty-Eight: Harold's Rogue and Jar."

Postscript

1. Sloane, "A Drum Is a Woman."

2. Placksin, *American Women in Jazz.*

3. Dahl, *Stormy Weather.*

4. Katherine Alleyne, "Portraits: Dottie Dodgion."

5. Gourse, *Madame Jazz.* New York: Oxford University Press, 1995.

6. Willard, *Wildest One,* 172, 276, 317, 318, 388.

7. Compiled by Wizard of Roz, May/June copyright 1996.

8. Edited, produced, and directed by Paul Boczkowski and Marie Wainscoat. All three films were aired nationwide on PBS stations. Originally issued in VHS, the film has more recently been uploaded to YouTube.

9. Dottie's almost ten-minute segment featured her quartet (Jackie Coon, flugelhorn; Eddie Erickson, guitar and banjo; Bryan McConnell, bass) in live performance from the Casa Munras Hotel in Monterey; an interview that concludes with her singing "Time Heals Everything" (words and music by Jerry Herman) a cappella; and footage of her behind the drums with Papa Jake and the Abalone Stompers on the deck of the Big Sur River Inn.

10. Wayne Enstice and Janis Stockhouse, *Jazzwomen.* Bloomington: Indiana University Press, 2004, 112–127, 243, 251, 353.

11. William Minor, *Jazz Journeys to Japan: The Heart Within.* Ann Arbor: University of Michigan Press, 2004, 99, 102.

12. Minor, "The Remarkable Dottie Dodgion," 2014.

13. De Barros, *Shall We Play That One Together?* 208–209, 213, 262, 283, 284, 285, 340.

14. Ibid., 208–209, 283–285.

15. Angela P. Smith, *Women Drummers/A History from Rock and Jazz to Blues and Country.* Lanham, Md.: Rowman and Littlefield, xviii, 205–207, 236.

16. Bill Dal Cerro and David Anthony Witter, *Bebop, Swing and Bella Musica: Jazz and the Italian American Experience.* Chicago: Bella Musica Publishing, 2015, 220–225.

17. Carolyn Glenn Brewer, *Changing the Tune: The Kansas City Jazz Festival, 1978–1985.* Denton, Tex.: University of North Texas Press, 10, 40, 42–44, 50, 79, 157, 163, 165.

18. Ann Barnett, "Dottie Dodgion, The Living Legend."

19. Kristin Bartus, April issue.

20. Aired January 16, 2008.

21. Produced by Margaret Howze, aired December 6, 2016.

Selected Discography

As a Leader

Dottie Dodgion Sings. Arbors Records ARCD 19128 (1994). Dottie Dodgion, vocals; Jackie Coon, flugelhorn; Eddie Erickson, guitar; Johnny Varro, piano; David Stone, bass; Gene Estes, drums.

Live at the Elkhorn Slough Yacht Club. Monterey Mattress Marque (2000). Dottie Dodgion, drums and vocals; Jackie Coon, flugelhorn and vocals; Bryan McConnell, bass.

This Is What I'm Here For. Envirophonic Records EPR-0302 (2003). Recorded live at Club Paxton, Carmel Valley, Calif. Dottie Dodgion, drums and vocals; Bryan McConnell, bass; Eddie Mendenhall, piano.

From the Heart. Monterey Mattress Marque (2007). Live at the Inn At Spanish Bay, Pebble Beach, Calif. Dottie Dodgion, drums and vocals; Marshall Otwell, piano; Nat Johnson, bass.

Dottie Dodgion Trio, Live from Kuumbwa Jazz Center. Santa Cruz, California (2015). Dottie Dodgion, drums and vocals; Martin Headman, piano; Heath Proskin, bass.

As a Side Person

Nick Esposito Boptette. 4-Star Records (1949). Nick Esposito, guitar; Claude Gilroy, tenor sax; Buddy Motsinger, piano; Vernon Alley, bass; Joe Dodge, drums; Cal Tjader, bongos; Dottie Grae (Dodgion), phonetics.

Unreleased Test Dub. Self-produced (1962). Jerry Dodgion, alto sax and flute; Eugene Wright, bass; Chick Corea, piano; Dottie Dodgion, drums and vocals.

Ruby Braff and His International Jazz Quartet Plus Three. Chiaroscuro Records (1972). Ruby Braff, cornet; Milt Hinton, bass; Dick Hyman, piano; Jerry Dodgion, alto sax and flute; Sam Margolies, tenor sax; Howard Collins, guitar; Dottie Dodgion, drums.

Wild Bill Davison Live at the Rainbow Room. Chiaroscuro Records (1973). Wild Bill Davison, cornet; Ed Hubble, trombone; Jerry Fuller, clarinet; Claude Hopkins, piano; George Duvivier, bass; Cliff Leeman, drums; Dottie Dodgion, drums (two selections).

Joe Venuti Quartet Live at the Colonial Tavern. Toronto. Unreleased private recording (1975). Joe Venuti, violin; Mike Longo, piano; Major Holley, bass; Dottie Dodgion, drums; Spiegle Willcox, trombone.

Now's the Time. Marian McPartland Sextet, Live at the Monticello Room, Rochester, N.Y.; Halcyon Records (1977). Marian McPartland, piano; Mary Osborne, guitar; Lynn Milano, bass; Vi Redd, alto sax; Dottie Dodgion, drums.

The 3rd Annual Delaware Water Gap-Celebration of the Arts. Cota LP 12" 1080 "Sweet and Lovely" (1980). John Coates Jr., leader and piano; Steve Gilmore, bass; Dottie Dodgion, drums.

Relaxin'. Jackie Coon Quintet, Recorded Live in Monterey, Calif. Eddie Graham Productions (1990). Jackie Coon, flugelhorn and vocals; Eddie Erickson, banjo, guitar, and vocals; Bobby Phillips, piano; Buddy Jones, bass; Dottie Dodgion, drums and vocals.

Larry Vuckovich: Young at Heart. Tetrachord Music (2000). Larry Vuckovich, piano; Jules Broussard, tenor and alto sax; Harold Jones, drums; Noel Jewkes, tenor sax, clarinet, flute; Josh Workman or Bob Basa, guitar; Nat Johnson or Buca Necak, bass; Dottie Dodgion, drums (one selection).

Index

cording by, 138–139; diagnosed with polio, 40–42; at the Dick Gibson Jazz Party, 197–198; divorce from Monty Budwig, 85–87; Dizzy Gillespie and, 141–142; Dottie Dodgion Quartet and, 158–160; as Dottie Grae, 43, 59, 87, 105; drumming lessons taken by, 66–70; early relationship with Jerry Dodgion, 84–90; at Eddie Condon's, 158–160; exposure to music in San Francisco, 15–16; feminists and, 133–134; first experience with drumming, 61–62; formal education of, 10–11, 26, 34–35, 40; at the Four Queens Hotel, 168–169; friendship with Eugene Wright, 91–95; at the Gate of Horn club, 148–149; Giaimo family and, 19–22, 27–28, 64–65; Grande Parade Festival and, 212–215; at Half Note club, 132–134; happy marriage years with Jerry, 171–172; Harold Land Quartet and, 112–116; Harry Bossi and, 39–40; in Hawaii, 184–185; on the jazz community in New York City, 161–166; Jerry and Dottie Dodgion Quartet and, 174–175; "Jerry's Girls" show and, 218–219, 224; with the Jimmy Rivers Jazz Band, 228–229; in Lake Tahoe, 149, 201–203; in Las Vegas, 102–106, 107–108, 117–122; "Late, Great, Ladies of Blues and Jazz" and, 223; later years in California, 239–241; life on the road with her father, 8–10; living in Los Angeles, 64–65; marriage to Bob Bennett, 71–73; marriage to Jerry Dodgion, 89–90; marriage to Monty Budwig, 77–83; Mary Lou Williams Kennedy Center Festival and, 237–238; media attention on, 243–244; meeting with William Morris Jr., 130–131; Melba Liston and, 209, 210–219; modeling jobs of, 44–45; at Mount Airy Lodge, 134–135; move back to Sacramento, 224, 227–228; move to Los Angeles, 199, 200–201; move to Monterey, 234–235; move to New York, 121, 122, 125–126; move to Pacific Grove, 237; move to Park Ridge, 167–168; in Munich, Germany, 196–197; in Perugia, Italy, 194–196; pet dog of, 11, 12; piano party and, 176–177; rape of, by

Ed Jensen, 18, 23, 39; recording of *Dottie Dodgion Sings*, 235–236; relationship with TD&L, 47–54; religious beliefs of, 24, 93; return to New York, 210–211; rhythm section lessons with Eugene Wright, 96–101; Ruby Braff and, 157, 177, 178–186; singing jobs in San Francisco, 36–37, 40, 73–74, 84–88; at Strollers Theater Club, 140–143; tap dancing by, 24–26; with the Thad Jones/Mel Lewis Orchestra, 207–208; at the Thunderbird Hotel, 117–122; Tipton family and, 29–32; troubles with Jerry, 189–190, 191; use of brushes by, 62–63, 74–75; at the Village Stompers, 149–150; as vocalist for Charles Mingus, 55–57; as vocalist for Nick Esposito, 43–46, 55–59; as vocalist with Roscoe Ates, 60–61; in Washington, DC, 202–209, 211–212; at the Women's Jazz Festival, 1978, 208

Dodgion, Jerry, 2, 3, 84–90, 117, 131, 132, 134, 155, 162, 183–184, 186, 231; with the Benny Carter Orchestra, 102–106; breakup with Dottie, 198–199; career decline of, in the 1970s, 188–189; Chiaroscuro sessions and, 183–184; demo recording by, 138–139; Dottie's relationship with Gus Mancuso and, 118–120; Jerry and Dottie Dodgion Quartet and, 174–175; marriage to Dottie, 89–90, 171–172, 189–190; move to New York, 121, 122, 125–126; move to Park Ridge, 167–168; in Munich, Germany, 196–197; in Perugia, Italy, 194–196; with the Thad Jones/Mel Lewis Orchestra, 159, 174, 188, 189, 194; unhappiness and drinking problem of, 189, 191; work with Red Norvo, 107, 109–110, 201

Dolphy, Eric, 113–114
Domber, Matt, 235
Donegan, Dorothy, 131, 143
Dorough, Bob, 4, 135–137
Dorsey, Tommy, 37, 120, 168
Dottie Dodgion Quartet, 158–160
Dottie Dodgion Sings, 235–236
Down Beat, 3, 172, 243
Down Beat Club, 88–89
Drew, Kenny, 88

DOTTIE DODGION is a trailblazing American jazz drummer.

WAYNE ENSTICE is a coauthor of *Jazzwomen: Conversations with Twenty-One Musicians* and *Jazz Spoken Here: Conversations with Twenty-Two Musicians.*

Music in American Life

Composing a World: Lou Harrison, Musical Wayfarer   *Leta E. Miller and Fredric Lieberman*

Fritz Reiner, Maestro and Martinet   *Kenneth Morgan*

That Toddlin' Town: Chicago's White Dance Bands and Orchestras, 1900–1950   *Charles A. Sengstock Jr.*

Dewey and Elvis: The Life and Times of a Rock 'n' Roll Deejay   *Louis Cantor*

Come Hither to Go Yonder: Playing Bluegrass with Bill Monroe   *Bob Black*

Chicago Blues: Portraits and Stories   *David Whiteis*

The Incredible Band of John Philip Sousa   *Paul E. Bierley*

"Maximum Clarity" and Other Writings on Music   *Ben Johnston, edited by Bob Gilmore*

Staging Tradition: John Lair and Sarah Gertrude Knott   *Michael Ann Williams*

Homegrown Music: Discovering Bluegrass   *Stephanie P. Ledgin*

Tales of a Theatrical Guru   *Danny Newman*

The Music of Bill Monroe   *Neil V. Rosenberg and Charles K. Wolfe*

Pressing On: The Roni Stoneman Story   *Roni Stoneman, as told to Ellen Wright*

Together Let Us Sweetly Live   *Jonathan C. David, with photographs by Richard Holloway*

Live Fast, Love Hard: The Faron Young Story   *Diane Diekman*

Air Castle of the South: WSM Radio and the Making of Music City   *Craig P. Havighurst*

Traveling Home: Sacred Harp Singing and American Pluralism   *Kiri Miller*

Where Did Our Love Go? The Rise and Fall of the Motown Sound   *Nelson George*

Lonesome Cowgirls and Honky-Tonk Angels: The Women of Barn Dance Radio   *Kristine M. McCusker*

California Polyphony: Ethnic Voices, Musical Crossroads   *Mina Yang*

The Never-Ending Revival: Rounder Records and the Folk Alliance   *Michael F. Scully*

Sing It Pretty: A Memoir   *Bess Lomax Hawes*

Working Girl Blues: The Life and Music of Hazel Dickens   *Hazel Dickens and Bill C. Malone*

Charles Ives Reconsidered   *Gayle Sherwood Magee*

The Hayloft Gang: The Story of the National Barn Dance   *Edited by Chad Berry*

Country Music Humorists and Comedians   *Loyal Jones*

Record Makers and Breakers: Voices of the Independent Rock 'n' Roll Pioneers   *John Broven*

Music of the First Nations: Tradition and Innovation in Native North America   *Edited by Tara Browner*

Cafe Society: The Wrong Place for the Right People   *Barney Josephson, with Terry Trilling-Josephson*

George Gershwin: An Intimate Portrait   *Walter Rimler*

Life Flows On in Endless Song: Folk Songs and American History   *Robert V. Wells*

I Feel a Song Coming On: The Life of Jimmy McHugh   *Alyn Shipton*

The University of Illinois Press
is a founding member of the
Association of University Presses.

———————————————

University of Illinois Press
1325 South Oak Street
Champaign, IL 61820-6903
www.press.uillinois.edu

Printed by Printforce, United Kingdom